JEWS AMONG THE NATIONS

By the Same Author:

The Case For Conservatism

Introduction to the New Economics

Law Without Order

JEWS AMONG THE NATIONS
A Message for Christians and Jews

Bernard Lande Cohen

Philosophical Library
New York

To Wife, Children, Grandchildren

"Happy are we whose goodly portion is the word of God and the law of truth, that need not fear research and testing from any side and in any manner."
—Nachman Cohen Krochmal (1785-1840)

Contents

JEWS AMONG THE NATIONS

CHAPTER I
INTRODUCTORY

This book is intended as an addition to the very large catalogue of writings that deal with the destinies of the Jewish people. But there is to be found within it a limitation which I have imposed upon myself. No attempt has been made in the pages that follow at entering into a careful and minute narrative. This is a task which in full measure has already been performed by a number of historians, both Jewish and Christian, to whose achievements I defer. This volume pretends to neither the depth nor the massive detail of a learned work; but as a book of critical reflections, it does break into new ground.

In writing of the Jewish past, I consider it to be imperative that its major episodes be related more intimately to the geography of Europe and Asia, as well as the principal movements of European and world history. Necessitated by this method is the supplementing of that which is definitely recorded with fresh interpretations as to cause and consequence. One is tempted to entertain the proposition "Logic requires it to have been that way, therefore it was that way." This approach to the uncertainties of the past, be it ac-

1

knowledged, is not without its dangers. It should be confessed that as regards some of the interrelationships hereafter to be propounded, arriving at any sure position is virtually impossible. Lacking documentary confirmation, it is often obligatory, for the time being at least, to content oneself with probabilities in place of firmly attested facts. Should it be proven that I have erred in any of the deductions presented in the course of this survey, this should be attributed to the fact that the objective which I have set for myself is a large one, and that the insights which may have come to me call for investigation by persons other than myself. No one is ever called upon to propound hypotheses previously unheralded and to completely verify them as well. Be it noted likewise that evidence that is no more than tentative is evidence, none the less, since it may for the time being be all that is available. Quite often, and perhaps more often than not, such evidence becomes fortified by later information. It is no great wrong to form opinions and impressions on the basis of cursory reading or even conversation. At the worst, this is a weakness that is forgiveable. That which is inexcusable is the obstinate refusal to alter one's theories or to discard them entirely in the light of freshly ascertained data.

Some doubt has been cast on our ability to really know about the past. It has been asserted that the records which have come down to us give indications of either partiality or incomplete knowledge of the facts which they purport to transmit. While it ought to be conceded that the emancipation of history from mythology is anything but complete, I would suggest that despite all the handicaps in the way of accurate assessment of what used to be, the major events covering almost the entire globe during the past several thousands of years are either known or in the process of becoming known. The story of mankind, departmentalized according to nations, professions, and institutions, is presently assembled inside an unspeakably immense collection of books, manuscripts, memorials, periodicals, and not least of all, newspapers. All these have been written up in a great number of languages, and are to be found scattered across the face of the globe, within the walls of public libraries as well as in private homes and other buildings.

In support of the sceptical attitude towards history, we are reminded of the huge number of early writings that have vanished, along with the store of information which they might otherwise have conveyed to us. I suggest that the seriousness of such lapses could be overstated. Due allowance being made for the fact that a goodly portion of what has been recorded as history has been marked by repetition and duplication, the loss to posterity resulting from writings that were either deliberately burnt or otherwise permitted to disappear has not been as considerable as one might suppose. The two surviving epics attributed to Homer, which the world will forever continue to read and to enjoy, have told us a great deal concerning the religion, mode of life and warfare of the Mycenaean period. It is believed, however, that alongside these noble productions, there existed at one time as many as thirty others of similar scope and equal grandeur. Even had these survived, it is not to be assumed that we would now be much better informed as to the character of that far-off millenium, beyond being filled in with accounts of battles, massacres, and crimes, in addition to those of which we are already extensively and tediously informed. Turning to the vanished literature of the Hebrews, it could be conjectured likewise that if we were to have before us the account of the reign of King Solomon as originally written down by Nathan the Prophet and Ahijah the Shilonite, and from which the account contained in the first book of Kings is probably derived, our knowledge of that reign would not necessarily have been substantially greater than it actually is. The French essayist,

Michel de Montaigne, once referred to the habit of the Roman Senate of consigning to the flames the writings of those individuals whom it intended to punish. On a more massive scale, one of many, was the setting on fire of 200,000 volumes of Byzantine writings by the Turks when they entered Constantinople in 1452. But despite all such wanton acts, both great and small, there is hardly any reason to suppose that the sum total of human knowledge suffered from the absence of additional commentaries on the laws, or lives of the saints, or discourses on religious dogma. Not everything that was written down in ages past was deserving of being passed on to later generations, an observation that is obviously true of by far the greater part of present day literature as well.

Those writings of the past, which time has preserved, have sufficed to provide our generation with that "ocean of facts" against which many historians are presently murmuring, and in which the risk of being "drowned" causes them to tremble. It is perhaps no exaggeration to maintain that the activities of mankind throughout the ages collectively occupy a greater volume of print than do the combined data of all the physical and biological sciences.

From this theorem a significant corollary emerges, and it is this: The most scholarly historian, in the course of an entire lifetime, is capable of assimilating no more than a fraction of what has been ascertained in his own immediate field of inquiry. Being a fallible human being, he has seen himself restricted to finding only those particular occurrences as have aroused his curiosity. Hence must his authority as a scholar be necessarily limited. He might have made of himself a specialist in ancient history, and yet be relatively ill informed as to what occurred a hundred years ago, or perhaps even a year ago. It must follow that for passing judgment or giving advice on any contemporary political situation, the professional historian is hardly more

4

qualified than is the average technician or accountant or businessman or lawyer.

A student who has recently earned his doctor's degree, after studying mediaeval history for about ten years, is likely to possess more total information about the world of mankind than his father, who during his high school years was able to master one or two history text-books, and then spent his further years in the dress business. But on the issues of a current electoral campaign is he better able to arrive at a sounder view of things than the father, whose reading has been confined to the daily newspaper, plus the occasional magazine article? Not necessarily, and this for two reasons. The facts about human existence that he has absorbed and his parent has not, are at best only remotely connected with the current issues. Aside from this, even though his total fund of knowledge may far excede that of the older man, this of itself does not make him more of an authority on a problem of civic responsibility. Knowledge per se is far from being the equivalent of wisdom. It is a moot question, that I shall not here go into, as to whether one makes himself a more useful citizen from immersion in texts books than from a conscientious reading of current news media.

Of what value then are the "lessons of history"? A distinguished historian has recently written "To enable man to understand the society of the past and increase his mastery over the society of the present is the dual function of history."[1] My comment is as follows: For history to enable man to understand the past is feasible enough; but by its means for anyone to increase mastery over the society of the present is expecting a very hard thing. In examining the problems of the present time, it is certainly possible to discover bygone events that offer interesting and perhaps even instructive parallels. But then will the relevancy of such examples be acknowledged universally? And above all, how many professional historians may be depended upon to bring such parallel instances to our attention?

In the Grecian city of Syracuse in Sicily, there lived some 2,300 years ago a young man by name of Dionysius. He was an ambitious young man, eager to do well by his native city, and more particularly by himself. Through resorting to a malignant brand of oratory, he was able to gain the ear of his fellow citizens, and to win many of them over to conspiring against the constituted authorities.

A near bloodless revolution in Syracuse thus having been accomplished, Dionysius became the despotic ruler of his city and the terror of those who had blindly trusted in him. Now here was a possible lesson from history that went unheeded in our own century. During the decade that saw Hitler gradually winning his way to the summit of power, there were in Germany hundreds of professors and lecturers in history who knew at least something of the career of this Dionysius. It did not occur to any of them, apparently, to suggest to their students and to the German public at large that the man they were then listening to with so much rapture bore a close resemblance to an ancient demagogue from whose career some warning could have been derived.

As to the lessons of history I now make one other generalized assertion, even though it could lead to some passionate contradiction. History, properly understood, negates the philosophical concept of "one world," and the insistence that all dwellers on God's earth are indissolubly joined together into one all-embracing family. It is a poetic overstatement, I would maintain, when we are told that the bell that tolls for one tolls equally for us all. To the contrary, history informs us, perhaps only in subtle fashion, that the fragmentation of the earth into continents represents something more than a geographical accident. Throughout all the ages, mankind has been divided into a host of individual sovereignties and closed-in economic systems, unaf-

6

fected in great measure by external fluctuations. As regards life in earlier centuries, this could hardly be a matter of dispute. But even in the late twentieth century, no radical change in this respect has arisen. Even nowadays, a disorder, political or natural, may devastate one country, and yet leave most of its neighbours virtually unscathed. An upheaval of one kind or other could strike the Chinese mainland for example. Residents in far-off Montreal or Montevideo might hear of it soon enough, and yet in their daily lives the repercussions of such a catastrophe could otherwise be nil. The fact that nowadays news—or rather some news—travels from one end of the world to the other with the speed of lightning, does not of itself throw down any of the walls, political, economic, and cultural, that continue to exist in global profusion.

I repeat the statement that despite all the advances in the techniques of communication, the world has not been so altered as to sweep away entirely the earlier barriers of separatism. Quite obviously, however, this notion of insularity of the peoples of the world is not to be insisted upon to the point of absurdity. That in some respects, the world does have the aspect of a single community is confirmed by the unfolding of a network of transportation, covering all the continents and embracing the far reaches of the inhabitable globe. Furthermore, dotted across the face of the earth, one must take note of between sixty and seventy financial centres, all bound together by the ceaseless flow of a common monetary stream, and again pointing to the interdependence of nations. And yet in the further analysis, this way of looking at the world must in turn give way to still another. On the one side, the world is an arena of combined and common effort; but on its reverse side it is one of unceasing economic and cultural rivalry, to say nothing of outright warfare both hot and cold.

To summarize this matter, in the make-up of every

nation, three noteworthy positions are discernible. First, a nation or state has the visage of a self-centred entity, bent on the preservation of its isolated culture and reducing its political and economic dependence on the outside world. Second, this segregated existence has been of necessity invaded to a greater or lesser extent, by ties forged with other nations. And finally, there is hardly a nation anywhere in the world that is not engaged, either subtly or overtly, in active rivalry with one or more of its neighbours.

From the foregoing range of contradictory tendencies, the Jews have been no exception. In respect to their isolationism, it should be remarked that they have had almost no contacts, friendly or otherwise, with the followers of Buddhism, Hinduism, Confucianism, Taoism and Shintoism. Even towards their immediate neighbours, Christian, Moslem, and pagan, such isolationism has manifested itself through not a few of their religious prohibitions. Be it added that marks of hostility towards other nations and religions are by no means wanting in their literature. However, the third element in their make-up, and certainly the most pronounced of all, has been their commitment to friendly co-existence and amicable relationships.

It has been found convenient to decentralize the boundless stretch of universal history into ancient, mediaeval, and modern, even though such decomposition does run into difficulties when treating of Moslems, Hindus, Chinese, Japanese and even in the case of some European states as well. As regards Jewish history, with its very long past, some analysis into distinguishable epochs is by all means imperative.

The year 70 of the common era, featured by the destruction of the Jerusalem temple, can be regarded as marking the summit of Jewish antiquity. As the terminal point of the Jewish commonwealth, this could not be considered as altogether a suitable date, inasmuch as the independent Jewish state had been brought to a close a century earlier. Perhaps the taking of Jerusalem by the Romans was a turning point not so much in the political sphere as in the religious. Through the destruction of the second temple, an unlooked for religious reformation was in effect inaugurated. Its immediate consequence was the abrupt discontinuance of the cult of animal sacrifices which, going back to the time of Moses, had in effect been a concession to the pagan atmosphere of the Middle Eastern region. The loss of political independence was in some manner counterbalanced by a purification of Israel's religion.

The second or medieval period in Jewish history which had its commencement with this passing of the old order can be said to have been dominated by the struggle with the Church, a struggle extending over many centuries. It was a struggle that went strongly against the Jews, and for them reached its lowest level during the late decades of the fifteenth century. For them, the Dark Ages coincided with the time of the Renaissance.

The third, though not final period, which for the sake of bringing it into some conformity with the history of Europe, might be designated as the modern, can be said to have commenced in the year 1492. This was a year that witnessed two major events, filled with future promise. I refer to the departure from Spain of the larger portion of its Jewish inhabitants and their resettlement under happier conditions, and also to the discovery of America, an event in which Jews had some participation. From both these events better times were heralded. The centuries that followed saw the building up of some political and economic strength, and constituted a preparatory period for the rebirth of an independent Jewish republic. Hence this phase of Jewish history can be said to have been terminated in the very recent past.

The fourth and final era of the Jews has had its beginning at the very threshold of the present with the establishment of the State of Israel in the year 1948. Since that year it has been distinguished by great events; among these, the renunciation of anti-Judaism by the Roman Catholic Church, as well as by virtually all the other Christian denominations.

II

While making no attempt at chronicling even a fraction of the immense number of episodes which together constitute the fabric of about thirty-five hundred years of Jewish history, I have sought to transfer the emphasis from a recital of particular events to a broad summarization of several dominant themes. Among these, not to be altogether omitted is the phenomenon known as "Anti-Semitism," even though the recurrence during many centuries of all manner of injuries and insults directed against one small nation and from so many quarters is too well known to require any considerable retelling.

Thousands of years prior to the advent of modern European and Asiatic nationalism, the Jews were already placed in a position of incurring the displeasure of other nations, the majority of them Semitic incidentally. Standing with Moses at the foot of Mount Sinai, they were by this very act placing themselves in a posture of inviting hostility. They gathered unto themselves no love when, having entered the land of Canaan, and for a long time thereafter, it was their practice to tear down heathen shrines, burn the Asheroth and cast down the Baalim. It was at that remote period undoubtedly that the charge of "deicide" hurled against them with great regularity during more recent centuries had its initial outburst. At a later time, when settled within the many cities of the Graeco-Roman world, they drew to themselves the unfavourable attention of their follow-citizens by their refusal to participate in the pagan rites and intertwined magic that constituted the essence of civic engagement. While rejecting the omens and polytheistic rites of the other inhabitants, they were in their turn rejected, as they were in later times for denying Christ and the sacraments. In connection with all this, a number of cautionary statements would be in order.

For a right comprehension of the Jewish past, it is incumbent to realize that the melancholy aspects of Jewish history find their parallels in those of all other nations. Suffering on a gigantic scale has been the lot of innumerable tribes, classes, and individuals situated in every portion of the globe. Victims of civil disturbance and interdenominational struggle have at times and places exceeded those of institutionalized warfare. It is, in this connection, curious to recall that many notable oppressors of the Jews have been equally if not more brutal in their treatment of their own brethren in the faith. Pope Innocent III of the early thirteenth century, of whom the historian Graetz has written that the great misery of the mediaeval Jews began with his edicts, did not actually order the death of any of them; but he was responsible for the massacre of many thousands of his fellow Christians in southern France by reason only of some small differences in Christian doctrine. King Edward I of England who merely told the Jews of his country that he no longer wanted them within his kingdom, became known in the latter part of his reign as "Malleus Scotorum" or "Hammer of the Scots" a nation with whom he was in agreement in all matters of faith. The Emperor Charles V, a most pious hater of Jews, instigated in 1527 the sack of Rome and the massacre of a goodly portion of its Catholic inhabitants. The pages of history are fairly loaded down with similar paradoxes.

All this being said, it would be a great error to portray

11

Jewish history as one long tale of unrelieved friction with the remainder of mankind. From of old, there were extended periods of amicable relations with other nations, and when Jews were the victims of no others.

If we except a number of incidents reported in the Acts of the Apostles, there were no violent encounters between Jews and Christians during the first three centuries of the common era. Things changed after that. The meek inherited the earth, as Christ himself had foretold; and from then on all meekness was forgotten. Even then, Jews continued to dwell peaceably enough in the midst of schismatic sects, such as Arians, Monophysites, Manichaeans, Albigensians, Nestorians. Nor was there much in the way of open hostility between Jews and Christians in places where both together lived under the yoke of Islam. Finally and above all, has the past century witnessed a steady improvement in the relationship of the Jews with nearly all the Christian denominations. Where the Church has been defeated, as in Soviet Russia, the Jews have certainly fared a great deal worse than before. The extermination camps of the Nazis were the works of men who had abandoned Christianity. Nor is it entirely correct to say that the German clergy both Protestant and Catholic failed to raise their voices against the death camps. The record indicates that many among them did. As regards those that failed to do so, silence in itself does not necessarily imply acquiescence, even if it does indicate a want of courage. Silence in the presence of crimes that others are committing is not invariably the equivalent of complicity therein. For holding either the Catholic or any other of the churches of today as blameworthy for wrongs committed by their representatives of bygone times, there is at the present time hardly any justification. It ought to be accepted as a sound ethical rule that nations and religions are to be weighed in the balance according to what they stand for at the present time, rather than what was practised by their forefathers and predecessors in ages past. I shall go one step farther. It is proper that all the wickedness of past ages be recorded, and neither forgotten nor excused. But I hold it to be a puerile exercise to do so in terms of animosity and diatribe. Expressions of hatred, where warrantable, should be reserved only for the living, and not for those long dead.

Jewish history, I repeat, should be written not as a dirge, and not as a catalogue of complaints against the world. Notwithstanding, it bears noting that no nation, so numerically small, has through the ages been called upon to weather so many threats to its existence and to live through one crisis after another century after century. This battle for survival, be it added, has been identical in most instances with their struggle as the bearers of a religious message. Of Judaism as a faith should it be reported likewise that the perpetuation of none of the world's main religions has so often trembled in the balance. During the Biblical period its continuance remained in suspense during a long drawn out contest with the polytheism of powerful adversaries. In a later era this effort at pushing back the frontiers of paganism was accomplished far more successfully by the newer faiths that were fashioned out of Judaism. But in their turn, these newer faiths were the repositories of fresh beliefs that for the parent religion were impossible of acceptance. In one respect, the agony of the Jews has been altogether unique. On the ground of religion alone, no other religious community anywhere in the world has had to endure so extended and ferocious a persecution.

It is my overriding purpose to inquire into the causes and circumstances of Jewish durability in the midst of so much hostility. I have tried to answer the question as to why it was that this people, having passed from one threat to another to their continued existence, were not persuaded to surrender their identity and to merge themselves with a dominant environment following the example of many other ethnic groups. I hold this mystery to be not altogether unfathomable.

The reconstitution of the state of Israel, certainly one of the most stirring events in world history, enhances this question. More than ever before is the need reiterated for a more intimate exploration of those hidden forces that made possible the linking together of Biblical Israel and the Israel of today, and over a hiatus of so many centuries, filled with dark and perilous times. How has this people, for so long divorced from a normal national existence, been successful in retaining its identity to remain a cohesive community, and in the end to reestablish a full presence? The recreation of Israel does indeed represent the fulfillment of a faith that never dies. And yet in terms of practical events any transcendental explanation that might be offered does call for some amplification on a more material plane as well.

In writing of those forces that have stood between the Jewish people and ultimate disaster, note should be taken of the fact that on a number of occasions throughout their extended history, and more especially perhaps in our own time, a climatic outcome to their existence was only narrowly averted. Since the very moment of its founding, the state of Israel, representing as it does the embodiment of all Jewish hopes for the future, has itself been hovering at the cross-roads of permanency and annihilation. It came very close to never being founded to begin with. Had the final defeat of the Nazis been delayed for as little as from three to six months, Hitler's "final solution" of the Jewish people would in all likelihood have been consummated. There remained alive within the various concentration camps at the termination of hostilities some half million Jewish men and women. Had these not been rescued, there would have been missing the most vital element that entered into the composition of the new Jewish state. To this newborn state there was at that time available no equivalent reservoir of manpower that would have permitted it to beat off the attack of its neighbours and to proceed thereafter in the laborious tasks of peaceful creativity.

For those who have eyes to see, it has become apparent that given the circumstances of our present day world, the continued survival of the Jewish people is no longer possible otherwise than through the successful building up of a political and religious center of their own. Historically, this was not invariably the case, however. It is my contention that had it not been for their dispersal during several centuries among many nations, and in many quarters of the globe, and had they been rooted to only one particular area they could not for long have maintained a separate existence.

Given the military technology of earlier times, their original dwelling place in Canaan was not ideally suited for defence against inroads by the superior numbers of their enemies. Had our forbears remained obstinately anchored to their ancestral home, exposed as they were on every side, they would in the course of the centuries have been gradually submerged by a series of irruptions from near and from far. They would in the course of time have encountered a fate similar to that of many other small nations of the Middle East, none of whom were actually cast out from their original dwelling places. Had the Jewish state not fallen first to the Babylonians and later on to the Romans, it would in succeeding centuries have been repeatedly pounded by the irresistible hordes of Arabs, Crusaders, Mongols and Turks. In their status of an immobile peasantry, for the most part, no readily available means to betake themselves elsewhere would have been open to them. Even had they survived physically through their descendants, they would no longer have been recognizable as a distinct nation and religious community.

In searching for an answer about the survival of the Jews, the decisive influence of their peculiar culture is not to be dismissed. The study of their holy books gave them the inner strength to withstand the contempt and the degradation meted out to them with great consistency; and which would otherwise have occasioned their moral collapse. Inevitably, the question raises itself as to the intervention of God in human affairs, a belief discarded in our supposedly enlightened age. The question as to the existence of miracles is likewise here implied. I would define as miraculous a salutary event that is perfectly natural in itself, but whose timeliness could not have been rationally anticipated. Of such miracles, be it said, there has been no shortage throughout the long course of Jewish history.

"Generals and statesmen have decided the fate of other peoples, writers and teachers have moulded the destiny of the Jews."[2] With this statement, I only partially concur. The records tell us a great deal of the prodigious labours of spiritual notables during the ages of terror. We hear of writers and religious spokesmen, at great personal risk to themselves, not only hurling back the shafts of Christian controversialists, but of going so far as to deliver their own broadsides on the Church. Counted among these were Rashi, Abraham Ibn Ezra, Maimonides, Moses ben Nachman, Joseph Albo, Isaac Abravanel, Kimchi, Lippman of Mulhausen, Abraham Troki.[3] The purpose of these polemics was to fortify the minds of harassed Jews who were being daily tempted to go over to the dominant religion for the sake of some easement in their lives. Such writings were certainly the means of maintaining the allegiance of Jewish young people especially in face of great pressure from without. It is my contention, notwithstand-

16

ing, that had the Jews in the course of their life and death struggle been obliged to rely solely on the words of their spiritual leaders, they would in the course of time have succumbed to the massive forces, both temporal and spiritual, that were arrayed against them.

In their struggle for survival, the Jews possessed defenders other than those provided by their scholars and sages. I refer to their worldly-minded men of affairs, who were not usually generals or statesmen, but whose strength lay in their being almost entirely wrapped up in worldly affairs. As far back as the patriarchal age, the Israelites were able to generate from their midst persons of superior energy and talent, able to enforce the world's respect, and by whom leadership was provided in critical situations. Joseph, who unlike his patriarchal forebears was not once in his lifetime favoured by voices from heaven, can be regarded as the prototype of the secular Jew raised up on high, who in time of peril was watchful of his beleaguered brethren. Within this same company were Mordecai and Esther. Of another Biblical hero, Nehemiah, a court functionary but of no ecclesiastical credentials, has it been written that his coming to Jerusalem in the year 445 B.C. was for the Jews of that period the equivalent in strength of a full army corps.[4] The historian Cecil Roth has given us this estimate of a Jewish purveyor of arms to the Emperor Charles V of Germany: "If with the advance of the sixteenth century, conditions in Germany improved, the former sequence of massacre being stemmed, and the Jews being brought more effectively than hitherto under the protection of public law, it is perhaps to Joselman of Rosheim more than to any other individual that the responsibility is due."[5] The foregoing example, while illustrative of my claim that the preservation of Judaism owes as much to the businessman as to the rabbi and scholar, contains none the less more than a touch of exaggeration. A more apt explanation for the subsiding of the German terror in the course of the sixteenth century was the relative fewness of the Jews then remaining in that country. Also the ominous rise of the Lutheran heresy resulted in at least a partial forgetfulness of such crimes as stabbing of holy wafers, violating statues of the Virgin Mary, and flavouring Passover dishes with the blood of Christian children. The Protestants, for their part, were too preoccupied in slashing away at their Catholic enemies to make much note of Luther's command to burn the synagogues. Also, not unconnected with this interdenominational fury that was soon to set the entire German world ablaze, was the growing social unrest of the lower classes, directed exclusively against the rich Christian moneylenders and monopolists. In Augsburg, the very citadel of Jacob Fugger, Lazarus Tucher, Bartholma Welser and Endres Imhof, a certain Geiler von Kaiserburg was holding forth, urging the extermination of these exploiters, whom he compared unfavourably with the vanished Jews.

But to return to my theme. In the pages that follow, I seek to present an illuminating view of the effectiveness of commerce, and its offspring moneylending, as instruments for maintaining the Jewish identity. It is my contention that rarely throughout the Dispersion has there existed a Jewish community that was not built upon a core of commercially minded individuals. Without the timely aid, both in substance and in influence, of wealthier Jews, on innumerable occasions, the number of massacres would have been greater, expulsions would have been more frequent, enslavements and imprisonments would have attained gigantic proportions. Schools and synagogues would have been rare and far between; and the chain of learned scholars would have long ago been snapped asunder. It was their aggregate wealth, both collectively and in outstanding individual instances, that made it possible for Jews to buy for themselves any degree of toleration. But once shorn of their well-to-do

18

members, their communities faced the world in all nakedness. It was Pope Sixtus V, whose pontificate was in the late sixteenth century, who observed that a poor Jew stood even less chance in the world than a poor pope.

Did commerce and money dealing take root among the Jews at a very early stage? The answer is that it is highly probable. The Patriarchs, be it remembered, were persistent gatherers of cattle, sheep, silver and merchandise, as were many of their Biblical successors. Abraham was by his neighbours designated as a "prince of the Lord," partly in recognition of his lofty character, no doubt, but not least of all out of respect for his worldly possessions. Throughout his long odyssey, the Jew has been a worshipper of things both spiritual and material; for him, the two being never mutually exclusive. Judaism is indeed distinguishable from nearly all the other religions, and notably so from its two daughter religions, for its emphasis on the primacy of man's earthbound existence. On the delights of the world to come it lays comparatively little stress. For the prophet Mohammed, one of the unpleasant characteristics of the Jews was their craving for prolonged earthly existence. "And thou wilt find among them greediest of mankind for life, and greedier than the idolators. Each of them would like to be allowed to live a thousand years."[6]

This love of life—earthly life be it emphasized—along with its ancillary gifts, has been a consistent manifestation of Judaism. The economist Werner Sombart in his work "The Jews and Modern Capitalism" had no difficulty in discovering within the Hebrew Scriptures numerous texts in which material possessions are extolled as a blessing from the Lord, and as the tangible means for salvation. It is certainly the case that, in sharp contrast to the Church Fathers, the Jewish sages of old at no time regarded the ingathering of wealth with censorious eyes. The Talmud is replete with dissertations on business, and even advises how

19

a prudent man ought to invest his money gainfully. In Judaism it is by no means a sin to be penniless, yet poverty is looked upon as a misfortune and one to be overcome by all honest means. Men born to wealth, like Francis of Assissi, Loyola, and Buddha, who of their own free will make themselves paupers, are a phenomenon altogether strange among the Jews.[7]

In the Jewish conception of things, worship of God and worldly activity exist together in close harmony. True worship being largely a matter of ethical behaviour in relation to one's fellowmen, what better occasion could there be for the show of allegiance to one's religion than in the day to day activities of the market place? To the question once propounded to his disciples by the Preacher of Grodno "Where should one look for a righteous man?" they answered with one voice "In the synagogue, of course." Back came his retort: "Not at all. If you expect to find such a person, go look for him in the place where there is buying and selling."

There have been generalizations as to the characteristics of the Jews, both flattering and unflattering. General opinion has supported the view of their high mental endowments and "their strong capacity for abstract thought, and also a special kind of imagination."[8] In the judgment of the French historian Anatole Leroy-Beaulieu "the Jewish mind is an instrument of precision: it has the exactness of a pair of scales." To all such hyperbole, no great credence ought to be attached. There is no proof whatever that in the mass Jews have a superior capacity for meeting tough situations than do Anglo-Saxons, Frenchmen, Dutchmen, Germans, or Russians. Individuals, both foolish and vile, have been no rarity among them. They are distinguished, none the less, by two prominent characteristics that have qualified a vast number for worldly success. These are characteristics which are traceable, I would maintain, to a religion whose essence is the promise of salvation, not in some future existence beyond the grave, but in this earthbound world.

That the "People of the Book" have throughout the ages shown an aptitude for learning requires no proof whatsoever. "With all thy getting get understanding" has been taught of old; and this exhortation has been listened to by the children of Israel since old times down to the present day. To be sure, education in itself is by no means synonymous with intelligence, nor does it invariably bring about "understanding," as recent times have shown only too clearly. None the less, it is not to be denied that education per se, no matter in what field, does tend to bring to the fore the hidden talents and aptitudes of the individual learner.

There is yet one other Jewish trait that derives from religion, whose importance deserves to be emphasized as well. Charity in Judaism goes well beyond the giving of "alms." Performing acts of benevolence on the largest possible scale, depending on the means of the individual, is the paramount requirement of the Jewish ethic. Now it is scarcely to be denied that the doing of generous deeds has in it some element of sublime egotism, inasmuch as the doer himself obtains a justified satisfaction. But how is one to be in a position to accomplish noble works, unless he has first acquired the means for so indulging himself? Hence, in the case of the pious Jew, added to his normal acquisitiveness common to the generality of mankind was this added incentive. Herein lies one of the secrets of Jewish wealth and power.

That Jews from time immemorial have been active as traders and moneylenders requires neither apology nor excuse. The theory that these callings were originally uncongenial to them, but that they were constrained to go in for them by adverse circumstances, has very little basis of truth. Individual Jews were motivated to go in for mon-

21

eymaking from approximately the same impulses as moved Phoenicians, Greeks, Italians, and Englishmen.

The wise Machiavelli once pointed out that warfare is of two kinds, that of armed warriors on the battlefield and that between men of the law in disputed matters before the courts. He might well have added as a third variety of warfare, the combativeness inherent in the realm of commerce, industry and finance. In the commercial arenas, where Jewish businessmen were summoned to display their strength and ingenuity in contesting with their Gentile competitors, the issue for the Jews went much deeper than that of struggling for customers. Consciously or unconsciously, they were in the forefront in a struggle on which depended the survival of their less favoured correligionists as well as themselves. An observer as acute as the great Thomas Acquinas saw in the commerce and moneylending of the Jews the main obstacle to their conversion; and therefore urged that these occupations be forbidden them. The drive for money and the inclination to go in for commercial pursuits, while all but universal, is certainly not present in equal degree among all nations and individuals. Among the Jews, this particular faculty for making love has been well to the fore, be it acknowledged. But let this further fact be considered. Neither your love of money nor your actual possession of it will ever get you anything or anywhere unless there be others to share this love with you. Jews have been worshippers of Mammon only because of their well-founded conviction that they had as fellow-worshippers their Christian and Moslem neighbours. The sanctimonious "Merchant of Venice" was himself far from indifferent to the charms of profiteering. His noble companions, Bassanio and Lorenzo, while completely innocent of all contact with the market place, were obsessed, nonetheless, with the hope and desire for riches. The moral is this: You do not have to be either a merchant or a

22

moneylender in order to harbour within your soul a highly developed thirst for ready cash or its equivalent. A first-rate example were the sixteenth century Spanish conquistadores who, while utterly removed from all taint of commercialism, were in their seeking for gold, completely uninhibited. A common respect, if not total reverence, for currency, which in ages past united into a single bond of fellowship Jews, Christians, and Moslems, embraces at the present time capitalists, socialists, communists, and anarchists, leftists and rightists, materialists and idealists, revolutionists and establishmentarians, those who dwell on one side of the Iron Curtain and those on its opposite side.

CHAPTER II

THE BOOK AND THE SYNAGOGUE

Even though it is my intention to deal largely with the political and economic aspects of Jewish history, it should be granted that for an understanding of the secular affairs of this nation—or, for that matter, of any other nation—its religious experience cannot be held at arm's length. The prophet Mohammed, to whom the commercial proclivities of his Jewish neighbours were by no means imperceptible, chose, none the less, to characterize them as "The People of the Book." It should be interjected that the favourable opinion of this nation thus implied stands all by itself within the pages of the Koran. Long ago, it was perceived by others as well that even as the demands of commerce tied the Jews to no particular country or region, so too was it as regards the diffusion of their book. Its potent message was adaptable to every clime to which it was borne and in whatever tongue in which it was conveyed. By the poet Heine this book was referred to as "The Jews' portable homeland."

The Jews call this book the Tanach; and by the Christians it is known as the Old Testament. The unique product of a unique people, it continues to influence the world. With the passing of the era of religious strife, the mind of the modern world has lost nothing of its sensitivity in respect to this ancient literary heritage. Never has the Old Testament been as well understood as it is at the present time. Its thirty-nine separate portions or "books" continue to be implemented by a massive international literature devoted to its critical evaluation, its interpretation and reinterpretation. The signal advances in philology, archaeology and history have shed so much light on both the material and religious life of ancient Israel that the Testament called "Old" has become all but a new book, filled with fresh interest, and throbbing with renewed vitality.

Of the contents of the Old Testament, approximately one-third can be regarded as historical material. To be taken into account are two distinguishable streams. The first, and lengthiest, is the sequence of writings extending from Genesis down to the second book of Kings, covering the entire period from the reputed founding of the world till the final overthrow of the Judaean monarchy. The second, and more sparing version of the same sequence of events is found in the books of Chronicles, Ezra, and Nehemiah. This account differs from the first in that it reaches into a later era. During the Persian period there were neither kings nor prophets whose deeds invited recording. As far as is known the returned exiles were for nearly three centuries involved in neither wars nor uprisings. Hence during this quiescent interval, Jewish history in the dynamic sense was neither made nor written. It can be said to have been resumed with the stormy events set forth in the three books of Maccabees. For some unknown reason, these latter writings, unlike the book of Esther in which an earlier and altogether undated deliverance is recorded, were not accepted into the final compilation of sacred Hebrew texts. We owe it to the Roman Catholic Church that in its own version of the Old Testament canon these essential writings, along with a number of others known as the Apocrypha, have been included and preserved.

In common with the early trend of all historical writing, those contained in the Bible bear out the observation of the philosopher Malthus that "histories of mankind are histories of the higher classes." While it is true that the Biblical account takes but little note of aristocracies as such, it does concern itself in large measure with a few chosen individuals, beginning with Abraham and ending with the last monarch of the house of David. Until very recent years, the activities and ambitions of ruling dynasties everywhere formed the main substance of all historical writings. Appropriately named, therefore, are the two books of Kings.[1]

Here too, credit is to be given to a group of Christian scholars who, as a result of a minute scrutiny of the nonhistorical portions of the Old Testament, have been able to reconstruct for us the daily lives and habits of the Israelites in respect to such earthly matters as housing, dress, household utensils, and daily vocations. Notable among these researchers was the German, Alfred Bertholet.[2]

"A considerable literary activity seems to have set in among the Israelites at about the founding of the monarchy. Prophets and seers began collecting and reducing to writing the records of their people, its history, its laws, and its songs. Some of these undoubtedly derive from earlier written sources. The people of Israel very early demonstrated a remarkable gift of writing history, a gift most unique in the ancient world."[3] In common with the historiography of later nations, the annals of the early Jews from their dim archaic beginnings, as set forth in the Scriptures, are founded upon a selection—possibly critical to some extent—of pre-existing memoranda. Their titles alone have survived. Thus the book of Jashar, mentioned in Joshua 10:13, could at the hands of the later compiler have

26

undergone some process of trimming down of uncertified anecdotes. Repeatedly cited, though not actually authenticated, are the "Chronicles of the Kings of Israel" and the "Chronicles of the Kings of Judah," both of them official recordings, inscribed by state secretaries in a fashion perhaps borrowed from the boastful rulers of Assyria. A work of similar character could have been "The Book of the Acts of Solomon" mentioned in the first book of Kings. Less officially oriented, though in all likelihood more candid, were the reports of the prophet Samuel, along with those of his disciples, Nathan and Gad, all referred to in 1 Chronicles 29:29. In the second book of Chronicles are contained allusions to the memoires of the disaffected Ahijah the Shilonite, as well as those of Shemaiah, Iddo, Jehu the son of Hanani, and most interestingly "a writing of Elijah the prophet." Not actually mentioned were writings that could have emanated from such notables as Elisha, Jehoiada the High Priest, and Shaphan, all of them finally woven into the Biblical account as we now have it.

The Pentateuch, of which more will be said later, was no exception to this process of developing a coherent record out of a distillation of earlier ingredients. Herein referred to is "The Book of the Generations of Adam" (Genesis 5:1) and also "The Book of the Wars of the Lord" (Numbers 21:14). The mythological wonders related in these antiquarian productions might well have been too much for the more sober Pentateuchal authors of a later period. Moses himself is credited with a number of writings, other than those relating strictly to his laws. Attributed to him is the account of the battle with the Amalekites (Exodus 17:14).

Not all the epigraphic material that has entered into the creation of Old Testament history has itself been forgotten. Identifiable in these final versions and readily traceable to them are the excerpts drawn from the known writ-

27

ings of Isaiah, Jeremiah, and Lamentations. Also, several of the Psalms can be said to have yielded their quota of information to the final tabulation of the Biblical account. Examples are psalms 78, 105 and 106, which in versified form are among the possible forerunners of the prose accounts to be found in the Pentateuch and the subsequent annals.

Among the historical books of the Bible, the role of highest repute and of utmost sanctity has been reserved for the Torah, translated as "Book of the Law" and more widely known as the Pentateuch or Five Books of Moses. It remains today, as in the past, the book not only of the Jews but of Christians as well. As regards its historical element, to be sure, its predominant concern is with the fortunes of the Israelites of old, otherwise designated as Hebrews, and more recently as Jews. And yet fittingly, the majestic narration of the book of Genesis starts out with the birth of the human race as a single undifferentiated family, speaking one uniform though unstated language, and distinguished by no divergences of belief.

For the first seventeen or eighteen centuries of the common era, there was for all writers of history, both Christian and Jewish, only one pathway leading back to the founding of the world, the path laid down in the opening chapter of Genesis. To both Sir Walter Raleigh and to his Jewish contemporary, David Gans of Prague, it seemed axiomatic to begin their respective histories of mankind with a restatement of the Biblical epic of creation.[4] While later historians have not been so ambitious as to go back as far as the world's foundation, the imputation contained in Genesis, that civilization had its inception in the lands of the two rivers has been confirmed by present day scholarship.[5] It was in this region that the Jews originated. They are today the most favoured heirs of that region's early civilization.

Did Moses Write the Torah?

Traditionally, the question of who wrote this or that book of the Holy Scriptures has not been one of controversial importance. No one has dogmatized about the authorship of the Books of Ruth, Daniel, Jonah or even Joshua, Samuel and Kings. It has been otherwise in the case of the Pentateuch. To deny their authorship to Moses himself is to this very day regarded as an offence against orthodoxy. And yet this dogma, if such it might be called, is based exclusively on a single passage in the Book of Deuternomy; "Take this book of the law, and put it by the side of the Ark of the Covenant of the Lord your God, that it may be there for a witness against you."[6]

Perhaps the first to suggest that the scripture bearing his name was not identical with the texts actually written by Moses was the mediavel commentator Abraham ibn Ezra (1092-1167). Martin Luther, in his introductory remarks to his German translation of the Old Testament, declared categorically that Moses was not the author of the Pentateuch. In passing, it should be noted that within the Christian world, at about that time, scepticism as regards anything connected with the Old Testament was somewhat less dangerous than any possible criticism of the New.

The reasons for maintaining that Moses was not the actual author of the Five Books are in fact overwhelming. Had he been the author it would have been natural for Moses to have written of himself in the first person, after the manner of other Oriental rapporteurs, including the prophets. Would Moses have written of himself that "The man Moses was very meek?" (Numbers 12:3). Neither would he have boasted "And there hath not arisen a prophet in Israel like unto Moses, whom the Lord knew face to face" (Deuteronomy 34:10). Such an appraisal could only have been written many years after his passing. We are informed that Abraham with his followers pursued the

29

captors of his nephew Lot "as far as Dan" (Genesis 14:14).
This territory, situated at the extreme north of the Israelite
domains, was settled and so named by members of the tribe
of Dan as a result of a filibuster described in the book of
Judges (Chapter 18). How could Moses have so designated
this particular region? Again, the verse "At that time the
Canaanites were in the land" (Genesis 12:6) could only have
been written long after the time of Moses. There is advice as
to the correct means for laying siege to an enemy city. No
fruit-bearing trees were to be cut down but others might be
"that thou mayest build bulwarks against the city that
maketh war with thee until it fail."[7] In the thirteenth century B.C. the use of engines in siege warfare was still unknown. Joshua made use of no such "bulwarks" in attacking
Jericho. Nor is there any mention of them during the siege
of Troy. What purpose could Moses possibly have had, in
the precious moments of the life that was left to him, in
detailing the long and irrelevant table of the descendants of
Esau, to be found in chapter 36 in Genesis? Also, how could
he have written at the end of this chapter "And these are the
kings that reigned in the land of Edom, before there reigned any king over the children of Israel?"[8] It is also of some
interest to note however that nowhere in the Pentateuch is
there to be found any reference to kingship in Israel having
been terminated. The significance of such an omission will
appear in a later chapter.

Almost endless is the list of passages to be found in the
Pentateuch that could not possibly have been written by
Moses. "And the Lord God said—Behold the man is become as one of us to know good and evil." Can this really be
reconciled with the general tenor of Hebraic lore? Would
Moses have countenanced the ease with which the glib
murderer Cain escaped punishment for the crime of frat-
ricide? Was it not the stern lawgiver who had recommended
in the case of such men "Thine eye shall not pity"? Are we to

maintain likewise that Moses credited serpents and asses with the ability of carrying on dialogues with their human companions? There are also passages in the early part of Genesis which are clearly of pagan origin. "And the Lord smelled the sweet savour" (8:21), "the sons of God saw the daughters of men that they were fair, and they took them wives of all which they chose" (6:12). Such insertions do not fit in with the essentials of the teachings of Moses.

Moses was Israel's greatest lawgiver and teacher. We are likewise justified in regarding him as a superb military leader and strategist. Are we obliged to look upon him as well as a writer of history? The writing down of historical accounts is not generally within the province of the lawgiver. The Torah, as we have it, contains much that Moses would not have considered as essential to his purpose. The Pentateuch is far from being merely a book of laws and of ethics. Both in literary content and in style, the narrative content of the Five Books are of a piece with those that follow immediately in the sequence of the Scriptures.

There is yet a further matter to be considered, over and above the question of substance. The Pentateuch is a highly compendious work, in sharp contrast to the conciseness of antique writings generally, not excluding those of the Greeks. In a remote age when the written word was a difficult art, would it have been possible for any one individual to have indited anything so extensive? From the internal evidence of the Pentateuch it is possible to form some idea of what Moses did write. Towards the end of the fourth book we read as follows: "These are the stages of the children of Israel, by which they went forth out of the land of Egypt by their hosts under the hand of Moses and Aaron. And Moses wrote their going forth, stage by stage, by the commandment of the Lord; and these are their stages at their going forth."[9] What follows in the balance of this particular chapter is a dry catalogue of place names, bereft of all artistry and literary embellishment. Such monotony of style is not unexpected of an age when prose writing was yet in its rudimentary development. This chapter in particular might well be a faithful transcription of what Moses actually wrote at the time. It is a landmark of primitive historiography.

We read that Moses "wrote upon the tables the words of the covenant, the ten words."[10] We are then informed that on completion of the ark of the covenant, Moses was commanded to place within it "the testimony (eduth)." This presumably again refers to the "ten words."[11] A further mention of this same object occurs in connection with the coronation ceremony some four hundred years later of the boy king Joash in the year 878 B.C. at which we are told that his benefactor and rescuer, the high priest Jehoiada, "brought forth the king's son, and put the crown upon him, and gave him the testimony (eduth)."[12] As to the precise nature of this inscribed tablet we are once again given some inkling in a text where we are informed, "There was nothing in the Ark save the two tablets of stone, which Moses put there at Horeb."[13] Even if we are to assume that matters other than the Ten Commandments were contained likewise within the Ark, not a great deal more could have been added. This receptacle measured less than four feet in length and no more than two feet in breadth.

We are later informed of yet one other document emanating from the hand of the Teacher. In the closing book of the Pentateuch, there is a reference to a separate recording by Moses of those enactments posterior to those delivered from Sinai. "These are the words of the Covenant which the Lord commanded Moses to make with the children of Israel in the land of Moab, besides the Covenant which he made with them in Horeb."[14] It is in connection with these later revelations, apparently, that we now come across several references to a "Book of the Law." It was this book that Moses handed over to the priests and Levites and which by them was placed in the Sanctuary "by the side of the Ark."[15] The King James translation reads "in the side of the Ark." Of this book, we are told likewise that by order of Moses, it was later to be copied "on great stones covered with plaster,"[16] an order finally carried out under Joshua.[17]

Now of these stone inscriptions the question that could be asked is this: Along with the ordinances, did these monumental columns include likewise the story of creation, of Adam and Eve, of Noah and the flood, the tower of Babel, of the Patriarchs and of Joseph? In other words, did these stones contain, along with the laws dictated by Moses, the early history of the Hebrews as well? This seems far from likely. There is no reason to assume that a permanent inscription of any nation's laws would be preceded by a lengthy discourse of its early history. The laws of Hammurabi did not go into the history of Babylon. We know nothing of course as to the sizes and numbers of the stones that composed the cairn at Mount Ebal; but something is known of the single stela of diorite eight feet in height upon which were inscribed the code of King Hammurabi (2067-2025 B.C.). It contained no more than 8000 words or the equivalent of 25 to 30 printed pages.[18] Technically this was no mean achievement considering the obduracy of the material and the very primitive instruments at the disposal of the early scribes. One is permitted to doubt that writing on the stones of Mount Ebal could have been very much greater in volume.

When was the Torah Written?

The value of the Torah and its grip upon many nations does not depend on the determination of its authorship. Doubts as to the origin of ancient writings can never be entirely resolved. Our appreciation of the splendor of the Homeric poems is in no way diminished by reason of the controversy still unsettled as to the existence and identification of its reputed author. As for the Pentateuch, far more momentous than the question of its personal authorship is that of establishing the approximate time when it first came to light, along with the circumstances surrounding its reception. Only by means of such an analysis can the way be cleared for a full understanding of the part played by the Torah in preserving the Jewish people from utter denationalization, and its religion from being engulfed under a sea of paganism.

As indicated in a great many passages in the Scriptures, the maturing of the religion that came to be known as Judaism followed a long and faltering course. It necessitated a long drawn out struggle within the nation itself, as well as repeated clashes with environmental forces from without. As a new way of life, Judaism was out of harmony with all that preceded it and all that surrounded it. Coming to the fore at a critical juncture, it is my contention that it was the Torah alone that swung the final decision against idolatry and in favour of the monotheistic faith. Before expatiating more fully on this theme, however, it is incumbent to dwell somewhat on the clearing of the way for this towering manifesto.

So transcendant a work as the Pentateuch could only have been launched as the culmination of a prolonged literary apprenticeship among the Hebrews. With none other than Moses was the written word first invested with sanctity and utilized as an aid to religious teaching. He went further by requiring the copying out of his ordinances as a means for popularizing his message. "And thou shalt bind them for a sign upon thy hand, and they shall be for frontlets between thine eyes. And thou shalt write them upon the door-posts of thy house, and upon thy gates" (Deuteronomy 6: 8, 9). Can there be any doubt that the existence of some degree of literacy among the contemporaries of the Prophet is here implied?

That the Jewish tradition of literacy also reaches back to the time of Moses may also be inferred. Berthelot has indeed noted the early affinity of the Israelites for the written word.[19] Doubtless their proximity to the Phoenicians was an influence not to be left out of account. The prophetess Deborah, in her song of victory, mentions the tribe of Zebulon as "those who handle the pen of the writer."[20] As the near neighbours of the Sidonians, such specialization might well have been expected of them. And yet they had no monopoly of their art. Gideon, in the course of pursuing his enemies, met up with a youth who was able to write down for him the names of the recalcitrant elders that he had marked out for punitive action. By the time of David, reading if not writing had become commonplace as witness his missive to the unintellectual Joab apropos of getting rid of Uriah.[21] Of the usurper Jehu, we are informed that "he wrote letters."[22]

It would, of course, be unwarrantable to maintain that literacy among the Jews was actually high in Biblical times. Note was taken by the Prophet Isaiah of the separation between those able to read and those who were not.[23] Beyond doubt the former were in the minority, perhaps only a relatively small minority. Yet for that remote period, and by comparison with neighbouring nations, their actual significance could have been considerable. Indirect testimony to the advanced literacy of the Israelites during the monarchical period is also furnished by the fact that among them, as far as we know, stone had ceased to be used for the recording of events. By way of contrast to the famous stone inscription of King Mesha of Moab of the ninth century, neither the kings of Israel nor of Judah chose to memorialize the events of their reigns by this antiquated process. The scribes and recorders whom they employed for this purpose apparently were able to make use of a more sophisticated material on which to record the happenings of their time. We are justified in maintaining that a more adaptible material, either papyrus or the smoothed upper-sides of animal skins, was available to the Israelites in some abundance. Likewise, along with such superior writing materials, the presence in greater numbers of both writers and readers could be inferred.

There is a further point to be noticed. Of great signifi-cance is the fact that, unlike those nations of the Fertile Crescent that swayed the destinies of the world, the Jews were at no time retarded in their cultural development by having to rely on anything resembling the unintelligible styles of writing represented by the hyroglyphics and cuneiform modes of expression. Did Moses himself make use of an alphabetical script? There is no reason to hold that he did not. Authorities on the matter are of the opinion that even before the time of Moses a convenient mode of in-scription had come into vogue in the Sinai peninsula and elsewhere in Western Asia.[24]

The historian Grote has observed that the early Greek inscriptions were rudely and unskilfully executed, and that the ability to decipher their imperfectly shaped lettering called for a laborious discipline.[25] Formation of lettering was highly individualized, punctuation was unknown, as was the leaving of interstices between words. That among the Hebrews the improvement in writing, reading and criti-cism had to follow a similar path could be safely conjec-tured. For example, the barren enumeration of names that found its way into the Pentateuch was a trait common to Greek, Assyrian, and Hebrew composition of the archaic period. Considering the degree of actual physical labor required, it is understandable how all early composition would be excessively curtailed as to matters of substance. Of the literary prophets, Isaiah was the first to write more copiously. In one passage, he also informs us of his intention of gathering into one collection all his writings for the greater convenience of his disciples.[26] There was no shorthand at that time for an oration to be taken down word for word by a listener. In Judaea, as in Greece, a speech had first to be written down by the orator himself, "with a pen of iron and the point of a diamond" (Jeremiah, 17:1). The prophetic harangue, much like the Grecian discourse, having first been inscribed and then recited in public, was only later copied out and passed around.

It seems to me not foreign to our subject to dwell once again on the material on which the Torah was first inscribed, a material which continues to be so used down to this very day. For the writing down of a long dissertation, the celebrated papyrus was not a convenient material.[27]

The maximum length possible for any papyrus scroll was about thirty feet, with a width of no more than ten inches.[28] The Gospel of St. Luke, as well as The Acts of the Apostles, are believed to have been first written on such scrolls.[29] However, the amount of writing contained in the Pentateuch is several times the amount in each of these New Testament books, and could not possibly have been included in a roll of this fragile substance.

Even if it might be too bold an assertion that the Jews were the first to make use of the processed skins of sheep and goats, it is certainly reasonable to suggest that they had a powerful enough incentive to adopt this medium in preference to any other. Unlike the Egyptian product, the skins of domesticated animals did not have to be brought to them from afar. In any event, the utilization of a native product could well have been forced upon them by a disruption in the established trade relationship between Egypt and Palestine brought on by the Assyrian invasions.

No literary creation, other than the Pentateuch, has

ever been known to have taken the form of a double scroll, whether made up of animal skins or any other material. By way of comparison, it is of interest to note that the Fathers of the Church, faced with the similar problem of presenting to the world the voluminous work of the New Testament, adopted in place of the double scroll the modern codex or leaf book, a device undoubtedly invented by the Romans, but certainly popularized under Christian influence.

Such was the Torah's unwieldiness that at the time of its first appearance and for some unstated time thereafter, it was suitable only for being read aloud a little at a time to an assembled group of worshippers. For more convenient handling and reading by devout individuals, it was later subtitled into five books of conventional size and format, since known as Genesis, Exodus, Leviticus, Numbers and Deuteronomy. Collectively, these came also to be referred to as the "Humash" from a root word meaning "five." The equivalent Greek term, Pentateuch, was the invention of the third century Church Father Origen of Alexandria.

The Pentateuch is among other things remarkable as the earliest composition of note in which poetry was abandoned in favour of prose. Throughout the primitive world, poetry was the common cultural denominator. In an age before books were generally known or were common, the role of the poet and balladier was supreme. The story of the going forth from Egypt is believed to have received an epic treatment, traces of which are discernible in chapter thirteen of Exodus.[30] Among the Hebrews, the transition from verse to prose followed a path nearly identical to that among the Greeks. Thucydides was the first to observe and to express emphatically the view that minstrelsy belongs in the realm of the imagination, making it an imperfect medium for conveying the factual.

It is unquestionably true that only through prose composition did history as a record of sober events attain its full maturity. Hardly at all suited to heroic declamation were the peaceful lives of Abraham, Isaac and Jacob. To mention but one example, the bargain entered into between Abraham and Ephron for the transfer of the cave of Machpela could scarcely have been taken as a lyrical event. And yet here and there within the Pentateuch, as indeed elsewhere in the sacred texts, a reversion to the poetical does indeed take over. Such passages, where found, are manifestly the derivation of an earlier age. Even like the Greeks, the Israelites had their "singing men and singing women" (Chronicles 35:27). They intoned their songs of brutality, of strife, and of victory, as for example in the song of Lamech, the triumphant crossing of the Red Sea, and the paean of victory on the capture of Hesbon. Persistent themes for cantillation were the benedictions of dying men, as were lamentations for fallen friends. The Pentateuch marks the onset of a relatively advanced age in which prose had become dominant; but one in which poetic power was not altogether diminished as it was to be later on in the New Testament and the Talmud.

The Assyrian Empire and the Torah

Much more than a culmination of a literary evolution among the Jews, the publication of the Pentateuch was an event rooted in a crisis that threatened to bring their history to an early termination. Its timely arrival was no less a decisive factor for the durability of Judaism than were the Four Evangels for Christianity and the Koran for Islam. The Torah was no haphazard whim of scholarship, but a deeply calculated measure in the face of a gathering storm for the perpetuation of a nation and of its message.

To enlarge our insight into the true origin of the Torah, and its contribution towards the survival of the Jewish people, it is necessary to view its coming in the light of a religious and political crisis of the late Biblical period. That the Torah came upon the scene in the manner in which I shall relate admits of no absolute proof; but I hold it to be a reasonable and probable inference, and one, moreover, that is countenanced by two salient texts. The first of these texts is from the second book of Kings. It is a report of a sensational find in the year 622 B.C., during the reign of King Josiah, the last effective ruler of Judah, and which profoundly shook the entire nation and its leading men.[31] The second is from a discourse of the prophet Jeremiah, a younger contemporary of Josiah, in which there is a reference to the central position which this book had shortly before assumed.[32]

A chain of events that should illumine this fateful period as well as frame it in firmer outline will now be examined. The thread of events that I am about to take up concerns the time when the kingdom of Judah became a client state within the sprawling Assyrian empire; and I make no apology for dwelling upon it at some length. Its really meaningful period when the Assyrians were too close for comfort took in a little over one hundred years, extending from the dissolution of the northern Israelite kingdom in the year 721 B.C. and terminating with the collapse of the Assyrian colossus. For the Jews of that particular century, the submergence of their state and the quashing of their political independence, proved to be the signal for an internal conflict with a resurgent paganism, a conflict sponsored by the pro-Assyrian party within the state.

Among the Semitic nations of the Middle East, the Assyrians were first in military organization, as well as in cruelty and pugnacity. In the very pages of the Torah itself is to be found some confirmation of their seeming invincibility, along with a prediction of their ultimate downfall. "And he looked upon the Kenite and took up his parable

40

and said: Though firm be thy dwelling place, and though thy nest be set in the rock, nevertheless Kain shall be wasted. How long? Asshur shall carry thee away captive. And he took up his parable and said: Alas who shall live after God has appointed him? But ships shall come from the coast of Kittim, and they shall afflict Asshur, and shall afflict Eber, and he also shall come to destruction."[33]

To a land which nature had endowed bountifully the Assyrians owed their preponderant might. Within its original borders were to be found all manner of raw materials requisite to ancient civilization—and for ancient warfare—such as iron, lead, and copper, together with wood for building. The fertile fields of this territory yielded a variety of fruits and crops, not only for the sustenance of the people but for the needs as well of an extended commerce.

Of the overwhelming economic power of the Assyrian country, which was the true basis of its military might, we shall be the more easily convinced if we recall their monopoly of one major article of commerce. This product was petroleum. Its centre of distribution for the entire known world was in all probability Nineveh, a city in the neighbourhood of present day Mosul. Variously referred to as asphalt, tar, bitumen, slime, it was a useful ingredient for such purposes as holding together bricks, for the caulking of boats, for lighting, and for sepulchral purposes. Additionally, it was in demand for medicinal purposes such as curing leprosy, rheumatism, shortness of breath, as well as for driving away snakes.[34] The Greek historian Diodorus wrote of this essential substance, "Whereas many incredible miracles occur in Babylonian country, there is none such as the great quantity of asphalt found there. Indeed, there is so much of it that the people who have gathered there collect large quantities of it."

The overwhelming economic advantages enjoyed by this nation did not in any way incline its rulers to the pursuit of peace. "I conquered the cities. I caused great slaughter. I took their warriors prisoner and impaled them on stakes before their cities" (Ashurnasirpal II). Other warlords of later centuries were not behind in doing likewise what to them came naturally. But nowhere among Crusaders, Mongols, Moslems, Nazis, Communists, can we discover so much candour in the recording of one's own infamies. The hatred aroused by these fantastic slaughterers proved often sufficient to overcome the terror which their savagery inspired. Their extreme brutality and disregard of the well-being of conquered peoples contributed largely to their final downfall.

Never was the tribute which they extorted from the vanquished sufficient to satisfy their avarice. On all the fringes of their empire, the rebellions against their tyrannical exactions were either alternate or simultaneous. For their war machine this entailed a continual marching to and fro over difficult country, equipped for the most part with only primitive arteries of communication. Weariness began to overtake the Assyrians while trying to extend their rule over the Arabs, whose force of camels provided them with the advantage of mobility over desert territory. A long drawn out and inconclusive campaign for the subjugation of Egypt completed their exhaustion.

Prior to the Assyrians, there could be no large-scale empire in the world since no force could hold sway permanently over a widespread territory. Much like those of the Vikings of a later century, the early adventures of the Assyrian kings were restricted to raiding and levying tribute and immediately retiring with their plunder. King Shalmanesser III (858-824) in the course of a long reign made three incursions into the lands of the west, winning victories each time, collecting immense booty, but yet being unable to hold on to the territories that he overran with such ease. Neither he nor his marauding successors were able to break into the fortified cities that stood in their path. Since the time of Solomon, buildings and city walls were to an increasing extent constructed of hewn stone, whose firmness and resistive power was far greater than that which was of unshaped rock. But the defensive advantage enjoyed by little nations was not to last for long.

The Assyrians were the originators of systematic military tactics. To successfully carry out their earlier forays, they invented a way of crossing rivers by means of temporary bridges resting on inflated animal skins. Then, around the beginning of the eighth century, they again revolutionized warfare. They were the first to apply the principle of the battering ram in shattering the walls of besieged cities. By means of sloping ramps of hardened earth and logs, they were able to advance moveable platforms against fortifications on higher ground. King Omri of Israel (890-878 B.C.) when building his new capital of Samaria had considered its protective walls of fifteen feet in thickness to be sufficiently massive. A late successor, Jeroboam II (781-740 B.C.E.), learning of the advance in military science on the part of the Assyrians, found it advisable to double this strength to thirty feet. For the Assyrians to breach this thickened wall and to capture and destroy Samaria no less than three years were required. It was a victory that brought them no gain whatever, and a costly experience whose repetition they henceforth showed some inclination to avoid.

The long drawn out and stubborn defence of Samaria really saved Jerusalem from undergoing a similar trial of strength. Profiting by the delay afforded him, King Hezekiah (726-697 B.C.), an able and energetic ruler, went about placing his city in a good state of defence. "He built up the wall that was broken, and raised it up to the towers, and another wall without, repaired Millo in the city of David, and made darts and shields in abundance."[35] The

Assyrians, on their part, seemed likewise to have learnt a lesson from the protracted resistance offered them by the Israelite city. They were none too eager for another Samaria. The encounter between the military colossus and the small Judaean kingdom resulted in some kind of compromise.

The Judaean king undertook the payment of a tribute which appears to have been not overly excessive. In other respects, his kingdom did not fare too badly. Likewise falling under the encroaching arms of the conqueror were the neighbouring Philistines, Edomites, Moabites and Ammonites, who had been raiding Hebrew territory, and who were from then onward effectively curbed.[36]

The Assyrian warlords, whose eyes were set upon the conquest of Egypt, found it to their advantage to have in their rear a reasonably prosperous and contented Judaean population. Adept as they were in learning about war and its lessons, they made the added discovery that for the carrying out of a distant plan of conquest far from their home centre a more advanced base was essential. Since they had failed to establish control of the sea route, Egypt could be approached not otherwise than by the more arduous land bridge.

Jerusalem was at the heart of a fruitful producing area; and also a transit city between east and west of some importance, more especially so after the elimination of its rival Samaria. For the protracted and difficult campaigns against Egypt that had to be carried out by the last of the Assyrian kings, Esarhaddon (680-668) and Ashurbanipal (668-626 ?), Jerusalem provided a convenient staging post for the assembling of mercenaries that were brought together from far and near. These constituted the bulk of the Assyrian army. Jerusalem was a point of concentration not only for men, but for equipment, food, and supplies. Finally, and by no means least of all, the holy city was recognized as an accessible resort for soldiers on leave, whither they could repair for rest and recreation, gambling and fornicating, as well for worshipping the gods.

Between religion and politics there existed an intimacy that was apparent even in the remotest times. One need not probe very deeply to discover that the pagan world was far from being devoid of religious fanaticism. Ordinarily, a victor in war would leave no means untried to have his gods accepted by the subject population. More especially was it a feature of Assyrian policy to impose the worship of their pantheon on all subject nations.[37] Next only to the payment of the imposed tribute, submission to the Assyrian gods was essential to the physical survival of the conquered. Among these deities, the god Asshur was held by his worshippers to be the true giver of the territories added to their dominions. He it was who had willed world dominion for his people. Hence was it deemed proper that in turn his reign should accompany that of his believers. As regards Sennacherib, to whom King Hezakiah finally made his submission, the records, by way of exception, ascribe to him some indifference to religious observance (Cambridge Ancient History, Vol. III p. 75). It would appear therefore that King Hezekiah's reign to the very end remained free of pagan interference. Both Hezekiah and Sennacherib ending their lives at about the same time, this stage of religious non-interference was brought to a definite close.

Since all disrespect to Asshur and to his satellite deities was to be punished with severity, it is not difficult to imagine a fresh confrontation between the conquerors and the Judaean kingdom, had not the former found a willing enough tool in the new Jewish ruler. It is a reasonable supposition that the grave threat to the survival of the Mosaic religion that welled up during the vassalage of the Jews to the Assyrians was the catalyst which accelerated the writing and publication of the Torah. In this situation the long reign of King Menasseh was in all probability the determining period.

Menasseh ascended the throne on the death of his father, the pious King Hezakiah, in the year 690 B.C. and reigned until 637 B.C., a reign of 53 years that was among the longest in history. Menasseh's grandfather, Ahaz, had been a collaborator of the Assyrians. This newest scion of the House of David considered it wiser to follow the example of his grandfather rather than that of his father. In his eyes, the policy of his father had not been too successful. Even though the capital and heart of the kingdom had escaped destruction, much of the surrounding countryside had been devastated and all but depopulated by the irresistible Assyrian colossus. King Menasseh was determined that, come what may, this was not to happen once again. Yielding in regard to worship to the whim of the suzerain seemed to him a not unreasonable price for an untroubled and prosperous reign. There were among his subjects a great many who thought so as well.

That Menasseh was from the first a fervent and dedicated convert to polytheism, requiring very little prompting on the part of his Assyrian patrons, appears fairly certain. From Assyrian records we also know that he accompanied and aided them in their Egyptian campaigns. Not only did he do homage to the Assyrian gods and stellar deities; but in deference no doubt to the motley throng of mercenary soldiers recruited from many parts of the then known world who were assembled in Jerusalem, he lent an all-embracing patronage to every conceivable heathen god, not omitting the Egyptian favourite, Amon, after whom his own son and successor to the throne was named. The Bible says of him that "he did evil in the sight of the Lord, after the abomination of the heathen" giving as an example the offering of his first born son as a sacrifice to Baal. The highly charged events of his long reign, as conveyed to us in the text, are greatly foreshortened. No more than seventeen verses are devoted to him by the Biblical historian in contrast to the far lengthier accounts which have come down to us of his admired ancestors David and Solomon. And yet sufficient details as to his reign are definitely known to enable us to draw a number of plausible deductions as to things not specifically stated. That his reign, though peaceful as regards external relationships, was marked by tempestuous events from within is expressly indicated. "Moreover Menasseh shed innocent blood very much, till he had filled Jerusalem from one end to another" (2 Kings, 21:16).

It is perhaps disappointing not to be better informed of these great disturbances. Notwithstanding, by a process of logical inference, some reconstruction of this vanished period is altogether feasible. To begin with, the mutinous outbursts that marked the reign of King Menasseh were in all probability political as well as religious. Be it recalled in this connection that, along with their inventiveness in the military sphere, the Assyrian warlords were likewise in advance of their time in their skill at organizing collaborationist cells within those states that had fallen a prey to them.

For a greater insight into the events of the troubled reign of King Menasseh recourse should be had to what the Scripture has to tell us of an earlier tool of the Assyrians, namely King Menahem of Israel (740-737 ?). To release himself momentarily from the pressure of the encroaching Assyrians, he undertook to hand over one thousand talents of silver. "And Menahem exacted the money of Israel, even of all the mighty men of wealth, of each man fifty shekels of silver, to give to the king of Assyria."[38] It is not to be doubted that the demoralization that set in throughout the northern kingdom, and which preceded its final disappearance, was induced primarily by a load of renewable extortion, and its all but inevitably inequitable apportionment

47

among the Israelite population. It is a reasonable enough conjecture that neither in the northern kingdom prior to its dissolution nor in Judaea at the time of king Menasseh did all "the mighty men of wealth" without exception contribute their just share in shouldering the national load. It depended, one may very well suppose, on whose side they happened to be and upon whose favour they depended. The ultimate burden, it may well be assumed, rested on the backs of the common people.

Not unrelated to the foregoing was the matter of war profiteering during the age of king Menasseh. The tribute of gold and silver so ferociously exacted of the people was not long in being put back into circulation by the Assyrian warlords. Much of it had to be doled out to a motley array of hired fighting men. Also, the variety of materials, both raw and fabricated, that was needed for the pursuit of war did not fall too far short of that available for the upkeep of a population at peace. War and revolution, often enough indistinguishable one from the other, have this much in common. Both entail a redistribution of wealth. "Imperialism," much like revolution, impoverishes some members of the state while others it enriches. Since very remote times, warfare has been a bonanza for merchants who knew how to keep armies equipped with all their necessities. Additionally, slaves and other booty taken by a conqueror had of necessity to be converted into hard currency. In the book of Ezekiel do we come across an early recognition of this interdependence of war and commercial enterprise. "Sheba and Dedan and the merchants of Tarshish with all the magnates thereof shall say unto thee, Comest thou to take the spoil? Hast thou assembled thy company to take the prey, to carry away silver and gold, to take away cattle and goods, to take great spoil?"[39]

Merchants from Jerusalem were not absent from the crowd of caterers that followed in the wake of the Assyrian formations and attended to their needs. The new class of army purveyors, whose ostentation and callousness awakened the ire of the prophets Isaiah and Mica, could well have originated during the seige of Samaria, when Jerusalem offered a convenient supply centre for the stalled Assyrian attackers. That King Menasseh was detested by the entire Judaean people was far from being the case. For his physical safety, he was undoubtedly dependent on a body of Assyrian guards. But likewise was he backed by a large pro-Assyrian party drawn from among his own people. This army of collaborators was composed mainly of an enriched mercantile community, for whom the Assyrian presence was highly advantageous. Altogether acceptable to these religiously insensitive men was the remaking of Solomon's temple into a heathen place of worship that duplicated in all respects the fanes of the surrounding nations. All the voices of protest having been muted, the abolition of the Mosaic religion came to be state policy. One could very easily understand that oppressive measures zealously pursued for well over half a century, accompanied no doubt by much destruction of sacred literature, would in the end have brought the Hebrew religion to the verge of extinction, and greatly have reduced the number of its proscribed followers.

We are entitled to read into the terse Biblical account a situation of utmost gravity brought about by the monarch's surrender to Assyrian paganism, as well as the despairing measures that suggested themselves to the faithful remnant of the Mosaic religion. It is a plausible enough deduction that those elements of the population who were revolted by the apostacy of the ruling class would begin to foregather secretly in private dwellings or improvised chapels. The holding of prayer meetings under prophetic guidance may have originated at about that time, if not earlier. From such clandestine assemblies there were to grow to fruition in after years the institutionalized places of worship known to both Jews and Christians.

Suspending for the moment any further observations in regard to the origin of the Torah, I am impelled to enter upon a digression in order to inquire into the origin of the synagogue as well. By so doing, I seek to make clear that almost from the outset Torah and synagogue were interdependent and intertwined. It is my contention that both the one and the other of these converging institutions arose at some time prior to the Babylonian exile, and in response to an identical crisis.

We cannot, of course, be certain of the precise time or even century when the synagogue began to take its present shape, any more than we are to speak with confidence as to the root of other establishments that have long been integrated to our society. Every beginning has its secrecy. Between the undated beginning of a thing and its actual coming of age, the time interlude could be substantial. At the moment when things new in human affairs make their first appearance, it rarely happens that there are acute onlookers present who take it upon themselves to record their immediate headway from the time of their infancy. Thus, there are no documents of any kind that recall to us the time and place when men began to worship in temples, build walled cities, perform ceremonial marriages, or when the first king was crowned and enthroned, or the first parliament convoked. Only as of the time of their relative maturity have we any awakening to previously unmentioned social and political constructions.

Says the Jewish Encyclopaedia (Funk and Wagnalls), "The origin of the synagogue, in which the congregation gathered to worship and to receive religious instruction connected therewith, is wrapped in obscurity. By the time it had become the central institution of Judaism it was already regarded as of ancient origin, dating back to the time of

Moses. The synagogue as a permanent institution originated probably in the period of the Babylonian captivity when a place for common worship and instruction had become necessary." (Vol 11, p. 619.)

I would argue that the thesis of an exilic origin of the synagogue would have to rest upon more solid ground than that advanced by the aforementioned authority. We are assured that it was the deprivation of a spiritual centre, symbolized by Solomon's temple, that created in the minds of the exiles the need for a substitute means of religious devotion. The etiology here is unexceptionable. But no less effectively could it be argued that this very compulsion became operative during the long drawn out reign of King Menasseh, which along with that of his murdered successor covered a period of nearly two generations. During the whole of this interval, the temple of Solomon bore the aspect of a pagan shrine; and could only have become an object of aversion to the pious and stubborn remnant of the monotheistic faith. It is a justifiable enough inference that for those who remained faithful to the Mosaic tradition a substitute for the defiled temple as the one and only hope of preserving religious knowledge would be looked upon as a condition for continued existence.

To assert that the synagogue came into being not otherwise than as a means of filling a sudden chasm resulting from the firing of the temple by the Babylonians is in effect a denial of any evolutionary background and possible stages of growth. Aside from the physical destruction of the Jerusalem temple, there were in fact a number of situations going well back into biblical times that might well have induced pious, though disaffected, individuals to join together unofficially for purposes of prayers, study and discussion.

It can be said with tolerable certainty that even before the time of the idolatrous Menasseh, the temple had ceased to command the deference of many. As far back as the times of David and Solomon, there were devout Israelites who had objected to the replacement of the simple tabernacle by an elaborate and costly edifice in competition with the heathen. Among them was the prophet Nathan, for example. Later on, nourished by the preaching of Amos and some of his followers, there developed a growing alienation from the bloody pomp of animal sacrifice. Hence would it be quite understandable that, since early times, dissidents such as these would have required for themselves quarters where in limited numbers they might assemble in secret. Of the prophet Mohammed it has been said that, early in his career in Mecca, when his life and that of his adherents were in daily jeopardy, he ordered congregational gatherings to be held in private homes.[40] It is a reasonable enough supposition that, during the persecutions instituted by king Menasseh, a similar answer would have been given to and by the faithful. In such clandestine prayer meetings, there might even have been room for anti-monarchical plotters, much like in the Jacobin clubs at the time of the last Bourbons.

In connection with the nascent synagogue, there is yet another matter which ought not to go unnoticed. A secondary impulse for its gradual incubation might have come about in relation with the so-called high places, in which the cult practices of the main sanctuary at Jerusalem were in some degree duplicated. Within the antique world, Jewish no less than pagan, divine worship was long held to be inseparable from the performance of animal sacrifice. Though frequently denounced as strongholds of idolatry, these secondary fanes had been left undisturbed even by earnest and devout kings. For the sake of the rural population as well as for those for whom regular attendance at Jerusalem was an imposition, they had to be tolerated as a practical necessity. The advent of new places of worship in which all cult practices were discarded rendered superfluous the continued existence of these suspected sanctuaries.

By its elimination of animal sacrifices and the introduction in their place of readings from the sacred writings, a new focus was given to Judaism by the synagogue. Within these popular assemblies, any Jewish man was entitled to conduct the reading, and if sufficiently articulate, to address his companions in the faith on matters both religious and political. And yet at no time did the synagogue actually disown the temple, even though the one was destined finally to supplant the other. Testifying to their underlying harmony was the later presence of the ark as part of the synagogue structure, in which to this day have been kept the scrolls of the Torah, in recollection beyond doubt of the vanished Ark of the Covenant.

Essentially a lay institution, the synagogue was the first of its kind in all religious and political history. Moreover, it could never have been fitted into the life of the nation were it not for the prior creation of a weekly day of rest, for not otherwise would any attendance of the common people have been possible. Through the synagogue, Judaism was forever freed from its nexus to a fixed political territory. By their very nature, such places of worship being adaptable to any land or city, it would not be rash to suggest that, their roots having first been planted in the land of Judah itself, they were sufficiently advanced in their growth to swiftly fill in the void left open by the loss of Solomon's temple. This was made all the more realizable by the fact that the Babylonian exile, be it recalled, came actually in two stages. Preceding the main exile in 586 B.C. was a preliminary deportation of the population in 597 B.C. Hence in our reconstruction of this epoch, some degree of orderliness can be seen to have accompanied the transplanting of the people along with its possessions, both material and spiritual.

In this time of uprooting, a scattering of independent

congregations was responsible for rescuing for posterity many, if not all, the sacred writings; and in very much the same way as were the apostolic collections of Christendom preserved during the turbulence of the Dark Ages by the churches and monasteries. It was within these non-priestly meeting houses that various writings, including those of the prophets, had been declaimed, pored over, and copied. Intoned as well were many of the psalms, these in later times to form the nucleus of the prayer book as evolved over the centuries.

Of only modest dimensions, and attended for the most part by the humbler elements of the Judaean population, the primitive synagogues were unlikely to attract much attention from annalists, intent mainly on the doings of kings and prophets. In their physical proportions, they were not among the architectural glories. They were in all likelihood comparable to those ancient prayer houses that one sees nowadays in the town of Safed in present day Israel. The ancient Dura-Europos synagogue unearthed not long ago on the bank of the Euphrates River is said to have looked much like a private home. In all probability, such were the synagogues of New Testament times. A tendency towards more pretentious edifices manifested themselves in a later period, and more especially so following the destruction of the second temple. One example of a more impressive structure now known to us was the synagogue of Capernaum, the ruins of which are presently in the care of the Franciscan brethren. Measuring some fifty by eighty feet, it corresponded approximately to one fifth the area of the famous temple of Diana, at Ephesus.

The use of the synagogue as a forum for the early propagation of Christianity is affirmed in the New Testament. By the time of the apostle Paul, the pre-eminence of the synagogue in Judaism was unquestioned. The books of the New Testament are replete with instances of Paul going from one synagogue to another within the Grecian world, proclaiming his new doctrine to mixed audiences of Jewish worshippers and their Greek neighbours who were regular attendants.[41]

By way of contrast to the New Testament, allusions to the synagogue to be found in the pages of the Old are scanty and somewhat dubious. There is indeed a passage in Jeremiah that speaks of the demolition by Nebuchadnezzar of the temple, the royal palace, and "the houses of the people" (batei' am). Some commentators hold this latter designation as referring to places of popular worship, re-calling that in after times these conventicles were indeed commonly referred to as "houses of the people." This may well have been the case; and yet the more literal meaning of the text suggesting "the dwellings of the people" cannot be dismissed. A less ambiguous mention is that to be found in psalm 74, which, read in its entirety, could be taken as descriptive of the havoc and disaster that accompanied the sacking of Jerusalem by the victorious Babylonians. There it stands written, in the King James translation, "They have burned up all the synagogues of God in the land" (verse 8). In another English version of the same text, namely that of the Jewish Publication Society of America, the original Hebrew "moadei el" is rendered as "meeting places of God."

The Torah

The idolatrous element among the Jews having long had their day, something was needed to turn back the tide in favour of the monotheistic faith. On the verge of despair, the adherents of Judaism sought for an answer. They found such an answer in a much-laboured-upon and freshly disclosed compilation, namely the Pentateuch. Dramatically revealed, its entrance marked an occasion both opportune and momentous. "On a modern view, the Pentateuch covers the close of one chapter of religion and history and the beginning of another, the break-up of one era and the dawn of a second."[42]

The time depth of this book may the more easily be gauged by viewing it as the inseparable companion of the synagogue, each being complementary of the other. On the one hand, the mere physical aura of the new double scroll, and the labour required for its reproduction, was such that were there not a suitable place for its reception already in existence, its effect on the hearts and minds of the Judaean populace would have remained minimal. As for the synagogue, its effectiveness too would have remained small, were it not for being appointed guardian of this new spiritual treasure, and the forum par excellence for its reading and interpretation to a wide circle of worshippers.

The restoration of the Mosaic faith after the long night of its discontinuance is not, however, to be inferred from theory alone. Pertinent to the Torah's first appearance are two passages to be found elsewhere in the Old Testament. The first and the more significant of these texts is contained in the second book of Kings, in which we are informed that in the eighteenth year of the reign of King Josiah, that is to say in the year 622 B.C.E., a "book of the law" came to light within the precincts of the Temple, and that both among members of the court and the population, a great furor was engendered by this find.[43]

An echo of this discovery is found in a discourse of the prophet Jeremiah, who some years later, after the passing of Josiah, reproaches the people for the non-observance of the precepts of this same book. "How do ye say 'We are wise and the law of the Lord is with us?' Lo, certainly in vain hath wrought the vain pen of the scribes. The wise men are ashamed, they are dismayed and taken: Lo they have rejected the Lord; and what wisdom is in them?".[44]

The authenticity of these texts has at no time been called into question. And yet many authorities have denied that the Torah thus referred to in these memorials of some twenty-six centuries ago is identical with the Pentateuch as we know it today, even though its essential unchangeability for at least 2,400 years is acknowledged none the less. In a later chapter, it is my intention to deal more fully with the claim that the volume brought to light in the reign of King Josiah was in fact nothing more than the book of Deuteronomy and that the completed Pentateuch itself, as we know it, came only two centuries later. But the mere restatement of the law of Moses, which is all that is meant by the word "Deuteronomy," would of itself have been no earthshaking event, as I shall later point out. It is my contention that the document brought to light within the temple during the reign of Josiah was an elaborate work, anonymously compiled by a consortium of priests and prophets, and presented as the work of the revered Moses for the purpose of insuring its acceptance by a historically naive public. This book, which according to the prophet Jeremiah was immediately reproduced and propounded, was none other than the full Pentateuch.

Unlike the terse and laconic inscriptions, previously known and which had long since ceased to be evocative of extraordinary attention, here was a formidable scroll, wound not around the familiar single staff, but around two staffs in the form of a double scroll. Nowhere in the ancient world had such a device ever been previously noted. Its very appearance fired the imagination of all beholders. Had it been shown at the time at Nineveh or Babylon or any of the sophisticated capitals of the Fertile Crescent, there too its advent would have created a sensation, if only by reason of its unusual format.

Altogether credible is the report of the heightened tension that followed on the heels of its disclosure, and the onslaught on the intrenched paganism which it immediately catapulted. To this fresh direction, the young monarch, a son and grandson of apostates, instantly gave the stamp of his approval and authority. For an entire nation, about to free itself from the hated Assyrian yoke, a source of renewed spiritual vigor was now visible. Written in a style and language that was at once fluent, vivid, and popular, the new spiritual treasure revealed with confidence the design and purpose of the God of Israel, in creating first the world, and then the Hebrew nation.

The Torah, which in translation has been inaccurately designated "the book of the law," consists of matters other than law. A mere tabulation of ordinances in the manner of Lycurgus or Solon, or even a fresh manual of moral precepts, would have generated among the people no exceptional response. In laws alone no nation has ever yet discovered a means of solace and gratification, no matter how just and proper such laws might have been deemed, and how superior to those of other nations. For his laws to have acquired the force of respect and authority, Moses the lawgiver had to be celebrated likewise as Moses the national leader and Moses the deliverer. Unaccompanied by a tradition of unique national greatness, laws are not likely to win for themselves much fervent support. What a sorely tried and beleaguered nation now behold in all its fulness was not only a crystallization of all the enactments attributed to the venerated personality of Moses, but a flattering account likewise of the giant figures of their early history, along with a promise of a benign destiny for their descendants. For a generation, standing at the parting of the ways, the chal-

58

lenge which now presented itself was one emanating from the Pentateuch in its entirety and in all its amplitude, and not from a mere fragment thereof.

Such was the mood of excitement called forth by these tidings that we are told of the entire nation being summoned into one place to be informed of its new destiny. "And the king went up to the house of the Lord and all the men of Judah and all the inhabitants of Jerusalem with him—and all the people stood by the covenant."[45] Be it observed that neither debate, discussion, nor dissent is here indicated. In this proceeding, a parallel with that of Athens and republican Rome deserves to be noted. In these latter cities, on the occasion of some momentous innovation about to be embarked upon, the entire population would be called together in open air assembly solely for the purpose of approving by acclamation a decision already taken by those in authority. In the semi-democratic republics of Renaissance Italy, such ratifications were known as Parliamenti.

The Pentateuch is here and there a mirror of events and ideas contemporaneous with the time of its authorship, or the times immediately preceding its authorship. Many of its passages, if examined closely enough, should assist us in determining the time of its arrival. Proof of its authorship not later than the time of the Judaean monarchy is furnished to us by a number of passages relating to kingship. "And it shall be when he sitteth upon his throne that he shall write him a copy of this law in a book out of that which is before the priests and Levites. And it shall be with him, and he shall read therein all the days of his life" (Deuteronomy, 17: 18, 19). An admonition of this kind would have been utterly wasted on the idolatrous Menasseh or his equally idolatrous son Amon. But it accords well with the high hopes entertained of the youthful Josiah. In yet another verse, the new king is warned that, since he is no longer

59

under the tutelage of Assyria, he depart from the improprieties of some of his ancestors. "Neither shall he multiply horses unto himself—Neither shall he multiply wives to himself—neither shall he greatly multiply to himself silver and gold."[46]

It is natural enough that within a book of such sweep and magnitude, and more appropriately at its closing, there be found, disguised in ancient oracular form, some foreboding of approaching evil, along with the promise of final deliverance. Since the time of the earlier destruction of the sister kingdom and the exile of its inhabitants, warnings of a similar fate for Jerusalem and its inhabitants had become insistent. Now a voice purporting to have come out of the remote past was meant to be taken as a confirmation of the gloomy anticipations of contemporary prophecies.

The powerful and sublime maledictions, supposedly uttered by Moses in the closing portion of the Torah, undoubtedly bear some relationship to the woes which had already stifled one section of the house of Israel. Verses 20-27 of the twenty-ninth chapter of Deuteronomy are to be seen as a lament over the fate of Samaria, and the terrible consummation of the northern kingdom. Increasingly apparent, by that time, was the failure of the national life, along with the fading out of the promise into defeat and exile. These laments and exhortations could only have been the contribution of some unknown successor of Isaiah. That Moses, in his time, could have had some forebodings as to his nation's future is believable enough. But more than likely, his main preoccupation, at the close of his life, was with the coming victories of his followers, and not with their ultimate discomfiture many hundreds of years later. Fulminations and threats about their future sinfulness and the stressing of ruin and damnation would at the time of Moses and Joshua have added little to the morale of a small people about to engage itself in a struggle against overwhelming odds. The imprecations so energetically voiced in the concluding part of the Pentateuch, no matter by whom uttered, would seem to fit well into the doleful portents that were current in the late Biblical period.

In the opening chapters of Genesis, no less than in those of the concluding book of Deuteronomy, is the imprint of Assyria upon the Jews clearly manifest. Obviously drawn from Assyro-Babylonian mythology is the story of Noah and the flood, as is part of the creation story itself, as well as the goings on in the garden of Eden. As a further clue for pointing out the time and circumstances of its creation, I am prompted to inquire into the extent of geographical knowledge evinced in the Pentateuch. From a reading of the tenth chapter of Genesis and its survey of the peoples, it becomes evident that such knowledge of the outer world, though anything but global, embraced a fairly extensive area of western Asia, northern Africa, and southern Europe, a knowledge certainly much wider than that which must have been current among the Greeks of the Homeric Age. To the author of the Iliad and the Odyssey, Egypt, for example, was but a name for an utterly remote and inaccessible territory.

Crowning this line of investigation, some comparison between Genesis and other of the Hebrew scriptures is informative likewise. About "the nations divided in their lands" (Genesis 10: 5) the writings of the prophet Isaiah show no more than a meagre knowledge (e.g., 11: 11). Isaiah's ministry confined as it was to an earlier stage of the Assyrian hegemony, his world in the direction of the rising sun extended no farther than the Zagreb mountains. Beyond Elam lay the land of the Medes; but of this latter country, Isaiah apparently knew nothing. Known to him were "the islands of the sea," but probably neither mainland Greece nor the coastal lands of Asia Minor; and certainly not the land of the Scythians to the north of the Black Sea

(Ashkenaz). Not having heard of such colonies of the Phoenicians as Carthage and Utica, planted but a few years before his time, he was naturally oblivious of the fact that "afterwards were the families of the Canaanites spread abroad."[47]

Going yet a step farther in the making of comparisons, we observe a substantial measure of concordance between the geographical knowledge contained in Genesis 10 and that exhibited by the prophet Ezekiel, with one significant difference, however. In the account of the nations to be found in Genesis 10, there is a mention of the Medes, whose territory was adjacent to that of the Assyrian empire, but beyond its actual confines. But of the Persians, a nation originally distinct from the Medes, and whose country was still farther to the east, there is no reference whatsoever in Genesis. Ezekiel, on the other hand, a prophet of exilic times, and the first Hebrew writer to do so, speaks of the Persians on two occasions.[48]

To generalize on this matter, the knowledge of the earth's inhabitants as exhibited in the tenth chapter of Genesis accords rather well with that expected to be within the ken of persons residing within the confines of the world's first great empire. This catalogue of lands, provinces, and cities comprises the territorial acquisitions of the Assyrian conquerors, along with those territories lying not too far beyond its confines in the several directions of the compass. "Under the common overlordship of Assyria, the lesser and less ambitious states were brought into close contact with one another."[49]

The Assyrian period was clearly for the Jews one of unprecedented international contacts. The armies of Esarhaddon and Asshurbanipal campaigning in Egypt comprised numerous recruits from many countries both far and near. Fighting men were assembled out of Asia Minor, the Aegean Islands, mainland Greece, Crete and

Arabia. As in the case of the Carthaginians of a later time, it was a precautionary measure on the part of the Assyrian warlords to hire soldiers from diverse countries, mercenaries who would possess neither the ability nor the temptation to form a common front against their employers. To the curious inhabitants of Jerusalem, these newcomers could well have brought with them a knowledge of distant lands previously unknown to their hosts. The earlier dwellers in Jerusalem had known of no western nation other than the Egyptian. Brought into close contact with other westerners coming from out of the north, they were struck by their superior height, physique and deportment. Be it here noted that the name Japhet derives from a Hebrew word meaning "handsome." "God will enlarge Japhet, and he will dwell in the tents of Shem."[50] As early as the time of King Sennacherib, the martial sons of Japhet had been very much at home "in the tents of Shem." As predicted, Japhet, in the course of succeeding ages, did indeed become greatly "enlarged." Before long, his sons were admitted into "the tents of Ham" likewise. The army of Pharaoh Necho, which at the battle of Megiddo routed the untrained army of King Josiah, was made up almost entirely of Grecian professionals.

Of the many locations obliquely touched upon in the tenth chapter of Genesis, the greater number were only faintly known to its authors, and hardly more so than by name. A more intimate knowledge is revealed however as regards both Assyria and its main antagonist Egypt. Preponderant attention is given to Assyria, its capital Asshur, as well as to others of its major cities. Acknowledged likewise are the early rudiments of this empire and its rise to greatness. "And the beginning of his kingdom was Babel and Erech and Accad and Calneh in the land of Shinar. Out of that land went forth Asshur and builded Nineveh and Calah, the same is a great city."[51] Duly noted is the Assyrian fondness for the chase. "And Cush begat Nimrod. He began to be a mighty one in the earth. He was a mighty hunter before the Lord."

In the muster of eastern cities, a more distinct reference is made to the most lustrous of them all. Babylon, throughout the Assyrian period, was by far the world's outstanding metropolis, as well as being noted for its ziggurat, the Etemanaki, known also as the Tower of Babel. It was the unhallowed rearing up of this tallest of all buildings of remote antiquity that was supposed to have occasioned the linguistic separation of mankind. Suggestive also of this belief was the actual diversification of tongues to be heard within this melting pot of the nations, where were congregated the traffickers of many countries. But Babylon's glory was not to endure forever. By the time of Ezra in the late Persian period, Babylon was no longer a city of much note and was well on the road to extinction.

In the Pentateuchal survey of lands and nations, some stressing of Egypt is to be expected likewise; all the more so since a Judaean army is known to have accompanied Esarhaddon's expedition into that country. Cognizance is indeed taken of that country's subdivisions along with territories adjacent to it. Listed are the Nile delta (Naphtuhim), upper Egypt (Pathrusim), Casluhim (?) "whence came forth the Philistines." Not omitted are Lehabim (Libia), Put (Cyrene), Cush (Sudan), and more distantly Caphtorim (Crete).

Before taking leave of my thesis that the entrance of the Torah is to be fitted into the framework of a specified turn of events in the fortunes of the Jewish people, one final observation enforces itself. The authors of the Torah, having advanced the belief that the primal unity of mankind had been suddenly and catastrophically shattered, proceeded to a listing of the successor nations and, naturally enough, in order of their own predilections. Noah, the secondary progenitor of the race, is the father of three sons—mention of Noah's wife, an equally pivotal personage, is for some reason omitted. Each of these sons became allegorically the father of a distinct family of nations. Shem, the assigned ancestor of the Hebrews, is the first born and obviously the chosen one. Least favoured is the youngest Ham; while in between, in order of preference and affection, stands the unoffending Japhet.

Now it is a known fact that in every capital city throughout the world at the present day, and in every one of its chancellories, there is to be found a listing of foreign nations in accordance with a threefold division. Some are classed as friendly, others as hostile, while a third knot are recognized as neither friendly nor otherwise, but neutral. Whether in peace or war, every nation thus estimates its fellow nations in all parts of the world. Now is it not reasonable to suppose that the Jews, while in the embrace of a vast empire and thereby made newly cognizant of many far-flung nations, would be disposed to view them all according to this same threefold differentiation?

The survey in the tenth chapter of Genesis opens with the family tree of Japhet. Consistently enough, Japhet is the forefather of a group of peoples with whom, by reason of their remoteness, the Jews of that time had no relations of any kind, whether amicable nor otherwise. Following these are next taken up the descendants of the ill-omened Ham. Here too there emerges a fairly uniform attitude on the part of the Jewish writers.

The enemies of the Jews, both contemporary and of the immediate past, are here detailed—the Canaanites, the Philistines, the Assyrians, and the Egyptians. A question here arises as to why a remote nation such as Cush should be bracketed along with those with whom Israel had come into conflict. The fact must be acknowledged that the Jews of old were not blind to the invidious distinctions of colour,

65

and not free of what is nowadays referred to as racialism. The term "Ham," be it noted, is revealing. It derives from a root word meaning alternatively "hot" or "brown." Those living in hot countries are automatically taken to be of a brownish texture. Hence were such inhabitants numbered among those to whom the Jews were averse, if only to a mild extent. "And the sons of Cush: Seba and Havila and Sabta, and Raamah and Sabetca; and the sons of Raamah, Shelba and Dedan." According to Hertz, all these tribal names denoted places on the east African coast or on the opposite shore of Arabia.[52] Finally, as regards the preferred Shem, "the father of all the children of Eber," a lack of balance does seem to emerge. In the eyes of their Jewish contemporaries, few indeed of these "children" would have been deemed worthy of most-favoured-nation treatment. But here too, a common tie with the Jews is brought out none the less. It is that of language. It was during the imperial period that the Jews became aware of a diffusion over a vast area of the Middle East of a host of languages cognate to their own, and of the more intimate cultural relationships between them. From this category Asshur, even though already ranged under Israel's foes (verses 8-11), could not be excluded. Such, moreover, was the augmented image of Asshur that to have included this power simultaneously under both sons seemed not unnatural.

CHAPTER III
THE BOOK AND ITS CRITICS

My present task is to consider a well-entrenched thesis on the origin of the Pentateuch; and one that is at variance with that which I have adopted in the preceding chapter. I now touch upon what is known as the Higher Criticism of the Old Testament, represented by a body of intellectuals whose debates have covered a span of over two centuries, reaching back to a time when assaults on things sacred first became permissible. The quintessence of this higher criticism—as distinguished from that of "lower" criticism presumably—is that nothing contained in the Old Testament, and more especially the Torah, is actually what it purports to be; and that invariably, the truth is other than that which is plainly recorded. But inasmuch as these critics have failed to form anything resembling a common front, any summarization of their opinions presents us with an almost unsurmountable difficulty. Among these "schools" there has gone on what might well be described as a struggle for survival, accompanied by some degree of vehemence and contention.

In this struggle, the palm of victory seems at length to

have rested with what has been known as the documentary or Graff-Wellhausen theory. "The delay in the triumph of the Grafian criticism was due partly to the hostility of Ewald and his school; but in large part to the development of his theory by Vatke on a priori grounding in accordance with Hegel's philosophy of history. It is only after a fresh and keener observation of fact that the new theory made rapid progress."[1] Other encyclopaedists have been less sanguine as to this "rapid progress." Says Chamber's Encyclopaedia (Vol. 10, p. 542), "The documentary theory of the main sources of 'J,' 'E,' 'P,' 'D' and their relative dates cannot be regarded as adequate to explain the numerous and striking indications of diversity of authorship, milieu and date; but it marked an important stage in biblical criticism and no other theory has yet been generally accepted." The New Catholic Encyclopaedia has likewise commented that "later scholarship has considerably modified the documentary theory."[2]

The examination of the Wellhausen theory, which to this very day has a respectable following, deserves to be carried out as objectively and as cold-bloodedly as possible. But since scholars, no matter how eminent, are as prone to bias as the rest of us, it would be blindness to leave entirely out of account their known aversions and antipathies. Wellhausen was not immune to the scholarly anti-Judaism that took hold in Germany during the closing decades of the nineteenth century.

The mediaeval Church had inculcated hatred of the Jews, while at the same time holding their scriptures in reverence. But the seventh decade of the nineteenth century witnessed the birth of a somewhat revised form of anti-Jewishness, pedantically known as antisemitism. Under the impact of an aggressive scholarship, a scorning of Jewish antiquity now took over. It was featured by an attempt to depict the Biblical antecedents of the contemporary Jew in a demeaning and even ridiculous light. The early Hebrews, a bellicose and despised tribe of barbarians, living in abject dread of their storm god Jehovah, pressed further and further into Canaan. In the end they appropriated unto themselves the god Baal, eventually synchronizing his essence with that of their own monstrous storm god. There was never such a person as Moses, while the story of the Israelite sojourn in Egypt was pure invention. Additionally, all the Jewish heroes, from Abraham down to Solomon, were nothing but humanized deities or mythological figures. Abraham and Sarah, Isaac and Rebeccah, Esau and Jacob, Joseph and Asenath were each and everyone of them nothing but personifications of gods such as Ra, and Hathor, and Thoth. Closely allied to the new antisemitism, much of this higher criticism was actually synonymous with higher anti-Judaism.[3]

Wellhausen himself, after spending many years in studying the Hebrew scriptures, was able to arrive at no other conclusion than that they were basically deceptive, and their ethical message largely spurious. In a concluding chapter entitled "Judaism and Christianity," he thus sums up the Hebraic contribution, "We meet with a pedantic ascetism which is far from lovely, and with pious wishes the greediness of which is concealed; and these unedifying features are the dominant ones of the system. . . . The ideal is a negative one, to keep oneself free from sin, not a positive one to do good upon the earth. The morality is one which scarcely requires for its exercise the existence of fellow-creatures. . . . Monotheism is worked out to its fullest consequence, and at the same time is enlisted in the service of the narrowest selfishness."[4]

That many Christian scholars of recent decades have entertained so low an opinion of a religion from which their own faith is derived seems altogether unlikely. None the less, among them, as among a great many Jews, the impression still persists that the Wellhausen and Graff analysis of the Torah into four identifiable sources of origin is still to be regarded as intellectually "orthodox." This judgment, for reasons which I shall now indicate, I consider to be faulty.

The Documentary theory, otherwise known as the Graff-Wellhausen, from the names of its most eminent exponents, is in large measure an extension on the findings of certain of their predecessors. It asserts that the Pentateuch, as we now have it, is susceptible of being analyzed into four distinct components. The first and earliest, supposedly a product of the kingdom of Judah of the ninth century before the common era, is designated, in the absence of any known name, by the letter "J" which stands for "Jehovist." It attaches itself to the belief that, throughout this literary fragment, the name for God was repeatedly given as Jehovah, to the exclusion of any other. Again correlating to the preceding is the second ingredient, designated as "Elohist" or by the letter "E," which stands for the consistent use of Elohim as the divine name. This fragment in its turn is attributed to the northern kingdom of the eighth century. The third ingredient is that portion corresponding to the book of Deuteronomy, whose discovery within the temple precincts in the year 622 B.C. is viewed as episodal and as a turning point. Coming forth and last is "P," which stands for Priests' Code, embracing all that is written in regard to temple ritual, the priesthood, and the festivals. The creation of this last component is in the post-exilic period, and is attributed to Ezra the scribe. It thus follows that the Pentateuch in its completed form, in contradiction to what I have attempted to prove, could only have originated in the time of Ezra or perhaps even later, and certainly not during the period of the monarchy.

It will be seen that the four components of the Pentateuch are here divided neatly by centuries, the first three

70

being placed in the ninth, eighth and seventh respectively, that is to say prior to the exile.[5] Be it observed that the documentary theory refrains from offering any explanation as to why it was that "J" and "E," having been early fused into "JE" and then followed at no great interval by "D" (for Deuteronomy), the appearance of the Torah itself in its full maturity had to be postponed for no less than two hundred years thereafter. To be sure, according to the theory under discussion, the Priests' Code had yet to come along. But then for the mere writing down of the rules concerning the sacrificial cult, the priesthood, the festivals and the Sabbath, was it necessary for all that time to have elapsed?

The distinction between "J" and "E" as denoting two primary documents, originating one in the southern kingdom of Judah and the other in the northern kingdom of the Ten Tribes, and distinguishable from each other mainly by a variation of the divine name, has permeated the thinking of several generations of scholars down to this very day. It is certainly easy enough to concede that at one time there were current among the Israelite tribes dwelling in different parts of Palestine more than one account of the same ancestral events. It would be entirely credible if we were informed that of Abraham or Joseph there were as many as four varying accounts in circulation, in much the same way as in the New Testament there has been incorporated four gospels, each portraying the life of Jesus, but differing somewhat in details. But what is much harder to accept as probable is that in one part of the land of the Hebrews, depending on its political separateness, there were writers who by design restricted themselves, in referring to the God of their fathers, to one name and to one name alone, while at the same time, in another part of the Hebrew-speaking world, care was taken to designate the same ancestral deity by a different name.

The Hebrews of the northern kingdom and those of the southern were as much one nation as the Athenians and the Thebans were one nation. To the extent that the inhabitants of both regions remained faithful to the religion of Moses, they continued to worship the same God, though referring to Him poetically by several different names. We find a confirmation of this in the Psalms, many if not most of them written prior to the division of the monarchy. By way of example, I quote one of the Psalms entitled "A psalm of David when he fled from Absalom his son" (Number 3, King James translation): "Lord (Jehovah in Hebrew) how are they increased that trouble me. Many are they that rise against me. Many there be which say of my soul. There is no help for him in God (Elohim in Hebrew) Selah. —Arise, o Lord (Jehovah) save me, o my God (Eloha in Hebrew)." The Hebrew monarchy having been divided in two, there was no likely agreement, tacit or expressed, that from then on the Creator was to be known by one name in the north and another in the south. To imagine such a thing would be no less preposterous than to suppose that on the division of Charlemagne's empire by the treaty of Verdun in the year 843, there was an understanding that from then on the founder of Christianity was to be called Jesus in France and that in Germany he was to be known only as Christ.

Undue significance has been made to attach to the use of one or the other of God's names. In religious writings such as are known at the present time, these names are used indiscriminately, and often in the same sentence. It is extravagant to assume, without proof of any kind, that in the early forgotten texts the fashion was otherwise. In Hebrew, as in English or any other language, it would be natural for a religious writer, and more especially for one accustomed to using poetry as his vehicle of expression, to vary his style and manner of presentation by alternately using every divine appellation known to him. The proposed tracing back to sources as to which there is no fixed knowledge is a most idle form of scholarship. It may on occasion be a worthy intellectual exercise to link that which has been written in some well-known book with material to be found in some earlier document, but only as long as that earlier document is still available for being consulted. When such a document no longer is to be found, or might never have existed, then such a literary adventure becomes futile beyond measure.

The preoccupation of the Higher Critics with their unverified preconceptions to the exclusion of all background conditioning is well illustrated by their schematic and even-handed allocation of their putative sources between the two Hebrew kingdoms. The Hegelian interpretation of all historical happenings, with its insistence on a balance of thesis and antithesis, would hardly have had it otherwise. None the less, the question could be raised as to whether the religious climate within the half-paganized northern kingdom was at any time suitable for the production of a literature based on the Mosaic faith, be it "J" or "E" or "D" or "P" or any other. "All knowledge of the law was forgotten until 621 B.C.E. when the Law was rediscovered."[6] As to the time and circumstances of such forgetfulness, some distinction must be drawn notwithstanding. Of the northern kingdom it was certainly truer than of Judah.

As regards the northern kingdom, the alienation of its inhabitants from the sanctuary at Jerusalem was purposely instituted by Jeroboam I when he first set up his separatist state. To all the succeeding royal dynasties of this kingdom, Jerusalem was no Holy City. It was an alien city to which neither visits nor pilgrimages were to be encouraged. And yet, nowhere but in the Jerusalem temple were there likely to be found a preservation of records from the time of Moses, on the basis of which further scriptural writings could have been created. It was in Jerusalem mainly that the Mosaic traditions were imparted, irregularly no doubt, to assemblages of the people; or else in the Judaean country-side by itinerant priests and Levites. These same priests and Levites, be it recalled, had from the very start been expelled from the seceding Israelite kingdom. During the gloomy and disastrous centuries that followed the division of the Hebrew commonwealth, it is abundantly clear that as regards the preservation of the rules and statutes of the Mosaic faith not much in the way of spiritual communication remained.

In accordance with the Wellhausen interpretation of challenge, response, and final synthesis, the two disparate versions of "J" and "E" were supposedly fused into a sublimated version designated as "JE." This later operation is said to have taken place sometime after the year 722 B.C.E., that is to say, following the ruin of the northern kingdom. In "JE" for the first time, the two principal and significant names for the Divine presence came to be employed indiscriminately. It was in the surviving southern kingdom, presumably at Jerusalem, that this synthesis is supposed to have been consummated.

To a non-dialectical observer a serious obstacle in the way of credulity here emerges. To Judaean compilers is attributed the reconciliation of these hitherto conflicting texts, the Jehovist and the Elohist. But to these supposed conciliators, the name "Jehovah" had of old alone been acceptable as the proper appellation of the divine being. What could now have induced these authors to abandon their one-sidedness for no other reason than that of accommodating a terminology which in their minds had long been associated with the sinful men of the north? Again, these pious and self-sufficient Judaean expositors of the words of Moses were already in possession of their own version of creation, of the fall of man, of the flood, of the lives of the patriarchs, and the going forth from Egypt. In this primary and forgotten text, we are asked to believe that

74

the heavenly Father had for long been referred to by one name exclusively. Are we to imagine that it suddenly entered the minds of these mentors of the Jews to deliberately discard, if not to actually destroy, all existing versions of the sacred writings long in their possession for no other purpose than that of belatedly changing over from Jehovah alone to Jehovah plus Elohim?

Pentateuch or Deuteronomy?

All are agreed that the coming to light of a "book of the law" within the precincts of the Jerusalem, as mentioned in the twenty-second chapter of the second book of Kings, was a momentous event, and marked a turning point in the destinies of the ancient Jews. It is only as regards the substance of this find that disagreement enters. Following in the footsteps of nineteenth century Bible reconstructionists, a respectable body of opinion, both Jewish and Christian, has assented to the belief that the document referred to in this celebrated passage was none other than the book of Deuteronomy, and not the full scroll of the Pentateuch, as I have maintained in the preceding chapter. Against this selection in favour of "D," it is now my intention to offer some arguments as they occur to me.

The unfaltering assertion that the discovery inside the temple premises, so rapturously acclaimed, related to Deuteronomy only, or, in the opinion of some, to the "nucleus of Deuteronomy," is patently at variance with the matter-of-fact reading of the Biblical text itself. It would seem to be a safe enough rule that in cases where no improbability is involved, a plain meaning ought to be favoured rather than one based on a forced exegesis. This is not always admitted, unfortunately. Thus are we told that "it is the consensus of conventional scholarly opinion that

Josiah's scroll was a composition of his reign and resembled Deuteronomy, though it was not co-extensive with Deuteronomy. Scholars call that hypothetical document 'D' (standing for Deuteronomic code). And while no two scholars agree exactly what it includes and excludes, virtually all scholars agree on its actuality."[7] It would thus appear that among these critics the only matter actually agreed upon is that something or other was found in the temple during Josiah's reign; but that this something called in translation "the book of the law" was not the Torah, despite its being called that in the Hebrew original. It should be conceded in this connection that in Jewish lore the word "Torah" is indeed subject to some ambiguity. Quite often it has been applied loosely as taking in all Jewish learning. But used in a more defined sense, it applies to a specified literary creation. This much is certain: At no time has the term "Torah" been applied so restrictively as to refer to one alone among the Five Books of Moses, standing in isolation from the others.

It is interesting to note that in connection with a predecessor of King Josiah, there is to be found one other reference to a "book of the Torah." It is to be found in the same second book of Kings.[8] Again, three other such citations occur in the book of Joshua.[9] How are we to take this? To begin with, all six of the so-called early prophetic books extending from Joshua to second Kings are generally conceded to be organically a single book and to have been edited at the same time. At the very least, the four books comprising Samuel one and two, and Kings one and two, are known to have been a single undivided composition originally.[10] Nor is there much room for disagreement as to the time of this later composition. It could not have been put into its completed form prior to the destruction of Solomon's temple nor, on the other hand, much later than the time of the death of King Jehoiachin, whose rehabilitation is its last reported event. The Book of Joshua-Kings was written, in all likelihood, prior to the fall of the Babylonian empire, a paramount event to which it would otherwise have referred.

Now to come to the point of my argument. We find in what is actually a single literary production as many as five distinct references to an earlier work, namely the "Book of the Torah." Always bearing in mind that to the author of Joshua-Kings its Mosaic authorship is taken for granted, the "Book of the Torah" as read out to the people by Joshua was not different from the "Book of the Torah" allegedly lost and finally uncovered in the Temple. To argue that the book of the Torah meant one thing for the time of Joshua, another thing for the time of King Amaziah, and yet another thing to the time of Josiah, would be much like saying that the Iliad mentioned by the Roman historian Tacitus was not the same Iliad previously cited by the Greek, Anaxagoras. Hence the question to be asked is this: Did the author of Joshua-Kings, in his fivefold mention of a "Book of the Torah" (or a book of the law), think of it as being the equivalent of the entire Pentateuch or merely of Deuteronomy?

It can be assumed that the unknown author of the second book of Kings, whose report of the finding of Josiah's scroll was not written too many years after that signal event, would have possessed some knowledge of its exact character. At the very least, he could not have been in the dark about its outward appearance, as to whether it was merely a scroll of known size or one much larger than the conventional, whether it was wound around a single staff or around two. Furthermore, the book thus discovered in the confines of the temple was not returned to its hiding place. It remained for later generations a most visible object. Likewise, would this annalist have known somewhat as to the contents of this find, as for example, whether its substance embraced the activity of Moses only, or the lives of the patriarchs as well. One further supposition would seem to be warrantable. The author of the second book of Kings, announcing or even retelling this notable acquisition, has told us likewise of its buoyant reception on the part of both the ruling circles and of the multitude. From a reading of the text of 2 Kings, chapter 22, it becomes obvious that whoever wrote it down not only fully understood the reason for this impressive response, but that he himself gave it his own warm support. Now what was there in this major phenomenon that so moved the entire nation, and the feverish activity to which it immediately gave birth? In the light of this question, let us once again refer to some details of the regnant Wellhausen theory.

With the statement that the exhibit inside the temple was a signal event and that it immediately set on foot a revivalist movement, the school of Wellhausen is in full agreement. These authorities are insistent, none the less, that all this ferment within the nation, along with the urge to reform and purification, was occasioned not by the Pentateuch as we know it, but merely by one of its fragmentary elements, standing in isolation all by itself. Now Deuteronomy or "D," in the framework of the documentary analysis, had been preceded by "JE," which in its turn was an amalgam of the two primeval writings "J" and "E." As to the character of "JE," it is not denied that it was approximately the equivalent of what is presently included in Genesis, Exodus, Leviticus, and Numbers, minus the ritualistic contents of the Priests' Code or "P" which was yet to be inserted. We are thus brought face to face with the fact that at the moment, during the eighteenth year of King Josiah's reign, when "D" came to light, the Jews already had before them many, if not most, of the religious ordinances and ethical precepts attributable to Moses. Deuteronomy, as its name clearly implies, is in fact no more than a repetition of the law. Hence, with perhaps only a few exceptions, its provisions were even then no more than a duplication of matters already set forth in "JE," and already generally known. The question to be asked is therefore as follows: What was there in the religious reformation allegedly set in motion on the discovery of "D" that could not have occurred equally under the impact of "JE"?

We are informed of the energetic measures of the reforming monarch designed to stamp out idolatry, inspired undeniably by the newly revealed book of the law. Yet it is pertinent to recall that Josiah was not the first of his line to move against heathenish practices. Of his ancestor, King Asa, it is recorded that "he put away the sodomites out of the land, and removed all the idols that his father had made."[11] As regards the "high places" mentioned for the first time in Deuteronomy, and which King Asa, apparently under the impression that they were not too blatantly pagan, had continued to tolerate, they too were done away with by King Hezekiah, the great grandfather of Josiah.[12] It will be seen that various measures of reform and purification undertaken at several intervals did not have to await the arrival of the book of Deuteronomy. The exhortations contained in writings antecedent to Deuteronomy could well have been sufficient.

The overriding emphasis placed by the Wellhausen school on the centralization of worship supposedly instituted for the first time during the latter years of King Josiah's reign is apparently founded on the following language found in Deuteronomy: "Take heed to thyself that thou offer not thy burnt offerings in every place that thou seest. But in the place which the Lord shall choose in one of thy tribes there shalt thou offer thy burnt offerings, and there thou shalt do all that I command thee."[13] But the alleged uniqueness of this commandment and the hypothesis of its performance by the King being traceable only to Deuteronomy are both undermined by a parallel passage to be found in Leviticus, where we read, "And thou shalt say unto them: Whatsoever man there be of the house of Israel, or of the strangers that sojourn among them, that offereth a burnt offering or sacrifice, and bringeth it not unto the door of the tent of meeting, to sacrifice unto the Lord, even that man shall be cut off from his people."[14]

There is indeed ample evidence, despite the Higher Critics, that ages before the time of Josiah, possibly as far back as the time of Moses, there existed, in law at least, but one altar in Israel, upon which burnt offerings to Jehovah were authorized. Throughout the wanderings in the desert, there was only one "tent of meeting" and not several. But even after the settlement in the land of Canaan, the predisposition in favour of a lone centralized place of worship is plentifully illustrated, even if it was not invariably respected in practice. We note, for example, the indignation of Joshua and his entourage over the report that the men of Reuben, returning to their homes in trans-Jordan, were contemplating the setting up of their own separate altar (Joshua, 22:10-34). The sanctuary at Shiloh, until its demolition by the Philistines, was for the Hebrew nation the one and only place of pilgrimage. Since there was but one high priest and only one ark of the covenant, any duplication of this sanctum would have been scarcely conceivable. And, by way of adding strength to this conclusion, the setting up of the two dissident sanctuaries by the secessionist Jeroboam at Dan and Bethel, was in itself an indication that prior to that time, there existed throughout Israel no rival to the temple at Jerusalem.

Were other reforms initiated by King Josiah similarly related to matters stated in Deuteronomy? There is no reason to deny this. However, again bearing in mind that Deuteronomy is mainly a repetition, all such reforms related to things contained in the other books as well. We read, "And the king commanded all the people, saying, Keep the Passover unto the Lord your God, as it is written in this book of the covenant."[15] There is indeed in Deuteronomy a command as to the observance of the Passover; but the more comprehensive ordinance concerning this festival is to be found in Exodus. Again, the zeal manifested by the king in extirpating all vestiges of paganism can be said to have been derived from any number of passages of "JE" and not necessarily from "D."

To deny the interpretation of the Higher Critics is not to deny the meaningfulness of that portion of the book of the law which later became known as Deuteronomy. There are to be found passages in the closing part of the Torah that are certainly explanatory of the times and suggestive of a situation calling for drastic reforms. Of some significance is the following: "Thou didst wax fat and thou didst grow thick. Again he forsook God who made him, and contemned the Rock of his salvation. They roused him to jealousy with strange gods, with abominations did they provoke him. They sacrificed unto devils, no gods, gods that they knew not, new gods that came up of late, which your fathers dreaded not."[16]

The reference here to the war profiteering of King Menasseh's time along with its accompanying spiritual degradation is clear enough. And yet even more indicative of the times is the reference in the book of Numbers to the trampling of nations by the Assyrian warlords.[17] There is room enough here for the opinion that the substance of Deuteronomy did appear during the late Assyrian period; but not necessarily in the guise of a single isolated tract.

That in the building of the Torah a distinct setting was reserved for one of its five subdivisions over and above the others is a view not well supported even by the character of Deuteronomy itself. Deuteronomy is supposedly set apart from those standing ahead of it by its oratorical style, having been composed largely of speeches delivered by the dying liberator and lawmaker concerning bygone events. Like the Greek historian Herodotus of a later century, the Hebrew narrator was not averse to reproducing from the mouth of his principal characters orations that were not actually made but could only have been imagined from the occasion. But the forensic style is by no means confined to Deuteronomy. Thus we find in the twenty-sixth chapter of Leviticus an oration quite resembling those of the end book. Here too is an address to the people heavy with passion, with a pathetic forecast of approaching evil, along with a hint of ultimate salvation. On the going forth from Egypt, Moses himself speaks to the people at some length.[18] Otherwise, throughout Exodus, Leviticus, Numbers, it is usually God who speaks while Moses is only the listener. But on this peculiarity alone the establishment of an organic separation as between Deuteronomy on the one hand and the remaining portions of the Torah on the other seems rather tenuous.

As an integral part of the completed Torah Deuteronomy does, of course, have its distinctiveness. Standing out in bold relief by reason of its passionate invocation, it serves as the epilogue to the entire work, in much the same way as Genesis serves as its prologue. To the extent that it enfolds nearly the whole of the Mosaic legislation, it does seem in a way to be capable of standing by itself, in much the same way as Exodus, Leviticus, and Numbers combined are capable of standing alone. Deuteronomy, as its name clearly implies, is a repetition of earlier statues. It might in fact be conjectured that the compilers of the Torah, in the course of their editorial labours, had before them for consideration a number of such restatements to choose between, some, no doubt, differing from one another in some degree. Be it noted, in passing, that throughout the Old Testament as a whole, repetitious material appears with some frequency.

If we are to accept the theory of the Higher Critics that the document so dramatically announced and greeted with awe by both the ruler and the population at large was in fact nothing more than a reiteration of laws and ordinances already known, we are indeed confronted by an inexplicable event. It is a forced interpretation to affirm that what was essentially a restatement of earlier doctrine would suddenly and spontaneously be received as fresh gospel, and capture by its very newness the minds and imagination of an entire generation. If the remaining books of what now constitutes the Pentateuch were already in existence, let us say, in the attentuated form of "JE" in accordance with the Documentary doctrine of precedence, the appearance of what was hardly more than a recapitulation would not have been looked upon as an exceptionally luminous event. It would have occasioned no furor whatever. To assume, on the other hand, that Exodus, Leviticus, Numbers and Genesis were really composed subsequent to Deuteronomy would be a violent contradiction of the natural flow to be observed between each of the five books, and as reversing the order in a highly artificial manner. Logical arrangement requires Genesis to come before Exodus, and Exodus prior to Leviticus and Numbers. Numbers, in its closing chapter, indicates clearly that the story of Moses awaits completion in a book that is yet to follow.

That Deuteronomy was always fifth in the series and never first emerges clearly. Deuteronomy in Greek means repetition of the law. But it is quite obviously more than that. It also forms part of a continuing narrative, and one that is carried forward into the later series of historical books starting with Joshua. Were it not read as a sequel to Numbers, virtually all that is narrated in Deuteronomy would be unintelligible. Thus do read, "Remember what the Lord God did unto Miriam by the way as ye came out of Egypt" (Deuteronomy, 24:9). How is anyone to know, or how were Josiah and his contemporaries supposed to know, what the Lord had done unto Miriam, without learning about it in an earlier segment of the Torah (Numbers, 12: 14)? Again, the carrying forward of a grudge against Moab and Ammon is enjoined because of their intrigues with Balaam (Deuteronomy, 23:4). There is the implication here that the episode with Balaam as reported in Numbers was already commonly known.

From the internal evidence of Deuteronomy it is difficult to understand how such a document, standing in isolation from the remainder of the Pentateuch, could have greatly lifted the mood of the nation, suffused it with fresh hope, and raised to a higher level of confidence in its own destiny. Let us take heed, for example, of the passage wherein it is recommended that the monarch keep by his side a copy of the book "and to read therein all the days of his life." A copy of what book? It would have been utterly frivolous to have suggested to a ruler that a simple scroll of undistinguished length would be so abounding in worthy contemplations as to hold his repeated and unceasing attention to the very end of his days. To a tired and bewildered nation, decimated by its enemies, there would have been no balm whatever to listen to such words as "The Lord your God hath multiplied you and behold you are this day as the stars of heaven for multitude."[19] Being reminded of the great victories over Og and Sihon and the smashing of Amorite resistance in a territory which had since been lost to them would have tended to neither consolation nor inspiration. A prey to foreign empires, with how much enthusiasm could they have hearkened to exhortations such as the following? "Behold I have set this land before you, go in and possess the land which the Lord swore unto your

84

fathers, to Abraham, to Isaac and to Jacob to give unto them and to their seed after them."[20]

By way of answer to the foregoing critique, founded on quotations from the book of Deuteronomy itself, it will be argued undoubtedly that, according to the documentary thesis, the document designated as "D" is not precisely the Deuteronomy as we know it. Hence passages which I have quoted from Deuteronomy need not have been present in its prototype, and would therefore not be relevant. In the words of Professor Gordon and others, "D" was merely "the nucleus of Deuteronomy" and not the Deuteronomy as we know it. In view, however, of the admitted ignorance of the exact contents of this lost original, and the extent of its supposed variation from its successor, such an hypothesis can be no more than a compounding of uncertainties. Moreover, to attach any kind of credibility to this apparently attenuated version of Deuteronomy would make it even more difficult to understand how it could have gained any kind of dominance over the minds of both the king and his subjects. The unearthing of such a document would not have been considered as exceptionally noteworthy, and would have occasioned neither consternation nor exaltation.

The early years of King Josiah's reign had witnessed no shortage of prophetical utterances, calls for repentance, and denunciations of the blatant animism into which the nation had lapsed during so many decades. The youthful Jeremiah had begun to preach to the nation some five years prior to the discovery in the Temple. The Judaean population, or at least its leaders, were at that time not unacquainted with the messages of Amos, Hosea and Isaiah, whose writings did not need to be rediscovered. By the eighteenth year of King Josiah's reign, it is by all means possible that any number of scrolls had already turned up, some of them secreted during the time of his father and grandfather. There were beyond these prophetic utterances both known and forgotten that were replete with forebodings of disaster along with promises of ultimate redemption. The contention that the relatively insignificant "nucleus of Deuteronomy" was all that was then wanting in order to bring to fruition the mood of national repentance, and the expulsion of the Mesopotamian "workers with familiar spirits, and the wizards, and the images of the idols," seems altogether far-fetched.

The sounder view is that the corrosive influence of Assyrian domination having done its work, nothing less could have availed to save Judaism from its threatened extinction than a premeditated work that towered above all other documents then in existence. To be sure, writings endowed with a sacred character were not wanting at that time, many of them noble and uplifting. But the prophetic literature, sonorous and distinguished though it was, could have appealed for the most part only to the more cultivated among the nation. For the ordinary Judaean its concern with the destinies of other nations meant little or nothing. The new times called for clarity of exposition rather than veiled and mystifying verse. The priests and Levites who, being without property, had the single-minded duty of instructing the people, were the natural guardians of its spiritual treasures. No other task was theirs than that of roaming the countryside and recalling to the common folk the traditions of their ancestors. From this class, in all likelihood, emerged those individuals who cast into written and coherent form the self-contained stories of the garden of Eden, the founding of the world, the flood, and the separation of mankind into nations. As an added preservative, the pious imagination of these men caused them to crown their labours by attributing the whole of it to the venerated name of Moses the lawgiver.

The task of this unknown group of earnest men, disenchanted with the monarchy, and perhaps the ritualistic observances of the temple as well, was to devise some method for the continuance of the ancestral religion in place of a dependence on the patronage and goodwill of a crowned head. They also saw the need to fortify the nation against the coming day of judgment, and to rescue it from the despair of an impending exile. Hence, one of the more significant facts to be noted concerning the appearance of the completed Torah was the impulse for gathering together the scattered oral traditions, the written memorials, the legal and moral pronouncements into one comprehensive and harmonious coverage. As a compendium of texts which would otherwise have gone astray, the Torah was the forerunner of such later collections as the enlarged canon of the Old Testament, the New Testament, the Talmud, and the Law Code of Justinian. In each of these, the instinct was the conservation against the ravages of the coming times of writings that were deemed worthy of being rescued from oblivion.

In saving the nation's cultural and religious heritage, the Torah was instrumental likewise in saving the nation itself. Its actual writing, which doubtless consumed many years of secret effort, coincided with a time of national degradation. The fall of the northern kingdom reverberated as a painful memory. As for the kingdom of Judah, it had been reduced to a mere satellite, and in size to little more than a city state. In the midst of all such calamities, the Jews needed to be informed authoritatively that they were the product of a tradition which their oppressors were unable to rival, that in truth they had been selected for a high destiny and set apart from other nations.

The death of the last noteworthy conqueror, Asshurbanipal, in 626 B.C. was the beginning of the end for the Assyrian Empire. With this hated and dreaded colossus shaken, King Josiah was successful in banning paganism.

Assyrian and Semitic deities imported under pressure were thrown out. But the termination of vassalage was to prove no more than transitory. The renewed period of independence was to last no more than about fifteen years, being brought to an end with the death of King Josiah at the battle of Megiddo. His successors became once again puppet rulers, first of the Egyptians and then of the Babylonians. With the loss of national freedom there came once again the reaction in favour of heathen worship. We have it on the authority of the prophets Jeremiah and Ezekiel that polytheism among the Jews was still very much alive on the very eve of the Babylonian captivity. None the less, its total and permanent disappearance from among the Jews was soon to come.

The few years of recovered independence, coinciding with the later years of King Josiah's reign, had witnessed a miracle. This miracle was the coming of the Torah, later to be known as the Five Books of Moses. It was this written word that finally turned the tide against idolatry among the Jews. To an inspired documentary, venerated as the legacy of Moses himself, the idolatrous party was left without an answer.

EZRA

I have espoused the view that on a plain reading of the text the passage in the second Book of Kings relating to the finding of a remarkable document some thirty-seven years prior to the firing of Jerusalem, and presented to the Jewish world as the "Saefer Ha'Torah," was in fact none other than the Pentateuch, approximately as we know it to-day. But for many scholars, a more involved exegesis seemed preferable. They have come forward with an evolutionary theory of the sacred book, which bears a strong likeness to the

Hegelian approach to development through thesis, anti-thesis, and synthesis. Supported by both Jewish and Christian scholars is the concept of a continuously growing Scripture, gradually filling itself out, and finally assuming its present form in about the year 444 B.C. when given its imprimatur by the scribe Ezra.

While acknowledging the authenticity of the announcement contained in the twenty-second chapter of second Kings, these savants have advanced the view that the portentous find therein reported was no more than a kind of springboard to the Torah. There remained still to be added one other of its elements. This latter ingredient, designated as the "Priests' Code," or by the letter "P," is reputed to have devoted itself to matters of ritual, such as animal sacrifices, the construction of the tabernacle, the functioning of the sacerdotal orders, and the regulations governing the Sabbath and the various festivals.

It is in effect acknowledged by these thinkers that, with the exception of this final ingredient, the substance of the Torah had indeed attained its fruition prior to the exile. For want, however, of this adjunct, the promulgation of the Torah as the irrevocable word of Moses had to wait a further lapse of two hundred years. Only with the attachment of this culminating portion, by Ezra, in all probability, was the stage set for the final editing of the Pentateuch as we know it.

The Priests' Code, or "P," along with the vague sentiment of dislike grafted upon it, is supposed to demonstrate the retrogression of Hebrew civilization from the high spiritual level which it had attained earlier with the coming of "D" and the words of the Prophets. It represented a turning aside of Judaism in the direction of a cold and petrified ceremonialism that in the long run was to call forth the protests and disclaimers of Jesus and the Gospels. Even if we are to accept the view that "P" came last in a series of documents that began with "J" and "E," it does not follow necessarily that a deterioration in the religious attitudes of the Hebrew nation is thereby denoted. The supposed antithesis between what was spiritual and uplifting in Hebraic lore, on the one hand, and that which was crassly sacramental on the other, could have been apparent since a very early time, from the actual existence of the temple ceremonial and from animal sacrifices. It was not the mere writing down of a manual of ceremonial observance, or the time of its writing down, that would in itself have demonstrated any such a departure from that which was higher to that which was lower in the religion of the Israelite nation.

In the Wellhausen hypothesis, the Priests' Code, supposedly of late composition, was surreptitiously inserted into a pre-existing design, and made to coalesce so cunningly with its matrix as to create the impression that it had been there from of old. "It has actually been successful, with its moveable tabernacle, its wandering camp, and its other archaical features, in so concealing the true date of its composition that its very serious inconsistencies with what we know from other sources of Hebrew antiquity prior to the exile are only taken as proving that it lies far beyond all known history, and on account of its enormous antiquity can hardly be brought into any connection with it" ("P," 10). An undistinguished role is here assigned, not only to the scribe Ezra, but by implication to the high-minded statesman Nehemiah with whom Ezra is known to have laboured in close and harmonious collaboration.[21]

Let the so-called Priests' Code be more carefully looked into. According to Wellhausen, it pretends to be something that it is not. It "tries hard to imitate the costume of the Mosaic period, and with whatever success to disguise its own."[22] The Priests' Code is supposed to have as its core the entire book of Leviticus.[23] Wellhausen's Priests' Code takes in as well portions of the Pentateuch both immediately preceding and following Leviticus. In sum, the Priests' Code begins with Chapter 25 of Exodus and goes on to Chapter 26 of Numbers, several of the intervening Chapters being omitted. The excepted Chapters are 32-34 of Exodus; and in Numbers, Chapters 11 to 15 and 20 to 25. No explanation is offered by Wellhausen as to why an otherwise uniform code should thus be penetrated by extraneous matter, unless we are to suppose that such intrusion of non-relevant matter was in keeping with the compiler's alleged intention "to imitate the costume of the Mosaic period."

The hallmark of the Priests' Code, according to the school of Wellhausen, is its emphasis of the ritualistic and ceremonial, to the exclusion of the ethical and historical, matters which are treated of in other parts of the Pentateuch. That the Pentateuch was injured by the inclusion of profuse and repetitious details of burnt offerings is not deniable. It should here be pointed out, however, that the enforcement of ritual and ceremonial was not the sole reason for the existence of the sacerdotal orders. Throughout the Mosaic legislation, the role of the Priests and Levites is not detachable from numerous enactments concerning popular education, sanitation, and justice. Notwithstanding, a closer reading of the entire Humash reveals a fairly wide dispersal of matters that are supposedly distinctive of "P." Thus, for example, in Chapters 12 and 13 of Exodus, which are not part of the Priests' Code, are laid down the ordinances of the Passover and the even more cultic rules for the redemption of the first born. Why should the observance of the feast of Tabernacles belong to the Priests' Code, while that of the Passover belongs elsewhere? To an objection voiced by one of his critics that in the book of Deuteronomy, or "D," there are references to the ark of the Covenant, an obviously ritualistic object, Wellhausen was driven to reply that the ark mentioned in Deuteronomy was a different ark from the one talked about in the Priests' Code.[24] We are thus reminded of someone who refused to believe that certain plays had been written by Shakespeare, because "they could have been written by another man of the same name."

Consider this conjunctive fact. The Temple of Jerusalem, that is to say, the temple of the return, began to be rebuilt in the year 520 B.C. It was completed and dedicated in 505 B.C. In effect, therefore, at the time of the coming from Babylonia of the fresh batch of exiles under Ezra, supposedly bearing in their hands the newly composed Priests' Code, the temple rites in Jerusalem had been in progress day after day for a period of at least fifty years. We are to suppose, accordingly, that during the decades that Ezra's sacrificial manual was delayed in coming, the priestly bureaucracy at Jerusalem had been carrying on helplessly without really knowing what they were doing.

The evidence clearly demonstrates the contrary. There had been in Jerusalem an earlier temple, built about six hundred years earlier in the reign of King Solomon. During this long interval, other shrines as well had been constructed, such as those by Jeroboam I at Bethel and Dan, to say nothing of the multitude of chapels throughout the entire land of Israel. We are in effect asked to believe that during all that time and with the undoubted need there was, prior to the arrival from Babylon of Ezra and his friends, no fixed rule of any kind to instruct the priests as to their duties, as to what they were to burn and what they were not to burn. We are supposed to overlook the fact that the prophet Ezekiel, who lived about two hundred years before Ezra, had written about the details of temple worship.[25] Also, in examining the opening chapter of the book of Ezra—which Ezra may not have written—we come across the following: "Then stood up—Zerubbabel, the son of Shealtiel and builded the altar of God, to offer burnt offerings thereon, as it is written in the law of Moses, the man of God."[26] As a final word on this matter, recent discoveries in Syria at a place called Ras Shamra have revealed texts of Canaanite worship that resemble closely fragments of Leviticus and Numbers relating to sacrifices.[27]

Let us now recapitulate the constituent parts of the Graff-Wellhausen Pentateuch. We are told that some time after the downfall of the northern kingdom in 722 B.C.E. the two primary components, the Elohist and the Jehovist, were welded into one sacred document designated as "JE." We are to surmise that this amalgamation was carried out for a devotional purpose, and that it was presented to the Judaean population as the work of Moses. About a century later, presumably after the discovery of Deuteronomy or "D," we are to believe that a newer and enlarged edition of the Book of the Law was presented to the nation superseding the earlier book. This newer book was JED. Finally, after a lapse of not less than two centuries, a major catastrophe having in the meanwhile taken place, there came to the fore yet another revision of the Torah, this time with some interpolated material which unaccountably had previously been omitted, and as to which an explanation for such omission is neither asked nor given. There were thus within a period of some four or five centuries no less than three different Torahs, each one swallowing its predecessor in the approved Hegelian sequence. This might have been historically the case; and yet it seems highly improbable.

Alternatively, it might be urged that there was never but one Torah, and that it was introduced ab initio some twenty-three hundred years ago by Ezra, or perhaps by some unknown contemporary of Ezra, as Spinoza once theorized. But, here again, we are told in effect that the Torah, as a single and unified canon, had to wait upon the arrival of the relatively unimportant and uninspiring Priests' Code. This despite the fact that, long before Ezra's time, there had come into existence the very extensive book of Joshua-Kings, a book which in logical sequence could only have been composed after the Pentateuch and not before it.

Scholars are virtually all agreed that the later historical books extending from Joshua to Second Kings, and inaptly termed "the early prophets," constituted one single work originally. We have here a unified scripture that is even more voluminous than the Pentateuch itself, and which at the same time gives evidence of having been inspired by a preceding book. It is impossible to escape the conclusion that Joshua-Kings was meant to be some kind of supplement to the Torah. The transition from one book to the other is seen readily enough as one goes on from Deuteronomy to Joshua. Also the second work fully resembles the first in spirit, in that it is equally moralistic. While the first deals with God's promise, the other records the fulfillment of God's promise. The second narration deals with the occupation of the land, the succumbing of the people and their final punishment, all foretold in the Torah itself.

Now this later work, unquestionably a product of Babylonia, ends with the rehabilitation of the deposed Jehoiachin. It relates nothing of subsequent events, such as the destruction of the Babylonian empire, the decree of Cyrus and the return to Jerusalem. Obviously, it was written long before Ezra's time, who lived some hundred and fifty years after the destruction of the First Temple. It is safe to assume, therefore, that to Ezra and his circle this latter work was known well enough. It was at the time of his arrival in Jerusalem generally known, if not to the Jews of Palestine, certainly to those of Babylonia. Now does it seem probable that at a time when the secondary book had for some time been completed and accepted, that the book which preceded it, and on which it was largely based, should all of a sudden become subject to a major revision?

Ezra was a figure of the late Persian period. His arrival in Judaea was during the reign of King Artaxerxes I (464 B.C.-424 B.C.). Of Ezra it was written that he was "a ready scribe in the law of Moses" and that he had "prepared his heart to seek the law of the Lord and to do it, and to teach in Israel statutes and judgments."[28] The suggestion is undeniable that the sage at the very outset of his career had before him an established body of canonical literature, which neither he nor his contemporaries doubted was derived from Moses, who had lived some nine hundred years before.

Now we are asked to believe, first by Spinoza and later by the Higher Critics, that this same Ezra, who since his early days had been occupied in providing his coreligionists with copies of what they did not fail to look upon as the authentic legacy of the great lawgiver, was at a certain moment brought to a realization that something of major significance had been unaccountably omitted from its composition. What crisis or necessity presented itself at that particular moment in Jewish history which could in any way have been dealt with by drastically changing an already established body of canonical literature? What end could have been served as a result of the abandonment of the then-existing Torah—or pseudo-Torah if you will—and the bringing in of a substituted version? Ezra himself, whose written memorial forms a portion of the book bearing his name, certainly makes no claim to having instituted so drastic a change, or of having discovered anywhere "a priestly code." On the occasion of the first return of the exiles, which took place almost one hundred years before the coming of Ezra, we are told of an altar being set up in Jerusalem in accordance with the command of the Torah.

95

The inference is almost irresistible, from this passage alone, that the law of Moses to which in his early youth Ezra had dedicated his life already contained a full dissertation on matters concerning ritual, festivals and so forth.

Consider likewise the disarray that would have ensued among the scattered Jewish communities of western Asia had an announcement suddenly reached them that the book which at least as far back as the time of King Josiah they had been venerating as the last word given by Moses was now to be discarded in favour of a fresh and unfamiliar version. The introduction of a Priests' Code having to do with temple ritual, priesthood, and burnt offerings where no such work had previously been known would by its very nature have been offensive to Jews living outside Palestine at least. They would have informed Ezra that since there was among them neither fane nor burnt offerings the proposed addition of a Priests' Code did not interest them at all. By what persuasive device could Ezra have managed to secure the unanimous agreement of the dispersed communities of Babylonia, Persia, Asia Minor and perhaps Egypt and Arabia that a major implementation of the traditional scripture had suddenly become necessary and that they were to put aside the existing version as no longer sacred?

The supreme argument occurs in connection with the Samaritan neighbours of the Jews and their version of the Torah. The Samaritans were a sect scorned by Ezra. Nothing could be less likely then that their version of the Torah, or any portion of it, could have been fashioned for them by the hands of their hated enemy. Of the Samaritan Torah it has recently been written that it is "a recension of the Hebrew text of the Pentateuch written in an archaic script evolved from the old Hebrew (Phoenician) writing. Its antiquity is attested to, inter alia, by the shape of the letters as well as the fact that a dot is placed after each word. Possibly the Samaritan Pentateuch dates back in its primary form to the time of Josiah, but it has been much altered in the course of the generations. It nevertheless constitutes the earliest witness to the Hebrew text."[29]

Before abandoning this topic, there remains to be mentioned two relatively minor difficulties that stand in the way of Ezra having had anything to do with the composition of the Pentateuch. Ezra lived at a time when the Jews, influenced by the teachings of Zoroastrianism, had already accepted some kind of belief in the after-life. Had his connection with the Torah been other than that of copier, arranger, and scribe, then surely some hint of this doctrine would have entered somewhere into its composition. Again, linguistic intrusions are recognized as affording some intimation as to the period of a book's authorship. I refer to one example. From the fact that it contains at least one word taken from the Greek, we infer that the Song of Songs, traditionally attributed to King Solomon, was actually composed during the Helenistic period.[30] Now Ezra lived at a time when Aramaic had either replaced Hebrew as the vernacular of the Jews or was in the course of so doing. Significantly, the biblical book that speaks of Ezra's activities is itself written partly in Aramaic. Had the composition of the Torah—or of any portion of it—been contemporaneous with the ascendancy of Aramaic, then surely some betrayal of this fact would have been discoverable in the text itself, as in the case of such writings as Daniel and Ezra.

There are excellent reasons for rejecting the hypothesis of the Higher Critics that Ezra was either the author or compiler of the Torah or any significant part of it. But that he made an important contribution towards strengthening its role in Jewish life is by all means to be conceded. In his native Babylonia, Ezra had served as a scribe. He was a member of a respected brotherhood, whose livelihood consisted in turning out hand-written copies of the sacred scrolls of the law, a profession, incidentally, that among Jews has persisted down to this very day. In his labours he was conscientious. We are informed of him that being in doubt as to the correctness of certain words of the text, he would indicate such words by placing points over them.[31]

In the religious life of the Babylonian Jews, in which Ezra grew up, the Torah and the Synagogue were between them primary and uppermost. But among the Palestinian Jews, the situation was not quite the same. The focusing of attention on the sacrificial rites of the rebuilt temple tended to a downgrading of both Torah and Synagogue. This comparative neglect Ezra saw as a threat to Jewish survival. To correct this was the mission that he laid upon himself. He reached Jerusalem in the year 458 B.C., carrying with him "the book of the law of Moses," and leading a group of new settlers who were steeped in it. The Talmud credits Ezra with having stemmed the spiritual deterioration of the people by reintroducing a knowledge of the Torah which they had all but forgotten.

For the more effective utilization of the Torah, he converted its unwieldy bulk into a division of five conveniently handled "books," each named after the first meaningful word of its text. The first is Beresheet (in the beginning) followed by Shemot (names) Vayikra (and he called), Ba'Midbar (in the desert) and Devarim (words). The corresponding Greek renderings are of course derived from the translation carried out in Alexandria on behalf of Greek-speaking Jews and known as the Septuagint. Again, these major divisions, often referred to collectively as the "Humash" or "the Five'" were in turn subdivided into some fifty-four "Parshiot" (portions), corresponding roughly to the cycle of the year and its Sabbaths. These Parshiot were of sufficiently reduced size to be conveniently fitted with the weekly Sabbath services in the synagogues. Joined by Ezra to these weekly readings were the "Haftorahs," short excerpts from the prophetical writings both the earlier and the later. An important task still awaited the scribe. This was changing the Torah from being written in the antique Phoenician script to what has been since known as the "Ktav Ashurit," or familiar Hebrew lettering of our time. His reason for so doing was clear enough. Resulting from the schism with the Samaritans, it was his intention to create what he hoped would be an effective barrier between the Torah of the Jews and that of the Samaritans which, except for minor textual variations, was identical with it.

CHAPTER IV

SOME PEOPLE OF THE BOOK

Prior to the Reformation, and everywhere throughout the Christian world, the reading by the laity of both the Old and New Testaments in any of the "vulgar" languages was prohibited; while to read them in Latin required the authorization of one's bishop. In Catholic Spain to even request such permission was to lay oneself open to the charge of heresy.[1] Of the Old Testament, which for a number of reasons it could not have repudiated, the Church was especially wary. In common with Judaism, the Church accepted the version of the world's creation, as found in Genesis. Further, man's disobedience in the garden of Eden was the basis of the Christian doctrine of the Fall of Man, upon which in turn is founded the redemptive power of the Saviour. Also allusions to the coming of a Messiah were held to refer to none other than Jesus. Hence the Old Testament was held to be prefatory to the New. But beyond all this, the Jewish testament contains nothing about a three-fold deity, nor of salvation in a world to come, nor inherited sin, nor vicarious atonement. Thus its reading by a doctrinally untrained Christian could well have resulted in the crime of

Judaization, against which the Church had to be constantly on guard. And finally, the Church being on the whole pacifically inclined could view with little favour the reports contained in Joshua and Kings of wars and massacres, realities with which its flock were already well enough acquainted.

Martin Luther, in his prefatory observations to his famous translation of the Scriptures, thought it necessary to give reasons to his fellow Germans for having bracketed with the Evangels and the Epistles, the testimony of the despised and rejected Hebrews. A few centuries later, the British and Foreign Bible Society set itself the task of conveying to many nations and in many tongues a knowledge of the New Testament; but soon realized that there could be no widespread reading of the New without the Old.[2] All this being duly noted, it remains to be underscored that without the sponsorship of Christianity, the Hebrew Scriptures would not have gripped the imagination of millions, and achieved their world-wide renown. By way of contrast, inside the Mohammedan world, no prominence has ever been given to either the Hebrew Scriptures or to the Hebrew language itself.

That the history of any nation is in some degree a recording of its most distinguished representatives finds an echo within the historical parts of the Old Testament. And yet the Hebrew Scripture bears this unique feature: The earliest personages singled out for mention were human beings of no nation, and whose country was the undivided world. These early cosmopolites, who were said to have bestrode a world of lawlessness and chaos, were the earthly counterparts of the divine adventurers of the Graeco-Semitic pantheon. They were perhaps identifiable with "the mighty men of old, the men of renown."[3] One might surmise that of the mythical successors of Adam and Eve originally more was told than a threadbare listing of names.

101

The "Book of the Generations of Adam," to which Genesis refers as one of its sources, could have been a compilation of lore dealing with such notables as Tubal, Cain, Lamech, Jared, Methusaleh, Enoch, and the rest. Each of these mythological heroes had his own trail of fabulous performances originally in the keeping of the bards of that primeval period. But along with those of the "Nephilim" or "fallen ones," by the more sober authors of the Pentateuch, their exploits might well have been discarded as too destitute of reality. Some degree of selectivity in regard to their source material ought not to be denied these early Biblical compilers.

Most eminent of these legendary stalwarts was Noah, a man who shunned evil, along with his three sons, no mention being made of the female members of his fortunate entourage. These men were at the same time the last of the ante-diluvians and the progenitors of a new and diversified mankind. The story of the near destruction of the human race is of course drawn from a non-Hebraic starting point. Among the hoard of the tablets exhumed from the library of Ashurbanipal at Nineveh towards the middle of the nineteenth century and finally deciphered some fifty years later was the epic poem of Gilgamesh. This tale of the adventures of Gilgamesh and his companions Enkudu and Utnapishtim is known to have circulated throughout the Middle East. Of Sumerian origin, it received additional currency during the period of Assyrian ascendancy. Gilgamesh, like Noah, receives a warning from on high of the impending destruction of the world by a massive inundation. "O man of Shurrupak, son of Ubar-Tutu, tear down thy house, build a ship, abandon wealth, seek after life, scorn possessions, save thy life. Bring the seed of all things into the ship. Let its dimensions be well measured."

The site of Noah's ark, where it finally came to rest, was supposed to have been Mount Ararat in Armenia. To discover this ark, the Tzar Nicholas II of Russia sent forth an expedition shortly before his overthrow in 1917. Needless to relate, no trace of this vessel's existence has been found, nor ever will be. A ship with the dimensions of an ocean-going vessel could not have been built in that far-off time, and certainly not by a labour force consisting of one man and his three filial helpers. To have captured and assembled in one place all the many different species of mammalia, reptiles, fowl, insects, spiders, beatles, earthworms, and protozoa would have required the legendary labours not of one Hercules but of a million. The settling and provisioning within cramped quarters of so many diverse creatures, many among them carnivores, would have presented quite a managerial problem for their curator. Thus cooped up, most of them would have fared no worse had they been abandoned to the raging waters in the first place. And finally, since no mention is made of any protective measures for the earth's plant life, the rescue of the animals alone would scarcely have constituted an act of salvation.

The long continued credibility given to this and to other myths, both biblical and non biblical, is illustrative of that observation of the sage Martin Buber to the effect that for religious life some mythology is essential. But this ought not to strike us too unfavourably. All myths tend to vanish in the course of time. But the fall of one system of mythology habitually paves the way for another. And this simple truth holds good not only as regards religious fables. In our own time, not a few authors, critics, publicists, and even historians, have indulged themselves in imaginary realities suitable only to their temperamental needs.

Among the salient discoveries of the nineteenth century are to be numbered the decipherment of both the hieroglyphic and cuneiform writings. Therewith were added two new fields of knowledge, that of the early Egyptians and that of the Assyro-Babylonians. By way of contrast, during this same century, nothing of much importance came to light on the history of the Hebrews. Findings relevant to Egyptian and Babylonian antiquities served to open new vistas into the environment of the ancient Middle East. But within this new framework of fresh knowledge of early times, those episodes narrated in the Hebrew scriptures did not seem to belong. Such being the case, Christian students of the Old Testament were not slow in voicing their disbelief in annals for which no external confirmation seemed forthcoming. Thus in the view of Edouard Meyer, Bernhard Luther, and R. Weill, the patriarchs never existed. The names attributed to them were in reality those of early and forgotten Semitic deities, humanized for the purposes of a contrived history. By other researchers it was held that the patriarchal names were not those of individual men and women who once lived and breathed, but of Hebrew tribes, around which personalized legends were invented. For all such extravagant hypotheses no malice should be attributed. Their underlying incredulity was excusable enough, given a situation when so much of the past having been laid bare, the antiquities of the Jews reported in only a single unrelated book lacked confirmation from any independent source.

Time has brought about a far more positive attitude towards that which the Bible has to report in connection with the patriarchs and their times. With the liquidation of Turkish rule over the lands of the Near East that followed on the heels of the First World War, administrative hindrances to the researches of European archaeologists were overcome. The more recent situation has been thus summed up by an eminent French authority, and I translate: "Since the termination of the First World War, archaeological research has taken on great strides; and not only in Palestine but throughout the entire Near East. This has resulted in a fund of knowledge and a fresh documentation that is vertiginous indeed. With it there has come about a fundamental change in attitude in respect to the Biblical side of ancient history. A veritable flood of studies has come to the fore, throwing fresh light on the Old Testament. Symptomatic of this efflorescence has been the important place assumed by the age of the Hebrew patriarchs. By and large, the present emphasis is on its historicity."[4]

ABRAHAM

With the story of Abraham, the nature of the narrative in Genesis undergoes a pivotal transformation. Genesis begins with its version of the world's creation and of an undifferentiated human society prefatory to its division into separate linguistic groups. Further on, the story narrows down to the fortunes of a single nation, of which Abraham is the fountainhead, it being acknowledged parenthetically that he is likewise the progenitor of several non-Jewish nations as well. Tradition and sentiment have tied him to both Christianity and Islam. He was, according to Eusebius of Caesarea and Hilary of Potiers, the first Christian, while the Koran treats him as the first Moslem.

Abraham has been identified as the founder of the Jewish nation in the purely geneological sense. Is it proper to regard him likewise as the founder of the Jewish religion? Abraham, be it observed, was chosen by God. Significantly, it is not stated that the choice was the other way, that it was Abraham who chose God. Nowhere in Genesis itself is it averred that Abraham was the original monotheist and that he was the first man in history to abstain from idol worship. Of the time of Adam and his successors it is reported that "men began to call upon the name of the Lord." Well before the time of Abraham there were those who "found grace in the eyes of the Lord," presumably by reason of their being free of taint of idolatry and polytheism. Enoch is said to have "walked with God," and Noah "was in his generation a man righteous and whole-hearted."[5]

There is nothing discoverable in the Biblical text itself that would indicate that the faith and religious practice of Abraham differed from those of his friends Abimelech, King of Gerar, and Melchizedek, King of Salem. Of these latter personages, it is nowhere indicated that they worshipped idols and multiple deities. Discernible in Genesis is an underlying assumption that the belief in only one God had been the norm since the foundation of the world; and that polytheism and idolatry were the aberrations of the wicked of later times. Of Judaism could it be said, inasmuch as its essence is the belief in one only God, that, unlike all the other religions, it is without any individual founder.

The Biblical account of Abraham and his wife Sarah, though not devoid of mythological asides, is altogether that of credible human beings. Abraham's character differs from those of Isaac and Jacob, as do these latter differ one from the other, and as there are character differences between their respective wives. Interestingly enough, none of the patriarchs are depicted as agitators and fiery proselytizers. Abraham himself was not held up as either prophet or wonderworker. No one is reported as having been brought to him to be cured of any ailment. Not to him and not to his son and grandson are miracles attributed.

Abraham's birthplace was in Ur, a very ancient settlement whose name simply meant "a city."[6] Ur was for quite some time the metropolis of the southland, a role later inherited by Babylon. In the overall pattern of Mesopotamia, the centre of gravity of political power was a gradual shifting towards the north. The urban settlements of the south were as tenuous as were the trading routes that changed with great frequency. For a period of somewhat more than one hundred years, that is from about 2090 B.C.

till about 1960 B.C., an empire is known to have existed with Ur as its capital. An invasion by the Amorites at the beginning of the second millenium is believed to have brought to an end this early empire along with the greatness and prosperity of Ur itself.[7]

To reconstruct the story of Abraham so as to detach from it all legendary particulars is not an impossible task. In all probability, the story of the patriarchs was handed down in the course of many generations in the form of heroic poetry. By trained specialists were these epics recited to the people on festive occasions. Poetry, far more than prose, lends itself to accurate memorization. For it a fair degree of permanence and unchangeability can be inferred. Among other nations, aside from the Jews, oral traditions are believed to have been transmitted, more or less intact, from century to century. Only in the eighth century B.C.E. was the art of writing introduced among the Greeks, even though the events related in the Homeric poems go back some four centuries earlier. The Rig Vedas of the Brahmins are claimed to have been composed about five centuries prior to the adoption of writing in India. Beyond a few fragmentary remains that found their way into the Pentateuch, no epic poetry of the early Hebrews is presently known to us. Its preservation was perhaps considered unessential once its substance had been gathered into the later book.

No explanation is offered in the Scripture for the departure of Terah and his clan from their natal city; but it can be inferred from the known power situation affecting that doomed metropolis. The plain of Shinar, though favoured by the richness of its alluvial soil, as well as by the caravan routes by which it was intersected, was greatly exposed to the predatory attentions of barbaric outsiders. With their mud foundations, the fragile walls of its cities offered no strong defence against the rugged mountaineers and fierce marauding tribesmen of the adjoining deserts to the east and west. Asshur, Nineveh, and Calah, already considerable cities on the upper Tigris valley at the time of the patriarchs, had been built originally by refugees arriving from such places downstream as Erech, Calneh, Hir, Hit, Uruk, Eridu, Larsa, Shuppurak, all prehistoric dwelling places of no great permanency. Ur in its turn came to be a good place from which to get away. Among those who had fled the slaughter of its inhabitants were Terah and his family in all probability. Following the northerly route along the Euphrates river, they arrived safely in Haran, a city some two hundred miles to the west of Nineveh. "And Terah took Abram his son, and Lot the son of Haran, his sons's son and Sarai, his daughter in law, his son Abram's wife; and they went forth with them from Ur of the Chaldees; and they came unto Haran and dwelt there."[8]

In Haran, as in Ur, old Terah remained to the end of his days a votary of the moon goddess, Ishtar, and a worshipper in her celebrated Temple of the Moon. Nor does the text imply that it was ever his intention or that of his family to further remove his dwelling to any other country. In the cuneiform tablets of approximately that period, Haran is cited as a thriving and prosperous city. Mentioned likewise in these Assyrian remains is the nearby city of Nahor, where dwelt Rebeccah and her parents. Haran was then inhabited by no less than three distinct nationalities, the Accadians, the Amorites, and the Hurrites.[9] Amid this confluence of religions and cultures, some occasion was afforded for the emergence of one notable individual of a bold and independent turn of mind.

Abraham was haunted by an inner voice. He felt himself being summoned by the mysterious and incorporeal God, the lord of heaven and earth. "Now the Lord said unto Abram. Get thee out of thy country, and from thy kindred

108

and from thy father's house, unto a land that I will show thee."[10] The founder of Islam, soon after a similar vision had come to him, saw himself compelled to flee his native Mecca. Under circumstance not altogether dissimilar, Abraham too was constrained to withdraw from a place of residence, whose tutelary deity he would no longer join in honoring. But unlike Mohammed, Abraham was neither a fighter nor a zealot. His severance from his kindred, though brought about by differences of belief, was effected without rancour. In after years, seeking for his son a suitable bride, it was to the city of his long forsaken kinsfolk that his thoughts were turned. Only in the third generation was the thread that had bound the Hebrew people to their cousins beyond the great river forever snapped asunder. Jacob had many sons; but not one among them did he send back to the land of the Aramaeans for taking unto themselves wives.

Abraham's career was all the more remarkable in that he lived at a time when it was rare for any individual to venture far from the place of his birth. In that primitive and chaotic age, there were not many ways of insuring one's safety after leaving the shelter of a city and its walls. But travelling alongside a herd of sheep and goats or cattle was at least a way of warding off starvation. Also, as a drover you were but one step away from being a trader and peddler as well. As a buyer and seller of almost anything, at least a temporary welcome could be had even among the inhospitable.

The earliest commerce, as an eminent German economist has pointed out, was made up of traffic between groups rather than among individuals.[11] Trade between individuals within the same clan or community was in the beginning non-existent. As one step further away from this nascent commerce on a group level, there arose the itiner-

109

ant hawker, who journeyed from city to city buying and selling on his own behalf, and not for the benefit of any group. As a trader, Abraham belonged to that category.

In the course of his moving about, it is not however recorded that he had occasion to be invited inside the walls of Schechem or Bethel or Salem or Hebron. This is understandable. Inside none of these cities were there to be found permanent market places for the reception of merchants. For such buying and selling as the inhabitants of these cities chose to indulge themselves, the open spaces outside their city gates proved sufficient.

Abraham's customers, in all probability, were for the most part the many Canaanite temples and shrines who were in need of a regular supply of sheep and oxen for sacrificial purposes—to the extent, that is, that they dispensed with human infants. As a dealer in livestock and doubtless of fabricated commodities as well, Abraham was able to acquire riches. It deserves mention, in passing, that the more common forerunner in ancient times of the merchant, with his accumulated store of capital goods, was the breeder and trader in livestock, and only rarely the lowly tiller of the soil.

Unless he happened to be a large and independent landowner, the grower of wheat and barley was hardly ever in a position to accumulate any kind of surplus that would have permitted him to branch out into more alluring enterprises. Apart from being subject to the regular attentions of the rent collector, he was unremittingly visited by predatory tax gatherers. The herdsman, to the contrary, presented for all those who would have exploited him a far more elusive target. Moving about from place to place, he was fairly immune from harrassment by constituted authorities. Quite often moreover he had at his call a retinue of muscular slaves, so that for this reason if not for any other he would be approached with some hesitancy.

110

The raising of cattle for the market, which involved selling and at least a limited degree of buying as well, constituted the earliest form of tradesmanship. It was a form of enterprise in which business acumen and knowledge of the world were of some advantage. At this calling Abraham and his immediate successors were sufficiently adept, as were so many of their descendants in the later Biblical period, such as Nabal and Barzillai. The philosopher Philo wrote that in his day, and presumably for many generations previously, the men of his nation were noted as grazers and stock-breeders, and as keepers of flocks and herds of goats, oxen, and sheep in large numbers. From such sources, the kings of Judah appear to have depended for much of their revenues along with their trading in horses, as alternatives to taxing the people. The true source of Jewish mercantilism can well be said to reach back to the very beginning of their recorded history.

Like Thales of Miletus and Solon of Athens, of a later age, Abraham travelled far in pursuit of both gain and wisdom. Abraham was a man of God. But likewise was he a man of the world. And like most of his descendants, he was far from holding in contempt material possessions. On leaving the paternal comforts of Haran, he became a dweller in tents. This was not entirely by choice. Having abandoned a place of residence where he was known, he was not likely to discover immediately some other city that would have been more tolerant of his non-conformist worship; unless, like the prophet Mohammed, on reaching Medina, he had chosen to become an agitator and revolutionary.

Many years were to elapse from the time of Abraham's abandonment of his father's hearth and that of his unnamed mother until he was enabled finally to lay down fresh roots in the new land that had been pledged to him and his descendants. His own narrow share of that prom-

111

ised land lay between Hebron and Beersheba. A trading centre of some note was Hebron. Standing at the cross roads of at least two caravan routes, it was a link between the coastal cities of the Mediterranean and the cities bordering on the Dead Sea, including the unblest Sodom and Gomorrah. Into this area a mixed population had been attracted, including Hittites, with whom Abraham had business relationships.

Reflections must have crossed the mind of the patriarch on the contrast between this parched countryside and the rich territory which in his youth he had forsaken. Yet he had no thought of retracing his footsteps, nor would he permit his son Isaac to go elsewhere in search of happiness. He now found himself in a land that was meagre enough, but not unfriendly. Abraham, in the evening of his life, and after years of toil and effort, now found himself "a mighty prince" at ease among well-meaning and respectful neighbours; and what was even more exceptionable, a great man without enemies.

The Bible does not portray the patriarch as either a saint or a holy man. Sufficiently revealed were certain weaknesses of character manifested on critical occasions. Yet a deep current of humanitarianism is visible in all that is related of him. He had a genius for friendship and for binding men to his side. Stopping for a time near Damascus, he is joined by Eliezer, later to become the steward of his household. A faithful friend Eliezer proved himself to be, more loyal than Abraham's adopted son Lot, with whom Abraham refused to quarrel. Later Abraham came to the aid of his ungrateful kinsman. In all his dealings, Abraham proved himself to be the good neighbour and the friend of his fellow men. Abraham's intercession on behalf of Sodom and Gomorrah was poignantly recalled in the aftermath of an episode of the last world war. In 1944, a number of German officers were frustrated in an attempt to rid the

112

world of Hitler. The leader of this failed conspiracy was General Henning von Treskow, a devout Christian and a penitent. Before dying by his own hand, he left a written memorial in which he cited the incident of Abraham pleading with God on behalf of the doomed cities, concluding prayerfully that in a similar extremity God would spare the sinful German nation for the sake of its innocent members.

JOSEPH

The sons of Jacob, though many, were as a group unimpressive. Among them Joseph alone inherited the resplendent qualities of his great grandfather Abraham. Frivolous and conceited as a youth, Joseph matured quickly enough once overtaken by adversity. Sold as a slave in Egypt, his talent for administration and proven trustworthiness soon gained for him a position of confidence. But once again misfortune befell him. He found himself trapped in an amorous intrigue initiated by the concupiscent wife of his patron and benefactor.

Here was a possible snare in men's lives, first noted in the Scriptures, and yet not uncommon throughout the ages, and one from which no victim has been able to emerge entirely unscathed. For Joseph to have succumbed to the wanton's endearments would have resulted in certain detection with the same direful consequences as in a later century overtook Thomas Culpepper, the luckless paramour of Queen Katherine Howard, the wife of King Henry VIII. And yet almost equally ominous has it always been for anyone in a dependent position to spurn the advances of an imperious and masterly female. So precarious a situation did present itself some centuries later to another descendant of Abraham in the person of Herod, king of Judaea. King Herod, a vassal of the Romans, had as his guest Queen Cleopatra of Egypt, who besought him gently but urgently to beguile the tedium of her stay. Her Hebraic host, who was well enough posted on the story of Joseph and the Potiphar woman, courteously resisted her importunities. The queen, believably enough, was deeply offended. On her return from Jerusalem to the arms of her true lover, Mark Antony, she reported the unforgiveable incident in her own version, as may be supposed. Herod, who was at that time the underling of Antony, was thereupon summoned to Alexandria for an accounting of his misconduct. Unlike Joseph, he escaped confinement in a dungeon, but the affair was costly to him none the less. The tokens of appeasement insisted upon by both the aggrieved lovers were far from trivial. Antony's lacerated feelings could only be salved by a substantial monetary concession. Cleopatra, whose hurt was even greater, would hear of nothing less than the transfer to her by Herod of all the coastal cities of Palestine. Be it added that unexpectedly Herod did not come off too badly in the end. In the contest that soon flared up between Mark and his paramour on the one side and the youthful Octavian on the other, the agile Jewish monarch knew exactly on whose side to range himself.

And now to return to Joseph. While languishing in prison, he met up with some distinguished company, one of whom later presented him to Egypt's ruler. This particular Pharaoh was an intelligent but harassed monarch. His nerves frayed by a narrow escape from death through poisoning, he was troubled nightly by a procession of nightmares. Joseph, who had been long enough in the country to form some estimate of its economic weakness and its total dependence on the fickleness of the Nile river, interpreted Pharaoh's vision of the voracious kine as a threat not to the dreamer's own personal safety but merely to the Egyptian realm. Pharaoh felt much relieved; all the more so as the means for reducing the impact of the coming hard times was suggested to him as well. Moreover, the idea of a vast hoard of wheat monopolized entirely by himself did not fail to have some attraction for him. Joseph, whose reputation as a highly efficient bailiff of one of the nation's large estates could not have been unknown, was obviously the man that Pharaoh could now depend on. Empty granaries, the property of the Pharaoh, were already in existence, having been built long before in anticipation of recurrent seasons when the Nile failed to rise sufficiently.[12]

In chapter 47 of the book of Genesis is depicted a social revolution in all its sorrowful consequences, a revolution engineered from above and not from below. The entire kingdom was transformed into a kind of disagreeable welfare state, whose alternative could only have been mass starvation. The entire population, both noble and commoner, is shown as having been at the mercy of the ruler and his chief minister who, in exchange for the means of sustenance, proceeded relentlessly to engross the national wealth, in precious metals, herds of cattle, and finally virtually all the land. Exempt from this massive transfer were the holdings of the priests, whom the government did not dare antagonize, and who continued to receive their victuals without having to pay for them.

The rural spaces came to be all depopulated, with their inhabitants concentrated in the cities. (Genesis 47:21.) The text, however, says nothing as to what happened to the people thus transplanted. It could be surmised that they were put to work as indentured labourers in building additional granaries, as well as in the construction of new fortresses and temples in honour of the gods, in about the same manner as the Israelites themselves were conscripted at the time of Moses. Parenthetically, it could here be mentioned that drastic and wholesale changes in land tenure mentioned in Genesis were endemic in early times. The

115

Grecian migrants, forcing themselves into Sicily and southern Italy, drove the existing inhabitants from their lands and put them to hard labour building cities like Syracuse, Agrigentum, and Rhegium.[13]

Now Joseph, twice risen to affluence and power in Egypt, made no effort during these years to communicate with his kindred back in the land of Canaan. His resentment extended apparently even to his father, who unwittingly had despatched him on an errand which forever terminated his carefree youth. Married to the daughter of one of the country's leading priests, he had become almost completely Egyptianized. Even his name had been changed. His two sons were being raised as Egyptian nobles. "And Joseph called the name of his first born Menasseh. For God said he hath made me forget all my toil and all my father's house."[14]

The account of the chance meeting and final reconciliation between the dry bureaucrat and his contrite brethren has in it the quality of drama and pathos which has gripped the hearts and minds of generations without number. Of this stirring episode, an American literary critic once wrote, "Many characters like the above, to whom only a few lines are given, are nevertheless unforgettable; whilst the more important personages Jehu, Ahab, Jezebel, Joab, are as real to us as the leading figures in American history."[15]

Before revealing himself to his brethren, Joseph asks himself: Had their denial of charity towards him been no more than an accidental act, or did it indicate in them a persistent note of wickedness? He tries them by informing them of his intention of keeping the sheltered Benjamin as his slave, while allowing the others to depart. Will these brothers of his now abandon Benjamin as they had once abandoned him? He soon discovers that they will not. "And he asked them of their welfare and said, Is your father well, the old man of whom ye spoke? Is he yet alive? And they

116

answered, Thy servant our father is in good health, he is yet alive. And they bowed down their heads and made obeisance."

"And he lifted up his eyes and saw his brother Benjamin, his mother's son, and said, Is this your younger brother of whom ye spoke unto me? And he said. God be gracious unto thee my son. And Joseph made haste, for his bowels did yearn upon his brother and he sought where to weep, and he entered into his chamber and wept there."

Over the span of many centuries, and with astonishing vividness, the functionary Joseph leaps to life before us as a man of feeling. Raising himself above the level of the self-seeking office holder, Joseph does not hesitate to approach his sovereign on behalf of his straitened family. A not ungrateful Pharaoh responds with warmth. "And Pharaoh spoke unto Joseph saying, Thy father and brethren are come unto thee. The land of Egypt is before thee. In the best of the land make thy father and brethren to dwell; and if thou knowest any men of activity among them make them rulers over my cattle."[16]

Finding sufficient living space for these outsiders, and for the pasturing of the extensive herds that they brought with them, presented no problem for a countryside but recently denuded of a goodly portion of its indigenous population. The king, acutely conscious of the fact that his original subjects bore him no great love, even though his measures harsh as they were had rescued them from starvation, knew that he could count on the unswerving loyalty of these new arrivals.

An episode in the history of the Jewish people, duplicating somewhat their coming into Egypt, occurred at the time of the Macedonian Ptolemies about a thousand years later. Like the Pharaoh who had favoured Joseph's kinsfolk by granting them important offices of state, the Greek-speaking conquerors of Egypt in similar fashion-found it to their advantage to rely upon the Jewish settlers in Alexandria and to encourage the building up of their community. We are informed of this successor of Alexander that "he enrolled many in the army, giving them higher than ordinary pay; and in like manner, having proved the loyalty of those already in the country, he placed under their charge the fortresses that he built, that the native Egyptians might be intimidated by them."[17] It was this same Ptolemy, the second of that name and known as Philadelphus, who in the third century before the Christian era had ordered the translation into Greek of the Hebrew Scriptures. Being in all likelihood among its first readers, the story of the Israelites in Egypt might well have given him the necessary assurance that the Jews and the native Egyptians were unlikely to fall in love with one another, so that the danger of their making common cause against his dynasty was not likely to arise.

Some observation on the economic and political implications of the Israelite descent into Egypt is here in order. Why did Jacob, who apparently was not short of silver to pay for his needs, find it necessary to send to Egypt for grain? Why did not the grain come to him in the regular course of international trade? The answer is that Egypt in the patriarchal age was a self-contained and virtually closed economy. Beyond olives, wine, and slaves, it required nothing from beyond its borders. Its one important article of export was not wheat but papyrus, a product for which the world had no great need, and which was only carried out of Egypt at rare intervals. With a huge army of non-producers to be fed, including priests, soldiers, and officials, Egypt's peasantry, unlike those of Roman times, had as yet no exportable surplus. It is an overriding fact that, in antiquity and in the Middle Ages, it was generally the policy of governments to discourage the export of food stuffs. As the Scriptural account would seem to indicate, foreign buyers of wheat were not especially welcome in Egypt, and like Jacob's sons were received with suspicion.

To be noted is the fact that the drought reported to have fallen simultaneously on Egypt and Canaan could not have resulted from a common natural cause. That of Egypt was occasioned by a failure of the Nile to overflow its banks in due season, a failure traceable to a shortage of rainfall in the Abyssinian uplands.

The drought that overtook the land of Canaan could hardly have been connected with this environmental failure. Though coincidental in time, the famines in both areas need not have been exactly contemporaneous. The one in Canaan was apparently not so disastrous as to have compelled Jacob and his clan to abandon their homesteads. Jacob, invited to migrate with his entire family to Egypt, apparently hesitated to do so.

"And God spoke to Israel in the vision of the night and said—fear not to go down unto Egypt, for I will there make thee a great nation."[18] The forebears of the future Jewish nation at that time numbered less than one hundred, fewer than the three hundred and eighteen retainers that Abraham had been able to muster.[19] Their likelihood of ever becoming "a great nation" would, to an observer of that period, have seemed altogether remote. At its lowest ebb was the morale of this diminished community. Bespoken in the text was the agony of its head over the loss of his favourite child, while the bruising impact of the guilty secret of his sons may well be surmised. Nor is it unlikely that some hint of the truth had not during the years imbedded itself in the embittered mind of the old man.

Sunk in apathy, the Israelite clan were eking out their existence within a bleak terrain, with no fresh land available to them to permit any expansion of their numbers.[20] By no means were the other tribal descendants of Abraham condemned to languish so ingloriously. These others such as the Edomites and Ishmaelites were enabled by aggressive means to carve out ample territories for themselves. The Israelites were restricted in their occupancy to lands that they had been able to obtain only by peaceful purchase, an unsure mode of acquisition for those times. Their apparent destiny lay in amalgamating with the other Hebrew clans or otherwise in being absorbed totally into the Canaanite environment. Only through some miracle could they have been rescued from the total oblivion that seemed to await them as a group—and that miracle was indeed forthcoming.

"And Israel dwelt in the land of Egypt in the country of Goshen; and they had possessions therein, and grew and multiplied exceedingly."[21] "And the children of Israel were fruitful, and increased and multiplied, and waxed exceeding mighty; and the land was filled with them."[22] Here indeed was the actual fulfillment of promise that God made first to Abraham and later to Jacob. Here indeed was a miracle. The miracle consisted in a population explosion that within a century or two transformed a handful of destitute tribesmen into a nation.

Like their descendants throughout the ages, these early Israelites were quick to avail themselves of the opportunities offered by their surroundings. But Joseph, now thoroughly integrated with his people, and whose farsightedness did not desert him in his old age, saw for them no future in Egypt. "And Joseph said unto his brethren, I die; and God will surely visit you, and bring you out of this land unto the land which he swore to Abraham, to Isaac, and to Jacob."[23]

MOSES

Moses, in the opinion of the German savant Edouard Meyer, was not an historical personality. Others of this school have propounded the view that even if he were not a mythological character, he was not the author of the laws attributed to him. These are extreme opinions which in their turn tend to raise some unanswerable questions. If the exodus of the Israelites from Egypt had not as its leader a man by the name of Moses, who then could such a leader have been? The insistence that it was Moses and none other is imbedded in a tradition that is altogether consistent and uncontradicted. As to this Professor Albright has written, "The Mosaic tradition is so consistent, so well attested by different Pentateuchal documents, and so congruent with our independent knowledge of the Near East in the late second millenium B.C. that only hypercritical rationalism can reject its essential historicity."[24]

Some marvelous tales have indeed surrounded the infancy and early life of the divinely appointed leader, the greater part of them not deemed worthy of credence by the compilers of the Pentateuch. In the cuneiform library of Asshurbanipal there has come to light a chronicle of the birth and early concealment of a remote Babylonian monarch whose reign dates as far back as 3800 B.C. but whose actual existence has not been doubted. As an infant, the early exposure of this future ruler is strikingly similar to that of the child Moses on the Nile River. The life of Moses was in the beginning threatened and more or less miraculously preserved, as was that of Sargon, Cyrus the Great, Romulus, and Jesus. That the stamp of romance was by tradition imprinted on the early lives of these notable men has not in any degree impugned their existence. The fabulous and the historical are in a great number of instances intertwined.

To be taken even less seriously is the assertion that while a person answering somewhat to the description of Moses might have existed, he was not to be credited with the promulgation of the laws attributed to him. There is an improbability about a lawgiver whose true identity has been

121

concealed, and for whom the name of another has for no visible reason been substituted. The Hindu code of Manu is attributed to a sage of that name; and one whose existence has never been questioned, even though scarcely anything is known of his life and activities. No one has ever suggested that Solon of Athens was a mere front for someone else, or that Lycurgus of Sparta was falsely credited with the performance of some other anonymous legislator. Of Moses, it is clearly enough stated that he wrote down his laws in a "book," from which copies were then made on stones as well as on the doorposts of innumerable households.

Present-day scholarship is no longer dubious as to the historical character of Moses, and that the laws attributed to him were his in the main. Was Moses ancient Israel's one and only lawgiver? Apparently not. Of Joshua it is written that, having laid down the sword, he devoted his later years to implementing the peaceful work of his master. "So Joshua made a covenant with the people that day, and set them a statute and an ordinance in Schechem. And Joshua wrote these words in the book of the Law of God; and he took a great stone, and set it up there under the oak that was by the sanctuary of the Lord."[25]

More plausible is the attempt made to separate those laws in the Pentateuch which are undeniably of Mosaic origin from older rules common since remote times to the nations of the Middle East.[26] According to this authority, the rules which can be safely attributed to Moses, or perhaps to Joshua, are the Decalogue, the institution of the Sabbath, dietary laws, the construction of the tabernacle, the role of the priests, redemption of the first born, the festivals, as well as the proscription of idolatry, necromancy, magic, worship of the dead, human sacrifice, sodomy, homosexuality, and sacred prostitution.

This above all should be emphasized: The authority of the Torah and its significance for mankind does not turn on

122

the question as to whether a particular ordinance or ethical prescription ought to be attributed to Moses or to some later prophet. Thus, for example, the Torah repudiates Oriental mysticism. "The secret things belong to the Lord our God; but the things that are revealed belong to us and to our children forever, that we may do all the words of his instruction."[27] This sage advice is attributed to Moses himself. But should we happen to believe that it proceeded from some teacher other than Moses, need our respect for it be diminished on this account?

While the tradition which accords unto Moses personally a priority among the prophets is by all means entitled to our continued respect, it should be underlined that the grandeur of the Hebraic code is independent of the identity of any of its propounders. To its reasonableness and humanity no parallel is discoverable either in the ancient world or in the mediaeval world. The historian Edward Gibbon drew our attention to the universality of torture among the cultivated Graeco-Romans. Writing of the magistrates during the period of the Empire, he observed: "They found the use of torture established not only among the slaves of Oriental despotism, but among the Macedonians who obeyed a limited monarch, among the Rhodians who flourished by the liberty of commerce, and even among the sage Athenians."[28] Contrasted with all this, the rule of the Torah, requiring witnesses to a man's guilt and witnesses alone. Thus was judicial torture automatically ruled out.

Unique among all the known codes of Europe and Asia, the Mosaic or Hebraic laws took no account of social stratification among the people. Even as these laws were announced as applying equally to the stranger and the home born, so did they apply equally to the poor and to the rich. There is a prohibition of any favouritism towards the rich; and what is altogether unique, all favouritism towards

123

the poor is discountenanced likewise. All holders of land were deemed to be on an equal footing, there being no differention of status as between landlord and tenant. And finally, there was reference to neither aristocracy nor warrior caste. A sacerdotal class there was; but socially it was less than privileged.

How did Moses come to be designated by the Jews of later times as "Moses our teacher"? Clearly, in order to become a teacher, one must begin by first learning from others. First and foremost, Moses had to be instructed in the traditions of his fellow Israelites, such as they were at the time, as to the circumstances of their having immigrated from the land of Canaan to Egypt, and above all of the promise made by God to the patriarchs that their descendants would inherit a country of their own. Without a fervent belief in this promise, no hope of redeeming the Israelites from their bondage in Egypt could have entered his mind. As a requisite for leadership, Moses needed likewise to acquire "all the wisdom of Egypt."[29] Along with this "wisdom," Moses imbibed the art of dissimulation. He was careful not to reveal to Pharaoh his intention of leading the departing Israelites to the conquest of Canaan. Pharaoh, who still regarded himself as the suzerain of Canaan, would not have liked that.[30] It was the sudden realization that came to Pharaoh and his advisors that the freed Israelites were in fact heading for Canaan that motivated the last pursuit.

It was as a pupil likewise that Moses acquired from his Egyptian teachers his skill in the military art. Joined to this art was the useful knowledge that came to him, during the years of adversity in the desert, of the geography of the Sinai peninsula. Well versed in military science, Moses was able to make some notable contributions thereto. Thus, do we find him solicitous as to the hygienic arrangements affecting his followers.[31] Negligence in this regard has

124

throughout the ages resulted in the destruction of innumerable military lives. In anticipation of the Greeks and Romans, he marshalled his warriors in divisions of ten and multiples of ten.[32] Likewise did he understand the necessity, not as yet generally recognized, of having his men march in formation, and trained in obeying the varying signals of the ram's horn. And finally, Moses showed himself to be a prudent leader in knowing when to attack and when to refrain from attacking.

Moses had at least some knowledge of legal codes in effect prior to his time. More especially was he acquainted with the celebrated code of Hammurabi, thanks to his sojourn during his latter years in the Transjordan country, which lay inside the orbit of Babylonian civilization. But he borrowed none of its enormities, such as the execution of thieves and cutting off the fingers of luckless physicians. Merciful in its treatment of thieves and all offenders against the rights of property, the Mosaic legislation was severe enough in ordering drastic punishment for all violence to the person, depending on their gravity. One of the curiosities of later teaching, both Jewish and Christian, was the renunciation of severity in dealing with violently disposed criminals. Much like in our own time, a vapid and exaggerated sentimentality substituted itself for the robust teaching of the great lawgiver. In later times, a magistracy known as the Synhedrin in the name of a rarefied and easygoing justice, flaunted its own flaccidity in setting up new rules for dealing with murderers.

From among the things that he did learn, Moses both accepted and rejected. There were features in the pagan civilization that he did accept. Of the Ten Commandments, be it said, all but two are of international derivation. The Torah could claim no originality in its outlawing of murder, theft, adultery, disloyalty to parents, and covetousness. Nor should it surprise us that portions of the temple ritual resembled closely that of Canaanites. In the main, he rejected. Moses spurned all the Middle Eastern deities along with their idols, the worship of the dead and preoccupation with the hereafter. He forbade necromancy and witchcraft, human sacrifice, homosexuality and sodomy, marriage between siblings, and the eating of animal food that he considered both unclean and undigestible.

As teacher, prophet, lawgiver, and military commander, time will never obliterate the memory of Moses. Be it said that a combination of these attributes could not have exempted him from the practice and recommendation of acts of cruelty. His precepts for dealing with fallen enemies are not easy to reconcile with humanitarianism though they were not out of keeping with the spirit of the times. For him co-existence with the heathen was the dashing of all his hopes for the permanency of a God-inspired nation and society. And yet neither Moses nor Joshua were addicted to warfare for its own sake. Unlike all the other militant prophets that history speaks of, the territorial conquest sought by them was limited to a narrow and confined area. Against such neighbours as Edomites, Moabites, and Ammonites, Moses forbade all acts of aggression, warning his people that the land of these nations had been conferred upon them by the same God who bestowed Canaan upon the Israelites.

Though Moses certainly conceived the God of the Israelites as the ruler of all the other nations, he was in other respects no "universalist." His sole and primary aim was the betterment of one small nation; even though his teachings to them were in later ages to prove acceptable to many nations aside from his own. "*The man Moses*" we are informed "*was very meek*" (Numbers 12:3) It was such modesty, one might infer, that stayed him from declaring himself to be everybody's savior, and as God's chosen Messenger to the entire world.

Even though Moses was well in advance of his time, we

should discountenance all attempts to portray him as an excessively modernized innovator and reformer. Thus are we informed that "he wanted neither priests nor sacrifices."[33] In the version of Rabbi Silver, the cult of animal sacrifice, supposedly rejected by Moses, was incorporated into Israelitish practice only in a later period, and then only under Canaanitish influence. In support of this view, he adduces a single passage from the prophet Amos. Speaking rhetorically in the name of the Lord, the prophet demands, "Did you bring me sacrifices and offerings the forty years in the wilderness, O House of Israel."[34] The implied answer is in the negative.

From this particular text no proof can be derived that Moses consistently abjured sacrifices. Even though desert conditions were unfavourable to the bringing of burnt offerings, the practice could conveniently have been instituted in the more comfortable surroundings of transJordan where Moses lived and taught for some time at least. We are informed of Joshua, who was assuredly under no Canaanitish influence, that he erected an altar on Mount Ebal.[35] To assert that Moses cast aside all burnt offerings runs counter to innumerable texts which both explicitly and by indirection advise us that he was very far from banning the practice. Should the attempt be persisted in of ascribing all this ritual to someone other than Moses, then likewise it would be necessary as well to disconnect Moses from the building of the tabernacle, from all the festivals including the Passover, the laws of uncleanliness with their expiatory rites, and the creation of the order of priests and Levites. But this is not all. Should it be decided that we are to set at nought everything written about Moses in relation to animal sacrifices and the priesthood, as Rabbi Silver proposes, why not go one step further and question everything else that has been attributed to him?

To maintain that Moses disallowed in categorical fashion sacrifices and libations is a contradiction of textual information on wholly insuf icient grounds. Moses was enough of a reformer to have cried out against most of the objectionable practices of his Egyptian and Semitic contemporaries. The Torah, in addition to suppressing human sacrifice—a radical enough move in its time—confined animal sacrifice to one central shrine and forbade its practice elsewhere. It would be more in accordance with the truth if to some later men of God were left the merit of being wholly opposed to this unseemly form of worship.

What kind of people were these that Moses was called upon to serve and to deliver from bondage? From the very outset, Moses did have some experience of their ingratitude and fractiousness; yet at no time did Moses waver in his affection for this people; and in the conviction that in the mass they stood for something that was worth perpetuating. Nor were they in the main so completely "stiff-necked" as to refuse to agree to a fresh manner of living, along with a new set of beliefs and religious observances. Only natural was their repeated "murmuring" under conditions of excessive desert heat, hunger and thirst, disease, snake bites, and all-round misery. "Yet a little and they will stone me," Moses reported at one time. But they did not stone him. That from one crisis to another they continued to have faith in his leadership in itself testified to their basic intelligence, fortitude and self-control. In Moses they recognized a teacher and a prophet who for himself required no comforts which they themselves were denied, and that in all their privations he suffered together with them.

The generation that chose to abandon servitude by following Moses into the unknown was of no servile mentality. Nor did they sinfully bring upon themselves the condemnation of perishing in the wretchedness of the desert as tradition would have us believe. They were no sinners; but the true sons and daughters of the covenant. They were in

128

fact the one and only nation of the ancient world, who, threatened with final and irrevocable enslavement, were enabled to experience the joys—as well as the miseries—of liberation. The exploited peasants whom they left behind were at no time influenced by their example; not under the animal gods of the Pharaohs, nor under the Koran of Islam.

It is a spurious interpretation that a generation that bravely confronted the "great and dreadful wilderness where there were serpents, fiery serpents and scorpions, and thirsty ground where there was no water"[36] was unworthy of entering the promised land. Such men and women were as much fitted for great enterprises as were the survivors of the concentration camps who in 1948 held off the Arab hordes. The men who readily abandoned the tainted fleshpots of Egypt, who accepted the commandments at Sinai, who learned to march in formation as disciplined warriors, and who stood up against desert tribes, did not degenerate into a useless rabble merely because at a crucial moment they accepted the majority report of a body of scouts telling them that an attack on the Promised Land from the open desert was not practicable. Moses showed himself to be of the same mind as the majority when he decided that the only way to break into Canaan proper was by first setting up a suitable base in the more liveable country of trans-Jordan.

In the opening chapter of Exodus we are informed about a turn for the worse in the situation of the Israelites concentrated in the northern province of Goshen. The Egyptians had for some time been vaguely fearful of invasion by migratory bands of seafaring men coming from the direction of the Grecian mainland. Their apprehension came to a focus when Knossos, the famed Cretan capital, was taken and destroyed around the year 1400 B.C.E.[37] The northern coastal region, where nearly all the Israelites happened to be concentrated, needed hurriedly to be put

129

into a state of defence. For storing a variety of supplies that a defending army would require, the twin cities of Pithom and Ramses were built and munitioned. Conscripted to perform the necessary labour were the Israelite inhabitants of the region along with others whose loyalty was suspected.[38]

Adding to the woes of the Israelites was the effect produced by a technological development which around that time had overtaken Egypt's building industry. Early buildings in that country, such as pyramids, palaces, temples, and fortresses, had been exclusively of stone. But stone could be quarried only in the upper valley of the Nile. By masses of slaves such stone blocks were drawn to the lower part of the country where much of the construction took place, a wasteful and inconvenient process. It was in the alluvial soil of lower Mesopotamia that the making of clay into bricks had originated.[39] This new material found its way into Egypt sometime prior to the age of Moses.

The making of bricks had about it this distinctiveness. Unlike all the other crafts of early times, their manufacture did not lend itself to small-scale enterprise within scattered workshops. Brick-making from the outset was a mass production industry that required a concentration of many workers in the immediate vicinity of the building site. "And the Egyptians made the children of Israel serve with rigour, and they made their lives bitter with bondage, in mortar and in brick, and in all manner of service in the fields."[40] It did not indeed take the masters of Egypt long to discover that for the production of these newer and more convenient building blocks both the raw material and the man power was to be had in the very district inhabited by the unwanted aliens.

This, however, should be noted. Despite their being oppressed and ill-treated, the Israelites at the time of the Exodus, had not become slaves in the fullest sense, as was

130

the case with the captive Negroes or the Helots of Sparta. Their family units were still unimpaired. Nor were they altogether bereft of their possessions. Pharaoh, in one of his unkept promises to permit the Israelites to leave temporarily, had stipulated "only let your flocks and your herds be stayed."[41] Throughout history and in various societies, there have been discernible stages between persons who were free and those unfree. The Israelites in Egypt were never reduced to the level of chattel slaves. But that their Egyptian hosts, the inventors of Negro slavery, were intent on reducing them to a like status they saw with sufficient clarity. They could not but see before their very eyes the processions of chained Negro captives brought in from the Sudan. Neither did it escape their attention that the lives of these unfortunates were exceedingly brief, that among them the adults rarely reached middle age, and that the children hardly ever attained manhood and womanhood. But on the other hand, to choose freedom meant the abandonment of a fruitful territory for one that was almost lifeless. Never perhaps in the annals of mankind was an entire people called upon to choose between such two desperate alternatives as confronted our ancestors on that memorable Passover eve.

The departure from Egypt can be said to have been the first of the many mass migration to which Jews have been subject in the course of their long history. Their situation becoming more intolerable from day to day, their final departure was in a sense an involuntary one. Between an "exodus" and an outright expulsion the line of distinction is not invariably a clear one. The problem that the departing Israelites were compelled to face was a twofold one. The first was where to go. It was certainly not their intention to wander about in the desert to the very end of their lives. Had they been told in the beginning that only their children and grandchildren were destined to reach the promised land, and that they themselves would all perish in the desert, few among them would have been persuaded to leave Egypt. Also, egress from Egyptian jurisdiction would have been difficult enough, even without the pursuit of Pharaoh's armoured brigade. The Egyptian border was habitually patrolled at nearly all available transits. To discover a place of easy exit, at which the defenceless Israelites would be free of molestation, required leadership as well as skill of the highest order.

The challenge presented to the Israelites leaving Egypt had some kind of a repetition thousands of years later in the mass evacuation of the Jews from Spain in 1492. Spain forms the major portion of a peninsula; but for the several hundreds of thousands of Jews who were given no more than three months to leave, it was for all purposes an island. The only overland exit was France, but France had for a century been closed to them. Somehow on that occasion the necessary amount of shipping as well as the passage money was forthcoming.

The Jews of Spain, who were no longer permitted to remain and to live with their religion, could easily have been locked in and compelled in the end to surrender to the fanaticism of the Church and the Spanish monarchy. On a relatively small scale, a fate of this kind actually did befall the Jewish community of the kingdom of Naples in the late thirteenth century. Following a rebellion which brought to the throne of that kingdom a member of the French house of Capet, things soon became impossible for the Jewish community, which numbered some 30,000 and formed about 3% of the population. Assailed by a frenzied drive for conversion on the part of the Dominicans, accompanied by threats of death, the Jews of that kingdom had nowhere to flee. The Italian cities of the north were closed to them. An insufficient number of ships being available for taking them to Africa or Spain, the greater number, in order to save their lives, allowed themselves to be converted.

A controversy worthy of some attention is that over the number of Israelites that accompanied Moses into the desert. Was it a large horde as the text would have us believe, or a mere handful as others have contended? In passing it should be noted that as regards the exodus from Spain, an event of comparatively recent times, there persists likewise a great uncertainty as to actual numbers involved, the estimate varying from about one hundred and fifty thousand to as high as eight hundred thousand. The Scripture speaks of a prodigious surge in the Hebrew population preceding the Exodus from Egypt. "And the children of Israel were fruitful and increased abundantly, and multiplied and waxed exceeding mighty, and the land was filled with them."[42]

There is no other textual affirmation that the Israelites in Egypt became so extended in numbers as to overrun the country south of the delta. The small number of settlers who arrived with Jacob were comfortably enough ensconced in the extreme northern province. It is impossible to believe, however, that they had this territory all to themselves. That the delta country had long been a haven for a considerable non-Egyptian population is a plausible enough suggestion.[43] Lending substance to this view is the affirmation that on leaving the Israelites were accompanied by "a mixed multitude."[44] But even allowing for this increment, the figure given of six hundred thousand men, not counting women and children, following Moses into the desert is unquestionably exaggerated. It is curious to note that the same emotional number is by the priestly chroniclers ascribed to the Crusaders crossing from Europe into Asia in the year 1097.[45] One might suppose, incidentally, that an army of such magnitude, even if inadequately equipped, would not have stood in any great fear of Pharaoh's pursuing chariots.

Generally in historical writings the epic treatment of events has been characterized by a carelessness as to numbers of persons involved. In a relatively small border affray, the Philistines were said to have mustered 30,000 chariots.[46] King Saul preparing an attack on the Amalekites assembled an army of 200,000.[47] For this miserable little campaign the actual figure could have been closer to 2,000. A force of Carthaginians that once invaded Sicily numbered 100,000 according to the Greek historian Timaeus. Another by name of Ephorus made it 200,000.

A sober approach to population statistics was until recent times not within the capacity of even learned authors. Montesquieu, in the year 1721, argued that the population of the antique world was at least ten times as great as that of his own time.[48] There was until quite recently no understanding whatever of the significance of birth rates and death rates. Also, there were deep rooted objections based on religion to the counting of men, and even more so to the counting of women.[49]

It is obviously a sound practice to shrink to credible levels the dilated figures that are to be found in the writings of the ancients. In respect to the Exodus from Egypt, a word of caution is required, nevertheless. By some critics, the quantum of refugees from Egypt has been reduced from a figure bearing comparison to the fabled sands of the sea down to a mere token, such as five or six thousand.[50] There are nonetheless weighty reasons for maintaining that the number of migrants that accompanied Moses in his desert wanderings was far from inconsiderable, even if it did not approach that given in the text.

Going into the desert of Sinai, with the prospect of remaining in its grip for some indefinite time, and with the assurance of having to engage in a war of conquest immediately on the termination of the adventure, was an enterprise that could not have been contemplated by a tiny group of desperate men and their families. Had their numbers really been so few, they would have succumbed quickly enough to the natural cruelties of desert existence. Further, it would have been impossible for a small force of wanderers, however skilfully led, to have made any kind of stand against the tribal enemies that they were certain to encounter. In sum, to have successfully survived "the great and terrible desert" required at that time an army of migrants that was neither excessively large nor excessively small, even though it would be rash to attempt any guess as to their actual number. Moses referred to his followers as being so numerous as to render it impossible to supply them all with meat.[51] Without a very substantial number of armed men, neither Moses nor Joshua would have been able to make the considerable conquests and settlements narrated of them.

A large number undoubtedly did set out from Egypt; but within a short time, a high percentage of them must have perished through pestilence, hunger and thirst. The attrition was great, as the text clearly indicates. Nor could it have been true that mainly the adults perished, while the children all lived to grow up and take their places. Arriving finally at the oasis of Kadesh Barnea, their number was so greatly diminished that an immediate onslaught on the Canaanitish cities of the south was deemed to be impossible of success. A sojourn in this somewhat more benign territory, where they "abode for many days," combined with the provisions for cleanliness and fresh rules for the avoidance of contagion, tended to restore their strength and numbers.

A probable exaggeration enters likewise into the number of years that the Israelites are said to have remained in the desert while moving from one stopping place to another. Forty is a consecrated number that occurs with some frequency in both the Testaments. Thus Moses was on the mountain for exactly forty days and forty nights. The same length of time was spent by Jesus in the wilderness.[52] In the book of Judges, the same perfected number is several times repeated. Also the period of rule allotted to both David and Solomon was exactly forty years for each of them.

The actual transit through the Sinai peninsula was in all likelihood of comparatively short duration, possibly a matter of three years or even less. Also, single incidents recounted in connection with this march are susceptible of being retold in a more probable sequence. For example, the spoliation of the Midianites as reported in the book of Numbers could have occurred shortly after the departure from Egypt rather than many years later as the text implies. The editing of this report as given to us required the Israelites to retrace their steps far southward for no other reason than that of carrying a war to a distant foe. It would be more natural to suppose that this encounter with the Midianites, who were in occupation of a territory presently forming part of Saudi Arabia, actually took place at a time while the Israelites were still lingering near the Gulf of Elat, on their way northward. The large booty in cattle that is reported to have fallen to them after the victory must have helped to alleviate somewhat the hardship of desert existence.

It is by all means probable that between the departure from Egypt and the crossing of the Jordan the lapse of years was considerable enough. At Kadesh Barnea, not only were the wanderers in need of an extensive period of repose after their terrifying ordeal of marching through a waterless desert, but the hard-fought victories against the kings of Bashan and Hesbon once again required a period of recuperation that could not have been brief. The story of the two and one half tribes being left in possession of a territory first conquered and occupied by all twelve, would indicate an increase over the original number of occupants

136

that could have born some resemblance to the rate of their earlier proliferation in Egypt. For such recovery of population, no small number of years would have been required.

Albright supports the view that the people, leading the easier life of a pastoral community, were in occupation of the east bank of the Jordan for a lengthy period, before venturing to cross to the other side.[53] The Scripture does in fact hint that it was in that country that Moses performed many of his labours. Of the goat selected for the Day of Atonement, it is written that he commanded, "Let him go for a scapegoat into the wilderness."[54] There is here a clear enough implication that the people ordered to carry out this ritual were not themselves living in any wilderness.

Four hundred and forty years is mentioned in the text as the duration of Israel's sojourn in Egypt. Some authorities question this figure, though others are inclined to accept it. Discounting the likelihood of any such protracted residence amid an unfriendly environment, Professor C. H. Gordon has commented: "Moses was the grandson of Levi, the older brother of Joseph. If Joseph lived to an old age, as he is reputed to have, it would be quite possible for him to have been alive when Moses was born. . . . Thus, the gap between the coming of Israel to Egypt and the birth of Moses, who led the Exodus, could be spanned by a single lifetime."[55]

Professor W. F. Albright, to the contrary, sees no reason to question the length of the Egyptian exile as given in the Scripture.[56] The Exodus is commonly believed to have taken place at sometime during the long reign of Rameses the Second (1301 B.C.E.—1234 B.C.E.)

Albright suggests as a probable date the year 1290. By adding 430 to this figure, the time of the entry of the Israelites into Egypt in the late eighteenth century before the common era would coincide well with the reputed patriarchal age at about the time of its termination.

Professor Gordon, reacting from an apparent exaggeration, would seem to fall into an opposite extreme. By reducing the stay of the Israelites in Egypt to less than a century, he makes no allowance for the expansion of a small family clan into a considerable nation. But likewise open to question is the traditional figure supported by Professor Albright. Starting with the first of the patriarchs, the lives of four generations of men are portrayed for us in considerable detail. Are we to suppose that thereafter, for a span of time covering at least fifteen generations, there was not a single Israelite prior to Moses who was worthy of some mention? That by the time of Moses there had been no such prolonged settlement of the Israelites in Egypt would seem to be confirmed as well by a closer observation of the Scriptural text. For each of the twelve tribes, stemming from the last of the patriarchs, no more than a few intervening generations are mentioned. Significant likewise is the announcement of a Pharaoh who "knew not Joseph." There is here a clean enough suggestion of a new ruler who not only knew nothing of the Hebrew foreigner and the benefit that he had conferred upon the realm, but that he did not even want to know about him. With it is the added implication that the ruler or dynasty that preceded this hostile ruler did indeed know Joseph, or at least of him. Hence it hardly makes sense to assume that there were in Egypt a succession of perhaps twenty-five rulers, spanning several dynasties, who not only kept alive the memory of Joseph, but continued unswervingly to remain well-disposed towards his kinsfolk.

Invariably, the ending of a particular era is better known than its beginning. Hence the time of departure of the Israelites from Egypt, though by no means accurately determined, is less controversial than the time of their arrival. There are grounds for believing that, apart from the obdurate monarch, the Egyptians were glad enough to see them leave. Their labour having been suf,iciently exploited in the building up of Egypt's northern defences, their further presence was no longer essential to that nation's economy. Pithom and Rameses, as strategically located cities, were in readiness as supply bastions in helping to repel an anticipated invasion from the sea, an invasion that materialized not long afterwards. Both for the Israelites and the Egyptians, the Exodus came at an opportune time.

The Israelite invasion of Canaan differed radically from earlier incursions of this country successively undertaken by Hittites and Egyptians and perhaps Babylonians. These latter were intended solely for the collection of booty and of levying tribute on a conquered and submissive population. Throughout history, in the case of virtually all expeditionary marches, there has been the option, in the event of failure, for the aggressors to return to the shelter of a land from which they had originally set out. For the Israelite invaders under Moses and Joshua, there lay open no such retracing of their footsteps. These were people who had run away from "a house of bondage"; and to this house they could have gone back only as slaves, and perhaps not even as such. The war of the Israelites with the Canaanites resembled in this respect that of their present-day descendants in their several death struggles with the encompassing Arabs. There is one further point of resemblance. The present state of Israel was made possible by the fact that, prior to the massive Jewish immigration, the territory to be settled was largely unoccupied. In somewhat similar fashion, the Israelite conquest of the country at the time of Joshua had been preceded by some three centuries of subjection to Egyptian rule. The Egyptian authorities, much like their Turkish successors of later times, were corrupt and rapacious. Their misrule, long continued, ended in a decline of the indigenous population. Thereby were

139

created here and there throughout the country empty spaces waiting to be filled in by newcomers. Of interest in this connection is the evidence uncovered by archaeologists that in the years preceding the coming of the Israelites under Moses, the territory of trans-Jordan was to a great extent unoccupied. The native population elsewhere was small likewise. The bastion that was Jericho, whose decrepit walls were easily thrown down, is said to have covered a land surface only somewhat larger than that of the Roman Colosseum.[57] Hatzor, to the north, likewise rated as a centre, was in all probability not much larger. A power vacuum, not only in Canaan itself, but throughout the entire Middle East, made it possible for the ancient Israelites to fulfill their destiny.

No more than partially realized under Joshua was the plan formulated by Moses for the total subjection and resettlement of the land of Canaan. On the cessation of the fighting "there remained yet very much land to be possessed."[58] The account of Joshua's campaigns, confused and contradictory as it is in some instances, makes it clear, none the less, that the cities of the level portions of the country could not be successfully breached by reason of their being defended by "chariots of iron."[59] A further if unstated reason was that this lowland section was comparatively heavily populated. Even much of the hill country to the north remained unsubdued. But by way of compensation, a large territory to the east of the Jordan had earlier come into possession of the victorious Israelites, perhaps unexpectedly.

To have taken at that time full possession of the entire promised land, as hoped for by Moses, and in the first rush of conquest, would have required a reservoir of fighting men that the Israelites simply did not have. In the course of each victorious encounter with the opposing Canaanites, Joshua's army, being of no great size to begin with, was bound to suffer some reduction in numbers, no matter how easy the victory. Added to this, the mode of conquest, followed by Joshua, was not such as could have lent itself to an enrollment of fresh recruits from among the conquered inhabitants. "There was not a city that made peace with the children of Israel, save the Hivites, the inhabitants of Gibeon."[60] Additionally, Joshua was throughout his campaigns dependent to a great extent on auxiliaries from the tribes that had established themselves east of the Jordan. In fulfillment of a pledge made to Moses these had crossed the river with Joshua; but a time did come when they could be detained no longer.[61] Permitted to return to their homes, their going away made all further conquests impossible for the time being at least.

Joshua's major successes were harvested mainly in the south country, the territory that coincided approximately with the later kingdom of Judah. It was here that the original inhabitants were extensively eliminated with the land all but completely filled by the invading Hebrews. Already living there were a number of tribes closely akin to the Israelites who had apparently not abandoned their homes at the time of Jacob's migration to Egypt. Such were the Kenites and Rachmeelites, who lent their aid to the newcomers and soon amalgamated with them. This transformation in the ethnic composition of the southern part of Canaan is comparable to the conquest of southern Britain by the Anglo-Saxon attackers by whom the indigenous Celts were all but exterminated. Conversely, as regards the more northerly portions of the country, its change-over from Canaanite to Israelite domination was comparable to the influx into Gaul by the Franks, who in the course of time were fused with the Romanized Gauls. The Israelite offensive had ground to a halt sometime before the passing of Joshua. "And the land had rest from war."[62] By a Canaanite chief named Jabin large-scale fighting between Canaanites and Israelites was apparently renewed some years later in the time of the prophetess Deborah. It again ended in the defeat of the Canaanites, and in all probability the loss of more of their territory to the Israelites.[63]

"And there was peace between Israel and the Amorites."[64] Such co-existence was of course punctuated by numerous incidents of a local character, as for example the murderous onslaught of a band of freebooters of the tribe of Dan on an unsuspecting Canaanite community far in the north.[65] Most spectacular was the capture of Jerusalem by King David. These were in effect isolated gains over a protracted period coming as the sequel to Joshua's original "blitzkrieg"; and constituted the secondary phase of the Israelite conquest of Palestine. This phase was not so much a process of annihilation of the original dwellers as their piecemeal subjugation and eventual absorption. Israelite penetration tapered off towards the north so that in many places, no doubt, it was an Israelite minority that surrendered their identity to the pagan inhabitants. Testifying to the absence of any strong Israelite presence was the later willingness of King Solomon to cede to Hiram, King of Sidon, "twenty cities in the land of Galilee."[66]

In the later historical books the remaining Canaanites are all but ignored. Instead these reports concentrate on conflicts of a totally different character—conflicts in which the Israelites were almost invariably under pressure and on the defensive. Following on the demise of their most formidable and successful general, the disunited Israelite tribes soon came under the sustained harassment of Moabites, Ammonites, and more especially the Philistines. The willingness of the hard-pressed Israelites to enter into some kind of amicable relationship with their erstwhile Canaanite antagonists, and for which they were roundly condemned by "an angel of the Lord"[67] was dictated by the sheerest necessity. Their alliance, or at least good under-

142

standing, with the Phoenicians which was of long duration dated in all probability from the period of the early Judges. To Israelites and Phoenicians alike, the Philistines were a menace. However, their entente would scarcely have been likely had there been continuing large-scale warfare with the remaining Canaanites, the near kindred of the Phoenicians.

Presence of large Canaanite enclaves defiantly asserting their independence could have aborted the later creation of the Israelite monarchy. But no such problem seems to have arisen. We do not know the exact limits of the new state created under Saul; but it undoubtedly embraced far more of the country than was taken over at the time of Joshua. Inside this unified state of the ten tribes, the northern Canaanites, though neither absorbed or expelled, held only a subordinate role. They are last mentioned in the Scriptures as having been compelled by King Solomon to perform forced labour. Notwithstanding, their influence within the secessionist kingdom of the north was considerable enough, as I shall seek later on to demonstrate.

CHAPTER V

THE MONARCHY

Unlike Moses, Joshua left behind no disciple of comparable stature. With his passing the line of inspired leadership was for some length of time disconnected. Not otherwise than through the institution of a monarchy would an orderly and automatic passing on of centralized authority have been possible following the Israelite conquest. But to both Moses and Joshua, as later on to Gideon and Samuel, kingship was an abomination. Moses would go no further, in providing for the future, than to require "Judges and officers shalt thou make thee in all thy gates, which the Lord thy God shall give thee, tribe by tribe, and they shall judge the people with righteous judgment."[1]

The loose tribal confederacy of the Hebrews following upon the conquest could be regarded as the embodiment of the polity envisaged by Moses, and as a mirror of his constitutional thinking. It was thus summed up by a writer of a later period: "In those days there was no king in Israel; but every man did what was right in his own eyes."[2] The anarchy and license here implied were both relative. The accumulation of rapine and private warfare among the Israel-

144

ites was for that uncouth period not excessive. Unlike those of contemporary Greece, the Israelite tribes were not held apart from one another by perpetual fears. Some intertribal strife and jealousy there was undoubtedly. More especially, the Jordan river served as a line of cleavage. But archaeologists, reporting on the remains of ancient city fortifications, have attributed a much smaller number to the Israelite period than to the preceding Canaanite.

The monarchical systems known and dreaded by the Israelites of that time was that of Egypt, where the king was also a god, and that of Asiatic countries, where he was a despot to whom all things were allowable. To neither of these patterns did the Israelite monarchy bear any affinity. Of the Israelite kings a conformity to the laws was insisted upon. David, in fear of exposure, attempted to "cover-up" a criminal liaison with the wife of a subject. King Ahab, in proceeding against Naboth, knew himself to be hampered by certain laws. For the disciplinary limitations imposed upon its rulers, the Hebrew commonwealth has received high praise. "Down to modern times no state has had a constitution in which the interests of the people are so largely taken into account, in which the duties, so much more than the privileges of rulers, are insisted upon, as that drawn up for Israel in Deuteronomy and Leviticus. Nowhere is the fundamental truth that the welfare of the state in the long run depends on the uprightness of the citizen so strongly laid down."[3]

The earlier kings, Saul, David, and Solomon, did make some moves to pattern their rule somewhat on the style of Oriental despots. Their successors, both in the northern and southern kingdoms knew better. We hear of not too many arbitrary death sentences, nor trumped-up accusations of treason, nor of confiscations. In instances when these were ventured upon, there was nearly always at hand some plain-spoken prophet to cry out about the matter, as

145

did Jeremiah who censured the intent of King Jehoiakim to build for himself a palace by means of forced labour. "Woe unto him that buildeth his house by unrighteousness, that useth his neighbour's services without wages and giveth him not his hire."[4] "Covenants" such as those entered into by rulers such as Asa, Jehoshaphat, Joash were in effect self-imposed constitutions, by virtue of which these kings bound themselves to rule according to the ancestral laws, by recognizing them to be applicable not only to their subjects but to themselves as well.

Nor were the people over whom they ruled ever remarkable for docility; and this also prompts the reflection that not even to their God were the Hebrews of old entirely submissive. We read of His decisions being questioned first by Abraham, then by Moses, by Jonah and by Job. "Enough," cries out the prophet Elijah, "I am no better than my fathers. Take my life." By the famous Rabbi of Berdychev, God is even addressed in bitter terms of reproach for having abandoned to their enemies his people Israel. In Judaism, unlike Islam, there is absolute surrender neither to man nor to God.

Government in ancient Israel differed widely from that of Egypt and the Semitic Levant. And yet, it would be erroneous to ascribe to the Jews of old, or even of later times, any great leaning towards democracy on the Grecian model. In the absence of kingship during the Persian and Hellenistic periods, there arose among them an aristocratic body of non-elective elders. Its title, if not its actual constitution, was derived from the Synhedrin or Senate of the famous League of Delos, constituted in the year 478 B.C. under the auspices of Athens. In the self-governing bodies of later times, as authorized by the rulers of Babylonia, Spain, and Poland, the oligarchical principle long remained dominant in their communities.

The pre-monarchical period of the Judges was one of

146

permissiveness in matters of worship, aside from its invitation to military helplessness and anarchy. As Moses was preparing to take leave of his people forever, he felt no inner assurance that they would in their later generations continue to honour his teachings. He understood clearly enough how one generation enters upon its promised land in victory; but that before long, the generations that follow settle down peaceably among the indigenous inhabitants, and accept their ways. Machiavelli summed up this problem when he wrote "The nature of the people is mutable; and while it is easy to persuade them, it is difficult to preserve them in their convictions once having won them over." The Israelites who stood at the foot of Mount Sinai, and fervently undertook to do and to listen, were at that time hemmed in by no neighbours to pull them in any contrary direction. The test, the prophet well knew, was only to come when this same people found itself immersed in a new environment and exposed to the cultural examples of powerful neighbours.

Moses, whose concept of civil government did not go far beyond that of setting up a theocracy, had made no provision for the enforcement of his religious code by any secular authority. To look after the religious guidance of the people, he had set up an hereditary priesthood. But in the war against a resurgent paganism, the priests proved to be no more effective than were the local "judges and officers" in the war against the Philistines. As rulers over the minds of their flocks, they were far less potent than were the Catholic clergy of mediaeval Europe. These latter, in the performance of their ecclesiastical offices, saw themselves unfailingly seconded by the zeal of kings, dukes, barons, and town councils. By the priestly contemporaries of Shamgar, Gideon, Jephtha, and Samson, such secular aid was not invariably forthcoming.

Those who are carried away by the notion that in the

long run things of the spirit inevitably prevail over what is called materialism should perhaps give the matter some further thought. In the wars of religion, or latterly in the struggle of contending ideologies, what is spiritual is not readily distinguishable from what is material. Hence, what are thoughtlessly labelled "materialism" and "idealism" are clearly not opposite forces. With the dubious exception of Buddhism, every so-called spiritual force that has ever been generated in the world has depended for its ultimate triumph largely on the secular arm, or, otherwise expressed, the conveyed threat of physical violence. To this generalization, the headway of Judaism over paganism in Biblical days was no exception.

The problems involved in regulating and inspecting worship in this half-legendary period of the Judges must have been formidable indeed. Religious practice varied from one locality to another, depending no doubt mainly on the degree of amalgamation between Israelites and Canaanites. Shrines were everywhere and sacrifices everywhere. Idols were set up in one place and destroyed in another. Often Baal and Jehovah were prayed to simultaneously. An instance of rare humour discoverable in Holy Writ is the anecdote, reported in the book of Judges, of the idol-worshipping Micah and his side-kick, the backsliding grandson of Moses. But equally so is there a reflection here on the rapid deterioration of the Israelite religion. Each man "doing what seemed right in his own eyes" meant in effect "whoring after the Baalim."

There is clear testimony that, with the creation of a monarchy in ancient Israel, measures were soon invoked to wipe out Canaanitish practices such as witchcraft. King Saul was wholeheartedly devoted to the monotheistic faith and its ordinances. Samuel would hardly have selected him otherwise. Even though we are informed of this by no text, it may well be supposed that on orders of Saul, David, and

Solomon not a few of the remaining Canaanite shrines were demolished.

The final and definitive abolition of idolatry was out of the question as long as the cult of animal sacrifices was carried out in all parts of the country and unchecked by any centralized authority. An effective means of control was brought about through the erection of a large and matchless shrine in one central city, with the building of any other at the same time discouraged. The Temple at Jerusalem did prove in the end, and after many vicissitudes, a positive contribution in the religious struggle. But costly as it was it could not have come into being otherwise than under royal auspices. In both the political and religious spheres the element of coercion which had lapsed since the time of Joshua was reintroduced in time to save the Israelite nation from falling apart.

It deserves to be noted, that in the change-over from what has been loosely termed a republic to a hereditary monarchy, there was involved neither a usurpation nor a "coup d'état." The advisability of such change had long been deliberated upon and, when finally decided, the national will was all but unanimous in its support. Not only did such sovereignty seem imperative in the eyes of those seeking surcease from foreign aggression; but on the religious front as well was it seen as urgently needed.

SAMUEL THE KINGMAKER

Samuel as both prophet and political leader was in the line of tradition of Moses and Joshua. Unlike the earlier "Judges," his authority seems to have been nationwide rather than confined to a limited tribal area. Though from childhood committed to a life of contemplative piety, he was not without some aptitude as a military commander. He managed to hold the Philistines in check, possibly with some support from the neighbouring Phoenicians, who were likewise under threat by these same attackers. Samuel's long ministry was the actual prelude to the creation of the Israelite state and monarchy. Grown old, he attempted to satisfy the need, then clearly manifest, of some orderly transference of authority by having both his two sons named to carry on the magistracy in his place. But the unfitness of these young men soon becoming apparent, the clamour for a totally new system of government became irresistible.

The Hebrew nation, in this dangerous and transitional period, manifested a great enough awareness of its perilous situation. Had Samuel died during the interval that the issue of the monarchy remained undecided, the leaderless nation, attacked from every quarter, would soon have been plunged into confusion and utter disaster. The course insisted upon by the bulk of the population was undoubtedly the wise one, wiser by far than the council of the unsteady and vacillating prophet. Drawbacks inherent in the institution of kingship that he eloquently conjured up before them, while undeniably real, did not sway them from a determination to live at long last under a strong government.

In the actual selection of Israel's first monarch, it was natural that a deciding voice should be exercised by none other than the venerable prophet, who had for so long guided the nation, and who alone enjoyed the necessary prestige to head off a possible clash between rival aspirants. That no rival candidate did present himself was in itself indicative of the esteem in which Samuel continued to be held, despite his unacceptable political philosophy.

The prophetic choice fell upon a young man of Gibeah, a city not far from Samuel's own residence at Ramah, and of a family probably known to him. Samuel may have been unnecessarily taken with the young man's good looks, "and there was not among the children of Israel a goodlier person than he; from his shoulders upward he was higher than any of the people."[5] A more thorough investigation might have brought to light the fact that he was also lacking in emotional stability and that he was given periodically to fits of "prophesying." In after years, when with alarming frequency Saul "prophesied in the midst of the house," those nearest to him would have some cause to tremble for their lives. A number of abnormalities marked the commencement of his reign. To his new subjects his outlandish method of invoking a general mobilization and call to arms must have seemed startling enough.[6] Following on some hard fighting, he capriciously and on pain of death ordered his men to refrain from eating.[7]

As for the departing tribune, pride and resentment began to gnaw upon his mind following upon the victory of his protegee over the Ammonites. His reduced status notwithstanding, he continued to look upon himself as the arbiter of moral conduct in the affairs of the newly created kingdom. But the final rupture between king and prophet was not slow in coming, as the young ruler acquired the habit and feel of power. Harmony between them came to an end shortly after Saul permitted himself to be diverted by Samuel from the main business of looking after the defence of his kingdom from the rampaging Philistines to the resumption of a tawdry feud with the insignificant Amalekites. Saul allowed himself to be talked into undertaking a needless expedition that had no relationship to the main security problem that confronted his kingdom. The operation resulted in the kind of victory that brought with it satisfaction to neither Saul nor the prophet. Samuel welcomed the homecoming Saul with dour reproaches. In language that was highly censorious he berated the young sovereign on some matter of sacred protocol, which to a

151

modern reader of the Scriptures can only appear as vexatious and absurd. The episode, quite expectedly, resulted in Samuel being chased from the royal presence and warned not to show his face evermore. The embittered old man, in whose eyes Saul had now become a false and fatal leader, set out to weave a filament of intrigue and treason, which had a prosperous outcome as it happened. Samuel's second choice, in his quality of kingmaker, was not the tallest among the people. But he was David.

Dating perhaps from the time of his break with the prophet who had befriended him and made him great, Saul's character began to take on an increasingly perverse turn. From a simple, modest, and disingenuous youth, the exercise of untrammeled authority soon transformed him into a suspicious and querulous despot, displaying the self-same qualities against which the opponents of royalty had warned. In typical oriental fashion, all sentiment of gratitude and affection vanished quickly from his mind. A group of women "came out from all the cities of Israel singing and dancing." The theme of these foolish and mischievous females was an improvised song about Saul slaying his thousands, while the hero David was slaying his tens of thousand. Enraged by such belittlement of his own homicidal abilities, Saul's affection for David was changed instantaneously into hatred, a sentiment which in the end contributed greatly to his own undoing, as well as the slaughter of thousands.

One of the accoutrements of royalty that Saul was not slow in instituting was a dependence on a network of tale bearers. Therewith was it possible for him to keep abreast of the going and coming of the restless Samuel, along with the whereabouts of the fugitive David. Even his eldest son Jonathan, for whom he entertained no love, and who did not conceal his disgust of his father's brutalities, was kept under surveillance. Saul's own sagacity was not of a high

152

calibre. In the endless and futile pursuit of the popular David, he exhausted his credit among his subjects. Kept well enough informed by his spies and sycophants of every change in the location of his quarry, nothing was told him until too late of an encroaching danger that was soon to destroy him.

The defeated and humiliated Philistines were preparing themselves for a fresh trial of strength. In forwarding their host onto the plain of Jezreel, they were accepting a risk of having to fight far from their home base of supplies. Otherwise, their choice of a battlefield was a good one. It was on level ground, thus permitting them to take full advantage of their superiority of numbers and in equipment. Also it lay in a territory that contained only a sparse Hebrew population, and where the Canaanites were probably inimical to Saul. The Israelite king encamped on a hillside saw his force hopelessly outnumbered. Perhaps once again he had attempted to recruit an army by using the same weird summons as in the earlier war with the Ammonites.[8] It did not produce a like result. The Israelites were no longer responsive to a ruler who had long forfeited their affection and trust by an act of genocide against the priests of Nob, by the betrayal of the Gibeonites, and by his vindictive pursuit of a popular hero.

THE KINGDOM OF DAVID AND SOLOMON

"Saul" wrote the German historian von Ranke "is the first tragic figure in history." Saul's early reign gave great promise; his later years were marked by fits of unpredictable rage and spasms of insanity, and closed in disaster for the entire Israelite nation. And yet this new experiment in monarchy was by no means the failure that the prophet Samuel had foretold; and it was to have a glorious re-

153

crudescence. "So all the elders of Israel came to the king in Hebron and King David made a league with them in Hebron before the Lord; and they annointed David king over Israel and he reigned forty years."[9] From the depths of despair, from their seemingly hopeless situation following the destruction of King Saul's army by the Philistines, Israel within a few decades climbed to a position of power and renown. Under David, Israel rose from a small rustic kingdom to an imperial sway extending from the Gulf of Aquaba to the Orontes River in northern Syria, and including every important territory on both sides of the Jordan river. The impregnable city states of the northern Canaanites, unsubdued since the invasion under Joshua, were all without difficulty incorporated into the Israelite kingdom.

All this was the achievement of David, a fugitive guerrilla fighter turned military and administrative genius. But conquest in those days, as in these latter times, was only possible when seconded by large material resources; and these resources David was able to command, once having extended his sway into the Negev with its wealth of copper and iron. "And David prepared iron in abundance."[10] Pressing forward to the Gulf of Aquaba, a sea route lay open to him athwart the Red Sea that beckoned to the remote shores of southern Arabia and East Africa. To David there fell the necessary means for providing himself with everything from a harem to a standing army. He created a civil service, he built fortifications and, something which none of his predecessors were able to supply themselves with, engines of siege for the reduction of enemy fortresses.[11] David's irresistible armies did not consist solely of Israelite levies, but were reinforced very substantially by mercenaries, recruited mainly it would seem from among the beaten Philistines, as well as trained professional soldiers from the island of Crete. The biblical text repeatedly

154

mentions among these auxiliaries the Cherethites and Pelethites and Gittites.[12]

David, who lived some three thousand years ago, was the first ruler of any nation, in fact the first human being, about whom there has come down to us a considerable volume of information. His fame transmitted by admiring and articulate contemporaries, the story of his life and exploits introduced the vogue of writing history in terms of individual royal biographies. Facts about his early life and adventures are believed to have been recorded by his early protector, the prophet Samuel. To the prophets Gad and Nathan, Samuel's disciples, we owe the fuller account of his reign.

More especially was David himself a poet and writer of lasting fame and distinction. Supplementary of what has been written about him by others, much knowledge can be gleaned from the many psalms and prayers attributed to him. From this latter source do we learn of disasters only narrowly averted, and otherwise unrecorded. On at least one occasion, David was seriously wounded in battle.[13] While still in the prime of life, he suffered an illness, during which he was given up for lost.[14] An attempt of secret enemies to poison him was only barely foiled.[15] We are informed likewise of an invading host from Mesopotamia that "made the earth to tremble."[16]

In radiant strength, David, encountering one danger after the other, prevailed heroically. Blessed he was with great sagacity and fortitude, and also with good fortune to a remarkable degree. But likewise do his own writings reveal the more sombre side of his character. As a fugitive with a price upon his head, we find him in the beginning wedded to what is nowadays referred to as the cult of the underdog. "And everyone who was in distress, and everyone who was in debt, and everyone who was discontented gathered to him."[17] Upon him was the moral pessimism of the ages that holds the rich guilty and the poor innocent. But how quickly does this view of life change with the repairing of one's fortunes. "Blessed be the Lord my rock, who traineth my hand for war and my fingers for battle—who subdueth my people under me."[18] A taste for glory and domination lifted him from great humility to great offensiveness. "Gilead is mine. Menasseh is mine. Ephraim is the strength of my head. Judah is my lawgiver. Moab is my washpot. Over Edom will I cast my shoe. Over Philistia will I triumph."[19] With overweening pride comes also a carelessness about human life, and an overpowering desire for vengeance. "Thou has also given me the necks of mine enemies that I might destroy them that hate me. . . . Then did I beat them small as the dust before the wind. I did cast them out as the dirt in the streets."[20]

And finally, with pride and cruelty there comes the troubled conscience, along with contrition and repentance for wrongs committed and hatreds incurred. "My strength faileth because of mine iniquity and my bones are consumed. I was a reproach among mine neighbours and a fear to mine acquaintances. They that see me without fled from me."[21]

The writings left by David, along with those of his contemporaries, such as Asaph, Heman, and Ethan, serve to instruct us as to the religious beliefs current among the Israelites a thousand years before the Christian era. They are revelatory of David's conception of the Supreme Being, which we are to assume he held in common with the majority of his fellow Israelites. Beyond any doubt, David saw in the God of Israel the heavenly father as well of all the other nations; and as the creator of heaven and earth and of all living things. "The earth is full of loving kindness of the Lord."[22] Be it added, however, for David, again in common with his fellow Israelites, faith in God did not include any belief in a life beyond the grave.[23] His enlarged view of the Divine, notwithstanding, David did not raise himself above a veneration of the ark of the Covenant as the symbol of God's presence among his chosen people. Also in common with the surrounding pagans, he believed in the performance of animal sacrifices.

Admiring historians have expatiated on David's ability of changing enemies into friends.[24] They have perhaps stressed this particular virtue too greatly. The son of Jesse was indeed successful in securing the attachment of a highly efficient band of foreign mercenaries, many among them recruited from Gath, a Philistine city with which he had carried on much warfare. These well-drilled professionals, drawn from both the cities of the Philistines as well as from the island of Crete, made it possible for David to score some notable victories over the untrained levies of his Asiatic neighbours, contributing greatly to the creation of his unique empire.

In a crisis with his own people, these foreign auxiliaries were also of great assistance in putting down the rebellion instigated by his son Absalom. One gains the impression that David's own Israelite veterans were none too pleased at favours that must have been showered upon these pampered foreigners; and that not a few among them gave vent to their displeasure in joining with the rebels. Moralizing upon this matter, it could be suggested that winning over enemies is good, provided that it does not entail sacrificing or neglecting one's friends. Be it as it may, David's supposed genius at converting enemies into friends seems at no time to have left him with any shortage of the former, if we are to judge by what he himself wrote in the psalms.

David's career was in the end bereft of all brilliance. His spirit was broken by the shocking and disgraceful conduct of his sons.[25] Compounding the agony of his closing years was an armed uprising instigated by one of them which all but resulted in his overthrow. The narrative of Absalom's revolt, which is also referred to in the psalms, leaves us in the dark as to the causes of this inglorious episode. The Biblical text, though none too explicit, points to some widespread disaffection among David's own people, though apparently not among the tributary nations. The account contained in the second book of Samuel of David's rule over Israel, as well as the extension of his rule outside Palestine itself, is but a digest of earlier records and is of poor literary construction. Yet the particular events there related, leading up to a profound discontent with his rule, can be made out with tolerable clearness.

Rulers in early times, and indeed for many centuries thereafter, were expected to exercise not only military and administrative functions but judiciary as well. A king or governor would spend a good part of his day listening to complaints from individual petitioners, adjudicating private disputes, and handing down punishments. We are informed that Absalom, substituting himself in this role for his aging father, was able to acquire a reputation for himself as an able and equitable judge of the people's grievances.[26] Thereby, he gained for himself an ever-increasing circle of admiring followers.

Now David, to the contrary, as we gather from several reported decisions attributed to him, was completely lacking in what we would call judicial temperament. To minor instances of wrongdoing, his reactions were choleric in the extreme. At one time, in his younger days, he had been offended by a wealthy cattle dealer by name of Nabal, who turned down his request for a gratuity. David was barely prevented from killing the man and despoiling him of all his possessions. The prophet Nathan came to test him on a hypothetical case of a wealthy man depriving an impoverished neighbour of his one and solitary lamb. David, too easily enraged, suggested death as the punishment for an unrighteous act that could easily have been corrected by means other than violence. Again, when the woman of Tekoa, at Job's instigation, propounds a problem to him as what should be done to a sole surviving son who had murdered his brother, David's reply was in flat contradiction to the rule laid down in the Torah.[27] An Amalekite came to him with a report of Saul's death on the battlefield, adding falsely with evident intent of ingratiating himself that he himself had been instrumental of putting the dangerously wounded king out of his misery. The man was not a murderer; and yet David ordered him to be killed; and in violation of the rule that one may be executed only on the testimony of at least two witnesses. David as king could well have acquired a reputation of judging badly.

Other grounds for discontent with David's rule had been building themselves in the course of the years. The one-time tribune of the poor and disinherited, once seated on a throne, required of his fellow Israelites that they prostrate themselves before him in imitation of the debased etiquette of the courts of Egypt and Assyria and China. Not in the presence of Moses nor of Joshua had any Israelite been expected to "fall on his face." In cataloguing the vices of royalty, Samuel had inadvertently omitted any reference to the foul institution of the harem, an Oriental implement of lust and intrigue, and which David did not refrain from adopting to his eventual undoing. The discontent of taxpayers compelled to carry the burden of such bloated and unsavoury domesticity can be easily enough surmised.

In other matters as well did David display little sagacity. Not unconnected with the dissipation of his popularity was his delivery to the Gibeonites for hanging of seven innocent members of King Saul's family. One is entitled to suppose that by a large enough segment of the Israelite population this act of moral cowardice was not readily overlooked. The Gibeonites had been ill-used under Saul, who had forgotten or ignored the pledge given these people by Joshua. No form of indemnification suggested to them by David would appease these implacable heathens, other than that Saul's kindred should pay the penalty of death that could not be exacted of their original oppressor. It was David himself who had selected the victims, being at the same time careful to exempt Mephibosheth, the son of his old friend Jonathan. Mephibosheth himself, a cripple but a man of honour, was apparently not grateful to David for thus sparing him while at the same time abandoning his kinfolk to an unjust retribution. While fleeing from Absolom, David was accosted by Shimei ben Gora, a relative of the slain victims, who reviled him as the destroyer of Saul's house. Knowing full well that the man had enough grounds, David told his entourage, "Let him curse."

As a practical leader and man of action, the career of David was clouded by no small number of deficiencies. Yet all that was good in him has never been forgotten. Unlike the founders of so many other royal lines throughout history, his rise to sovereignty was not founded on bloodshed. Refusing to take the life of his pursuer when he might justifiably have done so, he observed with great wisdom to his follower Abishai, "Destroy him not—as the Lord liveth, the Lord shall smite him, or his day shall come to die, or shall descend into battle and perish."[28] Not in all things was he so high-minded; and yet no moral perfectionist could at the time have become the unifier of a turbulent nation, the restorer of its dignity, and the conqueror of its enemies. In him ancient Israel was granted a brief moment filled with power, grandeur, and good fortune. By many other nations equally has the memory of David been honoured as "the man who was raised on high, the anointed of the God of Jacob, and the sweet psalmist of Israel."[29]

David's empire survived him, remaining intact during the entire reign of his successor, Solomon (circa 980-940 BC). We are told of this monarch that he possessed "a wise and understanding heart." For a shining example of his unusual powers of discernment into human motives, one need only read the latter half of Chapter 3 of the first book of Kings. Also in the wider arena of statesmanship he was, at least until his declining years, a prince of surpassing prudence and sagacity. He knew the art of kingship, and he knew how to correct its attendant insecurity. Finding himself challenged at the outset of his reign, he promptly orders the elimination of his dissatisfied older half-brother Adonijah as well as that of the veteran commander of the armed forces, the violently disposed Joab. The Florentine authority on statecraft, Messer Nicolo Machiavelli, had he also been a careful student of the Scriptures, might have discerned in Solomon a somewhat more delectable prototype for his celebrated treatise on "The Prince" than the abominable Cesare Borgia. Solomon was by no means a saintly character; but neither was he a tyrant. As far as we are told, his politically motivated executions numbered no more than three. Aside from these, no other acts of cruelty have been recorded of him, which for a reign of forty years was not too discreditable a record. Solomon waged no wars, perhaps from some innate love of peace, or perhaps from a just estimate of its attendant perils. Contenting himself with the considerable domain bequested to him by his father, he yet saw to it by means of a well-equipped standing army that no temptation be placed in the way of his neighbours to the south and to the north. "And Solomon had forty thousand stalls of horses, for his chariots and twelve thousand horsemen."[30]

Hardly less remarkable than his judicial acuity and

statesmanship was Solomon's far ranging intellect. "And Solomon's wisdom excelled the wisdom of all the children of the East and the wisdom of Egypt."[31] This extravagance of language need not dismay us, since the text does indeed give us examples of his scholarly attainments. Unlike the learned men of Egypt and Mesopotamia, he was not attracted to the lore of the heavenly bodies. But preceding Aristotle by some hundreds of years, Solomon made himself into an authority on natural history. "And he spake of trees, from the cedar tree that is in Lebanon even unto the hyssop that springeth out of the wall; and he spake also of beasts, and of fowl, and of creeping things, and of fishes."[32] We are told likewise as to his literary attainments. "And he spake three thousands proverbs; and his songs were a thousand and five."[33] Solomon is the reputed author of the Books of Proverbs, the Book of Ecclesistice, and Cantilations; and with perhaps more probability the 72nd and 127th Psalms are ascribed to him as well.

A question suggests itself. Solomon's reputed wisdom was of God, as the text informs us. But such science and scholarship as he displayed could only have come from his contact with others who were like-minded. Not in a vacuum of ignorant and uncouth courtiers could Solomon have acquired his knowledge and scholarship. Here as well, the text does not fail to shed some light. Names are even mentioned. "For he was wiser than all men; than Ethan the Ezrahite, and Heman and Chalca, and Darda the son of Mahol."[34] King Solomon, one might assert, belongs in the company of such crowned heads as the Emperor Augustus at Rome, and the Emperor Frederick II of Germany at Palermo, all assiduous in attracting to their court men of learning and versatility.

The versatility and energy of this gifted ruler were indeed considerable. "And King Solomon made a navy of ships in Etzion Geber which is beside Elath . . . and they came to Ophir."[35] It is certain that for the launching of the Jewish people into commercial prominence the long and peaceful reign of King Solomon was a historical landmark.

The line inaugurated by David and Solomon endured for nearly five hundred years, a good deal longer than might have been anticipated.[36] Following the passing of Solomon, a series of disasters befell his family and his successors. The copper mine in the south, discovered in all probability during David's lifetime, ceased being productive apparently before the death of Solomon. It was this fountain of riches that had financed the splendid courts of both founders, their standing armies, conquests, horses, harems, palaces, and, not least, the holy Temple at Jerusalem. Little enough of his power, wealth, and good fortune did Solomon bequeath to his successors. Added to the loss of the tributary states, as well as the defection of the northern tribes, was the invasion by an Egyptian army that devastated the land, sacked Jerusalem, and carried off much treasure.

That, despite such staggering reverses and blows to its honour and prestige, the house of David was able to maintain itself and later to gather to itself renewed strength was itself something of a miracle. Doubtless, the towering reputation of its founder counted in the balance. And yet, there were certain other things going in its favour. It soon shed itself of most of the trappings of despotism. The complete history of the House of David, though not unchequered, had little in common with the dynasties of Egypt, western Asia, the tyrants of the Greek city states, or the ruling houses of mediaeval Europe. In general, there was not much reported of its members in the way of licentiousness, wickedness, or cruelty. Nor were they often guilty of arbitrary arrests or executions. For their revenues, they appear to have depended mainly on the returns of their private estates, thus leaving them with few temptations to vex their

163

subjects with unendurable taxation. They built few palaces, prepared for their interment no luxurious mausoleums, and collected no women for their harems. They were not known to seduce the wives of the people. It is of interest to note that prophets, such as Isaiah, Micah, Zephania, and Nahum, who were sensitive enough to the social evils of their age, and who freely castigated the rich, saw little that was derogatory in the behaviour of these princes. With but few exceptions, the twenty successors of David and Solomon committed few of the sins of the celebrated founders of their House. The majority among them were commendable or at least tolerable human beings. A few were outstanding men.

Neither among the prophets nor within the nation at large did any anti-monarchical sentiments manifest themselves; and certainly not prior to the reign of the detested Menasseh. In but one notable instance was the dynasty in any real peril of being wiped out. King Jehoshaphat, one of its most sympathetic representatives, in order to bring to an end the strife with the northern kingdom, had permitted his son Jehoram to marry Athaliah, the daughter of Ahab and Jezebel. Later, this woman almost succeeded in exterminating her husband's family, including her own grandchildren. She thereupon introduced into Jerusalem the worship of Baal and the other deities of her pagan forebears. One grandson was saved from the slaughter, the boy Joash, who was rescued through the efforts of one of the princesses and the high priest Jehoida. At a favourable moment, this child was crowned king while, at the same moment, the screaming Athaliah was cut down by the soldiers.

On the life of small boy there for a time hung in the balance something more than the survival of the royal house of David. Had this dynasty been extinguished at that time, the survival of Judaism itself would almost certainly have been in jeopardy. From the defunct dynasty, a succession of upstart adventurers would have taken over; and in the ensuing struggle for power, the kingdom of Judah would soon have become a duplicate of the ill-omened monarchy of the north.

Among David's descendants, the last effectual ruler was the celebrated Josiah. A grievous error of judgment brought about the end of this estimable prince, and in effect the end of the house of David as a political factor. An Egyptian Pharaoh by the name of Necho, seeking to derive some benefit from the impending collapse of the decrepit Assyrian empire, and fearing the advent in its place of a vigorous new power, decided to rush his army to the assistance of the falling empire. The Judaean king, aware only of the record for weakness of Egypt's armed forces, was so rash as to oppose his passage with his own inferior and poorly trained army.[37] Unknown apparently to the ill-fated Judaean king was the fact that a short time previously Necho had gotten rid of his native soldiery and revitalized his armed forces by recruiting a fresh army composed of Greek mercenaries. These were, man for man, more than a match for any of the warriors of Asia.[38]

David's dynastic influence did live on for some time into the future. Down to about the tenth century, a scion of this family continued to be recognized as the legitimate and hereditary head of the Jewish community of Mesopotamia and accorded the enjoyment of both religious and secular authority. With an unbroken succession of almost two millenia, the descendants of David constituted at one time the world's oldest and most high-born family.

No date can be properly assigned for the dismantling of David's and Solomon's empire; nor is anything known of the actual process by which cities like Damascus, Ammon, Gaza, and Ascalon regained their independence. Efforts at shaking off Israel's domination must have been well under way during the later years of Solomon's reign; and coincided perhaps with the exhaustion of the fabulous copper mine, which was the economic basis of Israelite ascendancy. We may in any event safely infer that this falling away of the conquered tributaries preceded the actual bisecting of the Israelite kingdom. It is an acknowledged fact that states held together by no common bonds of allegiance begin to erode usually at their periphery. Also, the crushing burden of taxation, of which the revolting Israelite tribes complained, had in all likelihood been imposed upon them by an aging and not so wise Solomon in compensation for the lost tribute of the disengaged satellites.

This process of reduction and disintegration might have gone even a step further, and carried the Israelite nation back to the fractured and tribal sectionalism that preceded the institution of the monarchy. But, given the conditions prevailing in early antiquity, it was altogether inevitable for a severance of some kind to have taken place within the Israelite Confederation itself. The tribal confederacy set up under Saul and David was a consolidation made possible only with the continuing consent of its constituent parts. Particularist agitation for the withdrawal of such consent could not forever have been thwarted.

Prior to the coming of the Israelites, Canaan had at no time been a single unified territory held together by one centralized government; and in this respect, the contrast was great between it and Mesopotamia. Within the broad and flat expanse of the latter region, power flowed easily from one dominant city to another, each in its time extending its sway over a widening orbit. Finally, Nineveh was able to master the entire lowland region along with its adjacent uplands. By way of contrast, the topography of Canaan being unfavourable to large-scale consolidation of power, even conquest of one city state by another was fraught with difficulty. In a territory that was largely mountainous, and where transportation and communication were hindered by geographic barriers, a large number of viceroys, all able, devoted and unselfish, would have been required to insure a permanent centralized administration.

It is my contention that a pan-Hebraic commonwealth made up of all twelve of the Israelite tribes, though realized for a time, was anachronistic and in its very nature stood no chance of more than a temporary survival. The cloud which descended upon it in the latter part of Solomon's reign had to arrive sooner or later. The united Israelite kingdom, restored by David, was able to endure for the better part of a century only because a number of other principalities contiguous to it were brought likewise under his personal sway and that of his son. Be it recalled that David did not in the beginning of his reign show any inclination of becoming a conqueror of foreign nations. His early battles were entirely defensive and fought exclusively on the soil of his own little kingdom. Once having been crowned king of a united Israel, he was in effect given the choice by his heathen neighbours of being overcome and conquered by them, or himself turning aggressor and becoming the builder of his own personal empire. No in-between course was open to him. It was not otherwise than by subjecting some half dozen non-Israelite nations to his sway that he could insure several decades of repose for his own people. But this security vanished forever no sooner did these neighbours regain their freedom of action. Along with their independence, their normal bellicosity and antagonism to the Israelites came once again to the fore.

Be it remembered that the Israelites of old were in the minds of their neighbours held to be outsiders and interlopers in about much the same way as are their descendants living in the present-day State of Israel. Canaanites, Syrians, Moabites, Ammonites, Edomites, and Philistines, though certainly divided politically among themselves,

167

were like the Arabs of today bracketed by a common religion. Their culture formed a continuum, embracing a diffused system of both mythology and practice. In the religion of all Semitic nations—with the exceptions of the Hebrews, of course—divinity was conceived as the personified forces of nature in human form. Their deities, both masculine and feminine, were represented under various names such as Baal, Bel, Dagon, Ashera, Astarte, Moloch, Chemosh, Melkar, Ishtar, Adar, Tammuz, Sivan, Heshvan. Each god and goddess had his and her opposite, representing on the one hand war and pestilence, drought and destruction, and on the other hand life and blessing, love, birth and fertility. It was this well-rounded Semitic system, along with its attendant rites of human sacrifice, male and female prostitution, along with image worship, that the Hebrew newcomers had set out to subvert. We ought not to suppose that the proclaimed intention of the Hebrews to raze the heathen temples and pulverize the images did not evoke some passionate response on the part of those whose religious beliefs and practices were thus being assaulted.

It has been said that it was to the advantage of the Romans that at no time in their upcoming history were they compelled to wage two important wars at one and the same time. One could not lightly say that a unified Biblical state would have been equally fortunate. Had such a polity survived after Solomon, it would have floated about inside an endless sea of paganism. Such an enclave within an environment of total hostility would have been subject to incessant harassment by its neighbours acting singly or in concert, and would before very long have succumbed in the absence of some new military genius comparable to David. Its territory, along with its inhabitants, would have been parcelled out among its victorious and vengeful neighbours. For holding at bay a collectivity of such external foes, the Israelites of that time were equipped with no advantages whatsoever. The ability of the present state of Israel to quickly shift its armed might from one theatre of operations to another certainly had no parallel at that remote period. Likewise, unlike their present-day descendants, the Israelites of old enjoyed over their neighbours no superiority either of technological development, mass education, or fighting ability.

Paradoxical though it may seem, the very tearing asunder of the Israelite kingdom had the effect of forestalling any concerted action that might have been taken against it by way of a holy war. There being two Hebrew nations rather than one, and there being in evidence some difference between them as regards outlook on pagan worship, the latent fanaticism of the Semitic environment was without a steady target for its expression, all the more so since each of these successor states had now its own more mobile defensive organization along with its distinct diplomatic apparatus. The religious issue between the Israelites and their neighbours being thus thrown out of focus, secular issues assumed their customary precedence.

For the evolvement of Judaism, the discord of north and south that came to a head after the death of Solomon, thus proved in the end to be more positive than negative. By serving to make the international rivalries of that region more complicated than would otherwise have been the case, the longevity of both the Judaean and Israelite kingdoms was greatly facilitated. It is significant that in the two hundred years of their dual existence, the kindred Hebrew states were at no time assailed simultaneously by any one or more of their neighbours or by any combination of them, as would otherwise have been highly probable. While both these kingdoms were destined to disappear, the Ephraimite in the year 722 and the Judaean in 586, the supposition is by no means unwarrantable that, had the state created by David remained undivided, its termination would have

169

been closer to the earlier of these dates than to the latter.

"So far as the religious and intellectual life of the nation was concerned, there was no substantial difference between the two kingdoms."[39] The foregoing assertion deserves a flat contradiction. It is contradicted by everything that has been written as regards both kingdoms, and even more so by what may be known indirectly of them.

Of the original Israelite kingdom, prior to its division, the ethnic composition of its northern part was quite different from that of the south. A reading of Joshua's campaigns makes this fact clear enough. Joshua's major successes were confined to the south, many of whose cities were taken and their inhabitants totally destroyed to make room for the newcomers. There were hardly any such acts of genocide in that part of Canaan that later on was to form the secessionist kingdom of Israel. "But as for the cities that stood on their mounds, Israel burned none of them, save Hazor only."[40]

There were in the northern part of the country many empty spaces which the invading Israelites were able to populate without the indigenous inhabitants being dispossessed. Following this, a transition from bronze implements to those of iron facilitated the enlargement of these cultivable areas. The stage was thus set for a gradual intermingling of both nations; and of this fusion there are indications in almost every page of the book of Judges. "And the children of Israel dwelt among the Canaanites, Hittites, Amorites, Perizites and Jebusites. And they took their daughters to be their wives, and gave their daughters to their sons, and served their gods."[41] Thus the mother of Jephtha the deliverer was a "stranger." The hero Gideon may himself have been of part-Canaanite extraction; and it was only on reaching maturity that he renounced the worship of Baal. We are left guessing as to whether his fellow townsmen at a place called Ophra were predominantly Israelite or Canaanite, or an amalgam of both. What is clear is that as a community they were devoted to the Canaanite religion.[42]

In their religious orientation, the two successor kingdoms differed profoundly. Even though the early rulers of the secessionist monarchy did not actually countenance the re-establishment of the full Canaanite pantheon, by announcing their rejection of Jerusalem and its temple they fostered almost inevitably some restoration of pagan worship. "Whereupon the king took counsel, and made two calves of gold; and he said unto them, Ye have gone up long enough to Jerusalem. Behold thy gods, O Israel, which brought ye out of the land of Egypt."[43] It is here worth noting that the setting up of the paired "calves," one in Bethel and the other in Dan, was an idea that came directly out of Egypt, where the new Israelite king had long been an exile. The worship of two specially marked bulls, called Apis at Memphis and Mnevis at Heliopolis, had long enjoyed an extended national worship in the Nile country.[44] Jeroboam's manifesto on behalf of these neighbourly deities was followed promptly by the expulsion of the Aaronites and Levites who, gathering themselves together, migrated to the south.[45] They were accompanied by a substantial following "out of the tribes of Israel, such as set their hearts to seek the Lord, the God of Israel, came to Jerusalem to sacrifice unto the Lord."[46] Between the successor states, the religious cleavage here manifested was to remain unbridged to the very end.

That the transference of population brought about by this religious schism remained one-sided is altogether unlikely. Even though no text informs us of a reverse exodus from the southern kingdom to that of the north, there is reason enough to believe that inside the kingdom of Judah as well there was ample inducement for many of its inhabitants to seek more congenial dwelling places. Jerusalem itself, when first taken by David, had been peopled entirely by Canaanites. They were neither killed nor driven out, but were long permitted to remain undisturbed in their heathen practices and in possession of their chapels, to the scandal, one might suppose, of the more devout adherents of the monotheistic faith. To this era of tolerance and co-existence an end was finally made by King Asa (920-874 B.C.E.). "And Asa . . . took away the strange altars, and the high places, and broke down the pillars, and hewed down the Asherim."[47] The political consequences were not pacific but painful.

An imaginative approach to this religious attack upon his pagan subjects by King Asa should enable us to understand that it was not unconnected with the political quarrels that had set in between the two Hebrew kingdoms immediately following their separation. The struggles between their respective rulers, whose beginnings were undoubtedly personal and dynastic, could readily have been expected to raise certain doubts among serious-minded Judaeans. Into the minds of many who were being called upon to lay down their lives for the preservation of King David's throne, the thought might easily have entered as to whether a monarchy that showed signs of compromising with heathen practices differed greatly from its antagonist, and was worth fighting for. The issue of pagan worship in Jerusalem, with its shrines and idols and "sodomites," was thus forcibly brought to a head. King Asa, we may surmise, was given no option but to bow to the insistence of his more devout subjects, whose ranks had been swelled by the new arrivals from the northern kingdom.

In its turn, King Asa's interference with the religious freedom of many of his subjects undoubtedly had other repercussions as well. That many of the heathen residents of Jerusalem were in this way coerced into the dominant Jewish fold is by all means certain. But the inference could be drawn likewise that a great many others were not ready

172

to abandon their ancestral religion, and decided to betake themselves to the more congenial territory of King Baasa of Israel, whose army they might have swelled in an effort to avenge themselves against their oppressor. As an outcome the desultory feud between the two neighbour kingdoms burst into serious warfare. "And Baasa king of Israel went up against Judah and built Rama that he might not suffer any to go out or come in to Asa king of Judah."[48] Finding his situation desperate, King Asa bribed the Syrians to come to his assistance by advancing on the Israelites from the rear. For this unclean, though unavoidable, act of political realism, King Asa earned for himself the reproof of the prophet Hannanel, who was in turn cast into prison for his outspokeness.

The religious alienation of the northern kingdom, begun under Jeroboam, reached its culmination with the accession of Omri, an upstart probably of Canaanite descent.[49] Between him and a rival, Tibni the son of Ginath, there raged a civil war of four years' duration. "Then were the people of Israel divided into two parts; half of the people followed Tibni the son of Ginath to make him king; and half followed Omri."[50] In appearance no more than a commonplace struggle for power on the part of two rival adventurers, some element of religious warfare entered in all probability into this long drawn-out conflict, to which the Biblical text gives no more than a passing reference. Omri, as a wholehearted adherent of the Canaanite religion, was able to count on the support of the neighbouring Phoenicians.[51] His unsuccessful rival, on the other hand, apparently constituted himself the real or pretended champion of those Israelites who were averse to the further encroachment of paganism. Omri's new capital of Samaria built in 880 B.C.E. on an isolated hill six miles north of Schechem, the earlier capital, contained not a trace of the religion of Moses. Archaeological exploration of recent years has uncovered a network of shrines dedicated to the worship of the dead.

The tide turned strongly against the supporters of things Phoenician when Jehu, a soldier of great fervour, seized the throne of Israel. He soon proved himself to be a rhapsodical killer, his fury being fanned additionally by a fanatic named Jonadab ben Rechab. Not content with exterminating the entire house of Omri, he butchered as well the king of Judah along with a large retinue of his relations who happened to come his way. Apparently, this usurper's ambition was not confined to the throne of Israel. He aspired as well to supplant the House of David on the throne of Judah. In this expectation, he was forestalled by Queen Athalia, a lady no less energetic and murderous than himself.

Jehu's revolt had near-fatal consequences for the Ephraimite kingdom, which under his miserable rule came within a hair's breadth of foundering a century and a half before its time. By a massacre in one cunningly arranged encounter of many of the more notable adherents of the pagan cult, he not only succeeded in alienating a goodly portion of his new subjects, but he brought to a close the Phoenician alliance, which on a number of occasions had proven valuable to the Israelites. It was this rupture of a long-standing alliance that the prophet Amos had in mind when he reproached the Phoenicians for "not remembering the brotherly covenant."[52] Even more calamitous, the common front of Israel and Judah which had held in check the aggressive Syrians was from then on splintered likewise.

Jehu's wars with the Syrians were marked with disaster. That in their confrontations the Israelites were outnumbered can be readily assumed. Confirmation of this is to be seen in the Assyrian recording of the famous battle of Karkar in 854 B.C.E. in which mention is made of the numbers of the allied forces opposing the Assyrians, and in which the number of Israelites under King Ahab is given as only half that of his Syrian allies.[53]

Virtually unopposed, the Syrians were able during the feeble reign of Jehu to sweep through Israelite and Judaean territory, and to annex great stretches of the country on both sides of the Jordan.[54] To save himself and his kingdom from complete disaster, the once haughty usurper saw himself obligated to being inscribed among the vassals of the king of Assyria, and to beg his assistance in return for an expensive tribute. The biblical narrative leaves unmentioned this unhappy turn of events; but a bas-relief uncovered at Nineveh depicts either Jehu himself or perhaps his ambassador in the act of doing homage to the Assyrian warlord.

The stereotyped condemnation of the Israelite rulers, to be found in the book of Kings, spared neither Jehu nor any of his successors. The inference is clear that, willingly or not, Jehu or his immediate successor found it necessary to come to terms with the bulk of his subjects by bringing back the proscribed Semitic religion. Baal himself may have remained in bad odour; but his reputed consort Asarte was rehabilitated. Also, at the shrine at Bethel, the sacred bull—or calf, archaic sculpture was not always successful in portraying the more subtle characteristics of animal anatomy—continued as in former times to draw the respectful reverence of a host of suppliants. It is in connection with this reconciliation of the ruler and his semi-heathen subjects that we are to interpret the restoration of Israel's military capacity, and the later driving out of the Syrian intruders.

This much can also be affirmed with confidence: With the overthrow of the House of Omri, all political and economic co-operation between Israel and Phoenicia were brought to a full stop. They were never restored. Resulting from the mass slaughter of the votaries of Baal, a deity to which they were devoutly attached, the Phoenicians withdrew all aid to Israel at a time when it was most needed to sustain them in their struggle against the Syrians. In retaliation, the trading privileges and favoured-nation status enjoyed by Sidonian and Tyrian merchants domiciled in Israel was cancelled likewise. From this period stems the rise of a new Israelite plutocracy. "Ephraim indeed saith 'I am become rich, I have gained wealth.' "[55]

This newly enriched Ephraimite bourgeoisie were said to live in houses of hewn stone, built in the midst of gardens and fruit orchards. They were depicted as lying "upon beds of ivory, stretching themselves on their couches, and listening to the sounds of the vial."[56] Their wives were bedizened with precious stones and cosmetics. Such fastidious living, innocent enough by modern standards, was made possible, in part at least, by oppressive dealings on the part of these parvenues with the less fortunate of their countrymen.

To the prophetic mentors of the earlier Jehuites, the misdoings of these "mighty men of wealth" were either not visible, or else passed over silence. We do read of Elisha being appealed to by a woman whose children were about to be taken from her for non-payment of their father's indebtedness. Otherwise, Elisha was more concerned with dynastic politics than with social problems. An angry man, and also one of great personal vanity, his eagerness as a meddler even brought him to Damascus, where he helped engineer a political assassination. One of his successors, Jonah, the son of Amittai, the complacent counsellor to Jeroboam II, was also not unaware of the social evils which had followed in the wake of the new commercialism. But to him, likewise, the theme was too vexing. We discover some motive for his silence in the book that bears his name. Jonah thought it best to avoid entering into any conflict with men of influence and wealth.

Sturdier than Elisha and Jonah were Amos and Hosea, who had no fear whatsoever of antagonizing the high and mighty, and of voicing their low esteem of the new plutocracy. By Amos, these men were accused of "making the epha small and the shekel great, and falsifying the balances of deceit."[57] His disciple Hosea, of a similar view, observed, "As for the trafficker, the balances of deceit are in his hands."[58] It could be observed in this connection that when commerce was still in its nascent stage, the temptation was all but irresistible to exaggerate the weight of the gold and silver ingots given in exchange for an epha of wheat or barley, while at the same time lowering the true weight of the produce. This was especially the case when only one of the parties was in possession of a pair of scales and did the weighing by himself.

Cheating that was endemic to early tradesmanship was not the only malpractice. Incidental to commerce was the institution of moneylending. There were in ancient Israel or in any other country of that period no full-time dealers in money. The age of the professional moneylender and moneychanger came only later. To the successful merchant, lending of his surplus cash at interest was the only available means of investing it outside his regular business. To be sure, lending was not invariably a symptom of social disorder. But it did take on a nefarious aspect in instances where the borrower was unable to repay. The consequences to the borrower were equally grave, whether the loan had been made at a high rate of interest, at a low interest, or even without interest. The borrower and his family were in real trouble.

Now the lender to the needy among the Israelites was not as a general rule the Phoenician importer of pearls from the Persian Gulf or the exporter to Egypt of wine and oil. The foreign tradesman could not conveniently lend his money locally, since he arrived one day and departed the next, and might never again see his borrower to claim payment. His side-line business would more likely consist in the buying of enslaved debtors, buying them in the land of Israel and then selling them in one of the Greek islands, at the famous slave market at Rhodes, for example.[59] In Israel itself there were no slave markets, but the land of Israel was a source of supply. Moses had decreed that no Hebrew could be sold to another Hebrew for a longer period than seven years. But he had neglected to say anything about selling a Hebrew debtor to an alien who would resell him in a foreign country.

Who were the unfortunate borrowers? The borrower was a farmer who had suffered a crop failure, but whose hopes lay in a better year that was ahead when the loan could be discharged. But if that better year failed to come, his land was forfeited to the creditor who took possession without pity. Another class of borrowers were artisans. Handicrafts which had come to the cities of Israel at the time of the early monarchy were enhanced along with commerce in the later period of the Jehuides. Commerce and industry by their very nature were always meant to synchronize. The new rich had need of many fabricated products, among them such articles as many coloured garments, glassware, carved and inlaid furniture, curtains, and jewellry. All too often, however, such luxuries, turned out by inexperienced and newly risen Israelite craftsmen, failed to compete with the more aesthetically refined wares entering freely into the country from Babylon, Damascus, Tyre and Thebes. The incidence of failure among Israelite craftsmen must have been inordinately high. Failure to pay the money advanced to them for the purchase of their raw materials meant being unceremoniously taken into custody at the requirement of the creditor and consigned to a slave dealer.

Amos, a man of Judah, was appalled by what he saw and heard. Amos was no unsophisticate peasant, but a man of affairs. As a grower of livestock in his native city of Tekoah, he had seen much of merchants who had come to deal with him and their ways. He well understood the methods by which they went about overreaching the simple countryfolk, from whom they bought or to whom they sold. As an outsider, he was warned by the Israelite authority that all this was none of his concern. He was warned to leave the Israelite kingdom, and betake himself to his own country. He did so in all probability; but before abandoning his mission he had bound to himself at least one ardent disciple, a native Ephraimite by name of Hosea. The voice of prophecy, for the first time allied to the cause of social justice, first happened to be raised within the northern kingdom. But it soon communicated itself to the sister kingdom, where it was taken up by Micah, Isaiah, and others.

The "destroying of the poor" did not forever remain a feature of the Jewish economy. The protests of Amos and Hosea fell on deaf ears, it being too late for the northern kingdom to correct itself. In the south, the admonitions of the prophets were finally hearkened to but at a later period. At the insistence of the wealthy Nehemiah, who by his own conduct set them an example, the "nobles of Judah" agreed to forever relinquish the right of distraint on the lands and persons of defaulting debtors.[60] Thereafter, men of commerce acquired a new respectability. Neither in the later Wisdom literature, nor in the Talmud, did they again come under attack.

Turning finally to the kingdom of Judah, it was able, after the demise of Solomon's empire, to maintain itself for four hundred years, and for well over a century after the shades of night had descended on its sister kingdom of the north. For their respective fates there is to be seen some analogy to the division of the Roman Empire into two segments following the death of the emperor Theodosius in 395 C.E. The survival of the kingdom of Judah as a truncated state with a future of some hope was somewhat of a reminder of the continued and prosperous existence of the Byzantine Empire in the centuries following the prostration of its western counterpart.

The Judaean state, though militarily and economically weaker than that of the northern tribes was, all things considered, in a more favourable position for permanence, in that it was more secluded from powerful neighbours. For the greater part of this period, Egypt constituted hardly any threat. The raiding expedition of the Egyptian king Shishak during an interval of confusion following the secession of the northern tribes caught the Judaean kingdom off balance and unprepared. A follow-up intrusion a few years later met with a different reception, and was not repeated for several hundred years.

It was within the narrow confines of the Judaean kingdom that the religion known as Judaism became firmly rooted, and attained to an adult development. The Jerusalem temple proved the decisive factor in differentiating the religion of the Jews from that of their semi-Canaanitish kinsfolk of the northern kingdom. No fane of similar splendour was at the disposal of those among the dwellers of Judah whose leanings remained towards paganism; nor, be it added, for those faithful Israelites of the north who continued to oppose the official cults of the houses of Omri and Jehu. Solomon's temple was beyond doubt the strongest bulwark of the Mosaic tradition prior to the issuance of the Pentateuch. Its priests, in harmony with the prophets, a number of whom were of priestly descent, exerted themselves in reining in idolatrous tendencies on the part of the royal house.

The House of David, be it recalled, was partly of non-Hebraic descent, including among its forbears not only Ruth, the faithful proselyte, but heathen princes of Armenia and Tyre. Jezebel and Athalia were among its ancestry. While within this dynasty there were not absent some who did not escape the charge of religious treason, a remembrance of what its founders had stood for more often prevailed among David's descendants. Taken as a whole, this line of kings presented a favourable contrast to the unstable regimes of the northern kingdom; and without their presence, the religion of the patriarchs would have fared badly indeed. To King Jehoshaphat, and probably to others of his line, there came the idea of utilizing the services of priests and Levites in tasks other than in the performance of rites within the Temple, by sending them forth among the people as itinerant emissaries of the faith. "And they taught in Judah, having the book of the law with them; and they went about through all the cities of Judah, and taught among the people."[61]

Be it noted that among the Jews of Jerusalem the temple rite dwindled gradually into sheer formalism. Confidence among them in the efficacy of such propitiatory rites at no time approached that of the Greeks, among whom the engaging in a battle without some preliminary votive offerings was unusual. A perceptive understanding of the true nature of Temple worship in Jerusalem is conveyed to us by none other than Julius Wellhausen. "The Holy One of Israel sat enthroned not on the smoke pillars of the altar, but in the praises of the congregation pouring out its heart in prayer. The sacrifices were merely the external occasion for visiting the the temple, the real reason for so doing lay in the need for the strength and refreshment to be found in religious fellowship."[62] Significant is the fact that the earliest Christians, including Paul himself, accepted the sacrifical cult; and repaired to the temple at the hours of prayer. Jesus himself had a deep feeling of loyalty for the temple along with its ritual and had relations with it both in life and in thought.[63]

The Temple of Solomon, with its quadrangular enclosure, offered an area for large scale assemblage, much like the plaza of St. Peter's in present day Rome. It was the one and only location where a multitude of believers of like sentiment and spirituality were enabled to foregather. This is a point of capital importance. In and through public gatherings, sentiments of all shades, be they political or religious, become afflated and intensified. A flame that in the breast of the individual devotee burns but faintly is certain to be raised to a more fiery pitch once brought into communion with like sentiments openly shared within a circle of fellow believers.

Solomon's temple endured for about four hundred years. It was burned to the ground in the year 586 B.C.E. when the city fell to the Babylonians. But it could easily have fallen a prey to the flames at some earlier period. In the antique world, cities and their religious piles were repeatedly consumed by fire, if not through enemy action at least accidentally. The Jerusalem sanctuary, by comparison with nearly all those scattered throughout the pagan world, was of exceptionally long duration. But its end signalized the end of the Judaean state as well.

Between Jeremiah in Jerusalem foretelling doom and Demosthenes in Athens foretelling doom some affinities are obvious and some comparison is invited. Both were far-sighted orators whose counsel went unheeded. The Athenian democracy was overthrown by Philip of Macedon for its failure to act on the advice of Demosthenes, who urged preparedness while there was still time. Jeremiah, to the contrary, urged non-resistance to a force that could not be withstood with any hope of success. Both the Athenian and the man of Jerusalem were for the time and circumstances wiser than their audiences. As prophets of doom, they were equally detested by their obtuse listeners. Demosthenes, who had issued warning after warning to the Athenians, was later blamed for the city's misfortunes. So

182

too was Jeremiah, whose unpopularity remained great, and who declined to accompany his compatriots to Babylon. He was instead compelled by a gang of renegades to fly with them to Egypt, to a country that he had held in abhorrence, and to an unknown fate.

CHAPTER VI
JUDAISM VERSUS SEMITISM

The survival of the Hebrews as a distinct nation during centuries of submersion under Christianity and Islam has often been referred to as a miracle. But scarcely less miraculous was their earlier survival as a monotheistic enclave within an all-encompassing sea of Middle Eastern paganism. At the lowest and simplest level, the Israelite newcomers into the land of Canaan, in the process of learning from their settled neighbours the arts of husbandry and tillage, were in a situation to imbibe as well a veneration of the rustic deities of their instructors. More especially was it nearly impossible for them to hold at arm's length fashionable ideologies sponsored by rich and militarily potent neighbour states, by whom they were hemmed in. By way of and up to the present illustration, there would to-day be scarcely a communist movement anywhere in the free world were it not for the overshadowing presence of the armed might of the Soviet Union. Similarly, as long as there existed a militarily triumphant Germany, the cant of National Socialism was able to command world-wide sympathy and respect. Such was the case likewise with what was called

Fascism so long as Italy remained powerful and feared under the Mussolini dictatorship.

Except for one or two brief intervals, neither one nor the other of the Hebrew states had anything to fear from Egypt militarily. Hence the religion of the Nile country possessed no particular attraction, even for those Israelites whose inclinations were in the direction of the cruder forms of idol worship. There is no evidence whatsoever that would link a single Hebrew of the Biblical period to the worship of embalmed cats or crocodiles, or to the worship of the Nile River or to venerating Pharaoh as a god. But in the case of the far more dignified Semitic pantheon it was altogether otherwise. Patronized as it was by the masters of the then-known world, the allure of its mythology and ceremonial captivated even the mind of Greece. For it to have failed to make any inroads among the politically weak Israelites would have been surprising indeed. As regards the Ephraimite kingdom of the north, overshadowed as it was by Phoenicians, Syrians, and Assyrians, no more than a faint resistance to encroaching paganism was offered by a small minority of the Israelite population. Such resistance was far more efficacious inside the kingdom of Judah; but here too a strong enough minority held out in favour of official idol worship to the very last moment of the state's independence.

Between the appearance of the Pentateuch in the year 622 B.C.E. and the destruction by the Babylonians of the first Hebrew commonwealth, there was a lapse of some thirty-six years. During this period the victory of the monotheistic faith was once again in doubt. The successors of King Josiah, who was a near contemporary of the Athenian lawgiver Solon, were undistinguished rulers, or more correctly puppets, who proved unable and unwilling to carry forward his work of purgation.

The irate Jeremiah, who spoke to the nation during

this entire period of backsliding, complained of the resurgence of idolatry in Jerusalem itself as well as throughout the surrounding countryside. "For according to the number of thy cities are thy gods, O Judah."[1] For about a dozen years following the death of King Josiah, the Jewish kingdom remained under Egyptian control, and, by implication, under the spell of that nation's divinities, and especially, it would appear, of the mother goddess, Isis.

Lessons of the times, and of history, are hardly ever suf.iciently plain to be read alike by everyone. In the wake of any national disaster, observers and witnesses will invariably insist each on his own diagnosis. When after the defeat of Josiah the Jews were once again marked for calamity, there were among them not a few who were convinced that the chastisement which had befallen the nation was a visitation of the insulted deities of the Semites and Egyptians. "As to the word which you have spoken to us in the name of Jehovah, we will not listen to you. But we will do everything which we have vowed, burn incense to the queen of heaven and pour libations to her, as we have done and our fathers, for then we had plenty of food and saw no evil. But since we let off to offer to the queen of heaven and to pour out drink offerings to her, we have wanted all things and have been consumed by the sword and by famine."[2]

That among the exiles "by the rivers of Babylon" who found themselves compelled to labour in the broiling sun at the task of digging and repairing the canals there were to be found those who were still addicted to idolatrous beliefs admits of no doubt whatever. The prophet Ezekiel refers to Jewish women whom he saw weeping ceremoniously for the slain god Tammuz, whose seasonal resurrection they were soon to rejoice at as well. Also of the deportees from Jerusalem, there were those who preferred to separate themselves from the main body of their nation by seeking out Egypt as their new home. Having arrived there, they

186

were not slow in declaring their allegiance to the religion of that country.

A question to be asked is how it came about that the era of idol worship, which to the very end of the First Commonwealth had continued to anger Jeremiah and Ezekiel, was so drastically terminated as to no longer engage the attention of later post-exilic prophets such as Haggai, Zecharia, Obadiah, and Malachi? The answer is perhaps to be found in the ease with which the dissentient element among the exiled Hebrews were able, as never before, to dissociate themselves from their brethren by taking on the nationality as well as the beliefs of their new surroundings. Recusants who formerly were unable to isolate themselves from the rest of the Hebrew nation, once having been removed from their ancestral home, were henceforth privileged to go their own way and forever to disappear as Jews. Clear and irrevocable from then on was the distinction between those members of the Jewish nation who remained steadfast to their ancient creed and those who chose to apostasize themselves. Among the inhabitants of the fallen kingdom of Judah transplanted by Nebuchadnezzar were included a goodly number of idolators. Among those who returned to their ancestral homes following the edict of Cyrus, there were none. Through the combined forces of book and synagogue there had been forged a faith that was to remain unshaken throughout the ages.

A religious system sponsored by an irresistible Assyro-Babylonian master race could not for long have been spurned by a decimated and helpless Hebrew nation. But the exiles from the land of Judah were soon witnesses to a turning point in world history, which to all contemporary observers from near and far must have seemed astonishing indeed. To the omnipotence of the Semitic family of nations an end had been foreshadowed when in the year 608 B.C.E. the great metropolis of Nineveh had been reduced

187

to ashes. On the ruins of the Assyrian Empire there arose two others. The lesser of these was the recreated Babylonian Empire, which in effect was that portion not taken over by the conquering Medes. Its ethnic make-up differed hardly at all from that of its fallen predecessor, being likewise of the Semitic family.

During the brief interval of its grandeur, this neo-Babylonian Empire was in reality no more than a one man dominion, much like that of Hammurabi of earlier times. It lived under the shadow of its non-Semitic ally. The city of Babylon itself, in its ephemeral greatness, was the achievement of one man. "Is not this great Babylon that I have built for the house of the Kingdom, by the might of my power, and for the honour of my majesty."[3]

The great Nebuchadnezzar was above all a master builder: but apparently not one with a great deal of optimism about the future of his kingdom under his successors. He made of his capital a wondrous city, whose palaces and temples astounded the men of that generation, but whose costliness proved ruinous before long despite the gold and silver extracted from subject nations. A work of great squandering was the celebrated Hanging Gardens, motivated by considerations both political and connubial. The wife for whose caprice and edification they were erected at immense expenditure of wealth and labour happened to be the daughter of the Medean King Cyaxeres. Like Solomon of old, who was led into espousing an Egyptian princess, King Nebuchadnezzar sought, by the vain expedient of matrimony, to shore up an alliance that was inherently fragile and undependable. According to the anecdote, this lady felt herself constrained to pass her days tediously upon the hot Mesopotamian plain. She sighed for the forested uplands of her native country, to which she may have threatened to return, a step that for her husband could have been fraught with untoward political consequences. As a poor, though also costly enough, substitute she was privileged to behold this artificial mound of lofty terraces set with groves of trees, vegetation, and flowers. Even more devouring of treasure were Babylon's cyclopean walls of unrivalled dimensions. Forming a circumference, according to Herodotus, of sixty miles, their thickness was said to have been no less than seventy-five feet. For those who knew themselves to be genuinely secure, as for example the men of Sparta, no need was felt for mountainous barriers as a substitute for armed might.

By the prophet Jeremiah, the smallness of all nations in the eyes of God had been proclaimed.[4] A newly arisen world power was to engulf those nations of Western Asia which almost from the beginning of recorded time had dominated their surrounding world. The spectacular taking of Babylon by a nation stemming from the Iranian plateau, in 539 B.C.E., was followed a few years later by the overrunning of Egypt. Brought low likewise at about the same time were the lesser Semitic nations of the Levant. Prominent among these were the Phoenicians, whose coastal cities were reduced to servitude, first by the Persians and later by the Macedonians. After 550 B.C.E. the Phoenicians lost most of their seafaring trade to the Ionian Greeks, the Corinthians, and the Korkyrians. By land as well their commerce came to be greatly diminished.

For the Jews and for Judaism the eclipse of Semitic power and dominion spelt a great deliverance. It ought not to escape our notice that throughout the entire Biblical period the more persistent enemies of the Hebrews had been nations classified as belonging to the Semitic race. Genetically, the Israelites were obviously of that stock at least partially. "Thine origin and thy nativity is of the land of the Canaanites: the Amorite was thy father and thy mother was a Hittite."[5] But by their religious teachers the Hebrews had been summoned to cast aside all spiritual affinity with their racial kinsfolk. The story of Abraham is that of a man who broke sharply away from his tribal origin to set out upon a pathway of his own. And so it was with his descendants, who were from the very beginning and have been to this very day a nation *sui generis*. Throughout their early history, they formed no part of the Semitic bloc of nations, no more than they do so at this very day. Spiritually the Jews never have been Semites.

Bereft of its political buffer, the Semitic complex of polytheism, mythology, unspiritual and cruel belief and practice, long dominant throughout the Middle East, collapsed likewise. In proceeding to demolish the shrines of their defeated enemies, the victorious Iranians were far from backward. At the command of Xerxes, the celebrated temple of Marduk, long the pride of the Babylonians, suffered the identical fate once meted out by its votaries to Solomon's temple. "The Persians," Herodotus noted (1:131), "have not the usage of raising statues to the gods. Nor have they any temples nor altars. They regard these things as folly. The reason, it seems to me, is that unlike the Greeks, they do not regard the gods as having the same nature as men."

For the later prophets, who were the contemporaries of the new dawn, there was no longer the need to expatiate on the wrath to come. Malachi now was able to speak of the high esteem in which Judaism was beginning to be held, "For from the rising sun to its setting my name is great among the Gentiles."[6] Another of the prophets of the latter time discoursed with confidence of the approaching day when "many nations shall join themselves to Jehovah and shall be my people."[7] In due course the shortcomings of their ancestral polytheism became apparent to many individuals among the nations. Repeatedly was this pointed out to them in language which they could not fail to understand. Philo of Alexandria, who was well acquainted with the philosophy and theology of the Greeks, discoursed freely to his Greek readers and listeners on the superiority of Judaism. Josephus, the collaborator with the Roman conquerors, was nevertheless during his remaining years stamped with awe of the ancestral religion and was not reticent in informing his new patrons of its greatness. In the minds of Paul and the fathers of the Church, there was no doubt whatever as to the pre-eminence of Jewish doctrine and practice over the beliefs of the Graeco-Romans.

To be sure the time of Judaism had been slow in coming. The monotheistic faith had from the first been difficult to inculcate and to maintain. As regards any future existence, it held forth the promise of neither rewards nor punishments. It was related to a prophet whose tomb was unknown, and whose descendants and family were held in no particular reverence. To the ancients, worship without the aid of graven images was altogether unprecedented, and constituted an obstacle to comprehension. To a large multitude gathered together under open skies, the weakly intoned spoken word appealed less powerfully than the visible presence of the grandiose molten image. Hence David's conquests among the heathen had as far as is known effected no conversions to his religion. To Egyptians, Phoenicians, Syrians, Assyrians, Babylonians and Persians, the sacred writings of the Hebrews were long a matter of indifference. Nor was there any inclusion of them in the splendid library of Ashurbanipal set up at Nineveh. To the stationary mind of Asia, moreover, never a thought was given to having them translated.

This cold indifference to the Hebrew Scriptures and their message was largely overcome, even before the time of their actual translation into Greek, their contents becoming known to a widening multitude, who, though unable to read, were yet willing and able to listen. Be it noted that, within the ancient world, a book that told of matters celestial had its sway over the minds of people to an extent that it would be impossible to discover in a more sophisticated age. There existed during the entire Persian and Graeco-Roman periods no other book that could have told heathens how the world began, and about the origin of stars, animals, plants, and human beings. All that was related in the book of Genesis came to be believed by a vast number of non-Jews. "And in that day" Isaiah of old had prophesied "shall the deaf hear the words of a book."[8]

Almost coincidental with the prostration of the political and religious system of Semites and Egyptians was the disappearance of the greater portion of their literary achievement. Lost and forgotten for many centuries were the Ugaritic writings and those of Mari, as were many scrolls of papyrus, and at least 22,000 cuneiform tablets. Many of these lay buried in the ruins of Thebes, Nineveh, Babylon and other major cities. Of the epigraphic creativity of the entire Middle East, little remained extant beyond the Scriptural writings of the Jews, the youngest cultural representatives of that region. Such rival productions as still subsisted within the territories of the Middle East were written in a script intelligible to none but a few. The sacred books of Zoroaster also written in cuneiform, and not translated, constituted no threat to the popularity of the Jewish writings. The consequences that flowed from the Hebrew Scriptures thus making their way militantly into the wider world were political and economic as well as religious. Most significantly, it was above all among Greek-speaking people that the new presence of Judaism made itself felt.

Even though they might have known that much of their religion and mythology had come to them by way of the Semitic Middle East, the Greeks considered their civilization superior to all others. This conceit of theirs had some colour of justification, inasmuch as virtually all literature once emanating from Egyptians and Semites was no longer in anyone's possession. Though for the most part too vain to acknowledge anything of worth in the civilization of other nations, many of the Greeks were intrigued by their coming into contact with one other people as haughty and exclusive as themselves.

In Grecian character and civilization there were of course contradictory features. Very much in evidence were eroticism, homosexuality, drunkeness, glory in naked physical strength, all this according well with the spirit of its epic literature. For persons of this calibre, the Hebrew scriptures had something of jollification as well. The frivolous were titillated by sex scandals there related, as for example Reuben's amorous exploit with his father's concubine Bilha, a spicy episode not unlike that reported of the hero Phoenix.[9] Others, in love with things militaristic, were taken with the adventures of David, whose warlike prowess and amours they found to be in the Homeric tradition. To him their admiration went out for having won for himself a royal mate through the mass slaughter of his patron's enemies in preference to the conventional payment of the bride's price.

On the character of the Divine, the more serious among the Greeks had long been pondering. By Greek philosophy had before times been postulated the concept of a Supreme Being as an explanation and the source of the world's orderliness. To speak of Hellenic monotheism is certainly appropriate.[10] For such seekers, the Pentateuch now became visible as a source of creative religious power, and a writing to arouse their sympathetic curiosity. To their logical and scientific intellects, the answer as to the world's origin as revealed in the opening chapters of Genesis seemed not improbable.

Tormented as they were by questionings as to the existence of the gods, and in despair as to their worth and morality, these men belonged none the less to an age when capacity for faith and a readiness to believe were as yet unimpaired. For such minds it was invigorating to come upon a book from which polytheistic legendry had been rigidly excluded, and which presented a rational contradiction to the Orphic and Eleusinian mysteries. In the pages of this book they discerned nothing of the grotesque quarrels and rivalries among celestial personages, so pronounced in their own classical literature. Mythological accounts they did come upon in this newly discovered literature, but these were the mythical doings of human dwellers on earth and not of deities.

Other matters as well dealt with in the Jewish scriptures were close enough to the higher instincts of the more cultivated Greeks. To the politically advanced among them, there was much in their own treasured literature which to them was painful. "Homer and Hesiod" wrote Xenophanes of Colophon "have ascribed to the gods all things that are a shame and a disgrace among men, thefts and adulteries, and the deception of one another." Heraclitus added "Homer should be turned out of the lists and whipped and Archilochus likewise."

Such were the more blatant opinions. And yet undeniably, heroes such as Achilles, Menelaus, and Odysseus were glorified pillagers. To an enlightened generation, the Iliad, full of beauty and vivacity though it is, presented a tableau of political and social enslavement; and lamentably enough one to which the poet himself took no exception whatsoever. To the bard's evident displeasure, a private soldier, Thersites by name, has the temerity to arraign the unimpeachable leaders of the Achaian expedition, accusing them of indifference to the fate and well-being of the men under them. For so speaking up, he is promptly taken in hand by the noble Odysseus, who beats the man cruelly with his iron studded baton. The other soldiers, on whose behalf

Thersites had so boldly spoken, far from lending him their support, join in reviling him, all this to the reciter's satisfaction. To the consciousness of a later generation of Greeks, this inglorious episode was no longer edifying.

The translation of the Hebrew Scriptures into Greek, the first of known translations ever undertaken, set the stage for their popularization and, ultimately, for the spreading towards the West of the spiritual power of Judaism. In Rome itself, the later infiltration of Jewish ideals was of some vexation to poets like Ovid and Horace. To Seneca, a great philosopher and also a great slave proprietor, the observance of the Sabbath was altogether scandalous. Such a thing as a day dedicated to idleness, he protested, could only have been the invention of a criminal nation.

To the Jews themselves the appearance of the Greek Testament or Septuagint was a wondrous happening. No less than on the spiritual level, it spelt for them the opening of an era of political gain and economic acquisitiveness as well. In the Hellenized cities of the Asiatic interior, in those of the Aegean archipelago, on the shores of the Black Sea, and in continental Greece itself, the planting of new Jewish communities became greatly facilitated. Joining such nuclear congregations were converts from among the indigenous population, who had come under the spell of the Pentateuch and the Prophets. Along with actual converts, there were even wider circles of near converts, designated by their Jewish friends and neighbours as "Fearers of the Lord" and "Proselytes of the Gate." These latter were frequenters of the synagogues, in all probability contributing handsomely towards their construction and maintenance. Not to go unmentioned was the patronage of such friends and sympathizers in favouring the enterprise of newly settled Jewish merchants and artisans. The post-exilic prophets, who were testifying to the growing esteem for Judaism among the nations, were in effect announcing an infusion of new blood into the nation, along with a coincidental rise in Jewish collective wealth and influence.

Prior to the nineteenth and early twentieth centuries, when the Jewish population throughout the world soared in keeping with that of virtually all other nations, there have been two known instances when the Jewish population rose dramatically. The first of these, taken note of in the Scriptures, was the transition to nationhood of the small patriarchal clan transplanted to Egypt. The second was the period that followed the restored Jewish commonwealth at the time of the second Temple.

In all, about 49,000 of the exiled Jews are reported to have availed themselves of the permission given in the year 538 B.C.E. to return to the site of the demolished Jerusalem and to rebuild it anew. It has been suggested that those who did return were about one-tenth the total number of exiles.[11] According to this estimate, the total number of Jews throughout the world was then not far above one-half million. Contrasting with this insignificant figure, their number at the time of the destruction of the second Temple at the beginning of the Christian era was undoubtedly in the millions, even though some widely differing figures have been suggested. In the census of the year 42 C.E. ordered by the Emperor Claudius, the Jews were said to have been ten percent of the total population of the Roman Empire, or not less than seven million. This figure, which does not take into account the number residing in Mesopotamia, which was not part of the Roman territory, has been challenged as excessive. A contrary figure is four and one half million for all the Jews dispersed over western Asia, northern Africa, Greece, and Italy.[12] The conclusion that may be safely drawn is as follows: Even accepting the more modest top figure as the more probable, the growth of the Jewish population in late antiquity was such as to transform the nation.

Contributing towards this build-up was the accession of not a few proselytes, without whose aid the preservation of the nation would have been far less likely. Such converts came not only from among Greek readers of the Testament. Its later translation by Onkelos was intended for the benefit of Aramaic-speaking Gentiles who were converts like himself. Throughout Palestine, a goodly number of provincials, some of partly Hebraic origin, were won over to Judaism—some of them forcibly, be it added. Among Aramaic converts to Judaism may well have been numbered some of the forebears of Jesus of Nazareth. The motive that impelled the Jews of many communities to seek out converts to their religion differed markedly from that of their later Christian competitors. With the saving of individual souls the Jews were totally unconcerned. Under the tenets of later Judaism, one could continue to be a heathen and be received with favour into the next world, provided that he had conducted himself properly in the earthly world. The motive uppermost in seeking converts among the heathen was that of strengthening the Jewish position here on earth. There were those among the heathen Romans to whom this prospect was alarming. It was for this reason alone that, in the beginning of the third century, the emperor Septimius Severus issued his rescript forbidding on pain of death the conversion to Judaism of any Roman citizen.[13]

Expressive of the extensive infusion of non-Hebraic blood into the stream of Judaism is the following passage from the Talmud. "The Jews in the Roman diaspora compared as to their descent with those of Judaea are like mixed dough to pure flour; but Judaea itself is only dough compared with Babylon."[14] The relative indifference of the Babylonian Jews to proselytizing could have been due to their having been sufficiently numerous and confident enough in their own positions, so as to require no outside aid from newcomers.

It remains to be added that without the remarkable increment of their numbers during the Persian and Graeco-Roman periods, the Jews would not have been enabled to emerge viably from the fifteen centuries of struggle and attrition that awaited them. In the middle of the eighteenth century, when the age of persecution was visibly drawing to a close, the number of Jews living in Europe and Asia has been estimated at scarcely more than one million, or at most one fifth of what it had been in the opening centuries of the Christian era.[15]

PART II

The Jewish exiles carried off to the land of the two rivers did not share the oblivion that overtook their kinsfolk of the northern kingdom, or of the Hebrew-speaking Moabites, the destruction of whose kingdom is recorded in the forty-eighth chapter of the book of Jeremiah. To the prophet Jeremiah, the condition of his exiled people seemed by no means hopeless. His faith in the future of his brethren prompted him to write his famous epistle in which he counselled them, "Build ye houses and dwell in them; and plant gardens, and eat the fruit of them. That ye may be increased there and not diminished; and seek the peace of the city whither I have caused you to be carried away captive."[16]

In the lot of these deportees there was unquestionably a great deal of diversification. There were among them some who had managed to take along with them quantities of gold and silver bullion. These possessed the necessary wherewithal to follow Jeremiah's excellent advice about

198

making themselves comfortable in their new surroundings. But of the vast majority, it can be safely conjectured that their altered existence was, for the time being at least, hardly any different from that of the ancestors detained against their will in Egypt. Babylon, like Pithom and Ramses at the time of Moses, required a great deal of laborious building up. There is no reason to imagine that the life of an indentured construction worker was pleasanter in Babylon that it had been in Egypt. Ancillary to the work of building was that of making bricks. We are not specifically informed of the Jews newly settled in Babylon being compelled as were their ancestors in Egypt to labour at so uncongenial a task. But such mention would have been superfluous. There are no indications of persons—Jews or non-Jews—voluntarily going to Babylon for the jobs that were then available.

Babylon's population was in need of replenishing. Resulting from periodical epidemics, virtually all cities of the ancient world were from time to time faced with the problem of a thinned-out population. Babylon itself was all but destroyed by the Assyrian king Sennacherib in 689 B.C.E. The revived capital of a proud monarch, it required not only an infusion of new dwellers, but also new temples, palaces, and gardens, to say nothing of gigantic fortifications. Its ruler understood well enough a principle of good statesmanship that was in a later century expressed by Machiavelli in one of his "Discourses." "Those who desire a city to achieve great empire must endeavour by all possible means to make her populous; for without an abundance of inhabitants, it is impossible ever to make a city powerful. This may be done in two ways. Either by attracting population by advantages offered, or by compulsion." Machiavelli, who lived at a time when Jews, far from being persuaded or forced to settle in any of the cities of western Europe, were being driven from them, must have viewed with some mixed feelings the current violations of his maxim. In his own city of Florence, as it happened, the Jews were welcomed by the ruling Medici family, and more especially by the great Lorenzo.

There were tasks awaiting the deported Jews elsewhere than in the city of Babylon itself. The incessant salinization of the intensively irrigated soil of the surrounding countryside, along with the silting up of the canals and the weakening of their dikes, required a large and steadily replenished supply of labourers. As conscript labourers, the exiles were not concentrated in a single place. Thus the youthful Ezekiel was to find himself "among the captives by the river Chaibar." The river Chaibar, a tributary of the Euphrates about four hundred miles northwest of the capital, formed part of a route much frequented by caravans.[17] In part, such additional and supplemental watercourses seem to have been intended as means for stemming the onrush of an invading force.

"By the rivers of Babylon, we sat down and wept." These "rivers" were the canals that required to be dug out and dredged. It was a task that did indeed give rise to much weeping.[18] Throughout the ages, and as recently as the time of the Stalin dictatorship, canal building has been exceptionally costly in human blood, sweat, and tears. No records are available as to the number of Judaean captives whose lives were thus expended "by the rivers of Babylon." But, by way of a suggestive analogy, one hundred and twenty thousand Egyptians were said by Herodotus to have lost their lives during the digging of a canal for connecting the Nile to the Red Sea. Hardly less costly in lives, it might be supposed, was the canal ordered by Nebuchadnezzar to be built from the city of Babylon to the mouth of the Euphrates river on the Persian gulf.

The stern Nebuchadnezzar, whose mania for building meant a life of hardship for Jewish as well as other deportees, was succeeded by a milder ruler. The release from captivity of the deposed King Jehoiachin, as reported in the final chapter of second Kings, had as its issue a more sympathetic treatment of the fallen monarch's former subjects. The canals having been excavated and the fortifications completed, the conscripted Jewish labourers became free to create a new life for themselves.

As in Egypt at the time of Joseph, there was room enough in the land of the Two Rivers for new settlers. The countryside had suffered grievously during the period of Assyrian domination. Hence derelict lands now made fruitful by the newly restored watercourses called for fresh settlers. Jewish agriculture was reborn in a region which rampaging Assyrian bands had once laid waste, lands from which much of the original population had in 709 B.C.E. been uprooted and transplanted to fill up the empty spaces in northern Israel in the days of Sennacherib.

Jewish commercialism as well became in the course of perhaps two or three generations sufficiently acclimatized within the major cities of the Empire. Its rise has thus been expounded upon by a recent writer. "The Israelites could have chosen no better training college. Babylon was an international centre of trade, industry, and commerce, was the great school for the cities and capitals of the whole world."[19] One of the main things that the Jews learnt from the Babylonians was the permissibility of lending at interest. Among Assyrians and Babylonians this had always been acceptable. While the Jews were certainly in need of some additional tutoring in the ways of business, so too were their Babylonians hosts, apparently. Both the Babylonians and the Jews had to learn from the Lydians the advantages of coined money over the older system of making payments with ingots of precious metal.

A further observation is in order. Babylon, prior to the coming of the Israelites, did not suffer from any shortage of native-born traffickers. We are informed that even slaves were engaged in carrying on business.[20] An intrenched mercantile oligarchy, then as in later ages, has not been known to welcome any attempt on the part of a body of strangers and newcomers to intrude upon its preserves. However, only a short time was to elapse before all such jealousies were to be swept away. To the Persian conquerors, both Jews and Babylonians were alike subject nations. It was with the overthrow of the Babylonian Empire that the age of the Jewish merchant arrived.

The prophet Jeremiah in his advice to the exiles of Babylonia urged them to acquire gardens and vineyards. He did not advise them to become merchants: but that is what a great many of them came to be. The upsurge of commercial activity by the newly enfranchised Jews must have been quickened even further as a result of a disaster that befell the old established Babylonian patriciate. In the year 520 B.C.E., Babylon revolted against the newly crowned Persian king Darius. The retaking of this impregnable city as a result of a grotesque stratagem provides an anecdote which I am tempted to recall. I quote verbatim from the historian Grote.

"Darius assembling all the forces in his power, laid siege to the revolted city, but could make no impression upon it, either by force or by stratagem. He tried to repeat the proceeding by which Cyrus had taken it at first; but the besieged were found this time to be on guard. The siege had lasted twenty months without the smallest progress, and the Babylonians derided the besiegers from the height of their impregnable walls, when a distinguished Persian nobleman Zopyrus . . . presented himself one day before Darius in a state of frightful mutilation; his nose and ears were cut off, and his body misused in every way. He had designedly so maimed himself 'thinking it intolerable that the Assyrians should thus laugh the Persians to scorn,' in the intention, which he presently intimated to Darius, of passing into the town as a deserter, with a view of betraying it—for which purpose measures were concerted. The Babylonians, seeing a Persian of the highest rank in so calamitous a condition, readily believed his assurance, that he had been punished by the king's order and that he came over to them as the only means of procuring for himself single vengeance. They intrusted him with the command of a detachment, with which he gained several advantages in different sallies, according to previous concert with Darius, until at length the confidence of the Babylonians becoming unbounded, they placed in his hands the care of the principal gates. At the critical moment, these gates were thrown open, and the Persians became masters of the city.[21]"

Cf Babylon's leading citizens, three thousand, according to Herodotus, were promptly crucified on orders of the revengeful conqueror. It was ordained likewise that each year thereafter five hundred castrated youths were to be forwarded to the Persian court at Susa as slaves. Babylon became an unprivileged city, with its taxation the highest among all twenty of the satrapies or departments forming the Persian empire. Its final strangulation both as a residential city and a trade metropolis was ordained.

That Jews were prominent among the chosen successors of the Babylonian merchant princes so attainted and despoiled is a compellable enough inference. The city itself, constructed out of sun-dried bricks, slowly and gradually crumbled into dust. Its Jewish inhabitants along with the others gradually transferred their residence to other parts. Significantly, the great Jewish trading house of Mourachu, whose records have been rediscovered as dating about a century after the exile, show its location to have been in the neighbouring city of Nippur.[22]

A great many Jewish families preferred as their abode the capital city of Susa, among them the parents of Esther and Mordecai and Nehemiah. Abandoning the declining city of Babylon in the year 444 B.C.E. "some of the children of Israel" decided to follow Ezra and to resettle in Jerusalem. The vast majority, however, chose to remain settled in the vicinicty of the neglected metropolis within the narrow strip of land between the two rivers that forms the southern portion of Mesopotamia. In large numbers, they came to be concentrated within this region that long continued to be known as Babylonia. Through this corridor lying between the Euphrates and Tigris rivers, and touching upon the Persian gulf, there flowed much of the trade between the Middle East and India. Under the favoured treatment by Persia's rulers much of this trade was confined to Jewish enterprise.

But yet Persian rule had its serious limitations, and before long involved economic stagnation. Assyrians, Babylonians, and later Persians remained wedded to a cumbrous and incomprehensible form of writing which from a commercial point of view alone was a hindrance to effective trade and communication. These nations had of course heard of a more efficient form of writing invented by the Phoenicians; but then it was disdained as the offering of a small and despised minority nation and hence unworthy of acceptance by a great empire.

Also the Persian rulers were fond of gathering in the tribute of their distant provinces, as we infer from the book of Esther and other sources. Not knowing how to employ this treasure gainfully, it was stored and immobilized in their several royal palaces. It remained for the Greeks, flowing into this area in the wake of Alexander's conquests, to convert this sterile hoard into creative capital. "When one sees in countries like Mesopotamia and Syria a luxuriant crop of cities taking the place of unstable, sometimes nomadic and Bedouin-like communities which had hitherto lived their unprogressive lives in these regions, one realizes what a complete change was produced by the Hellenic foundations and how much their influence transformed the atmosphere of Oriental life."[23]

Fructified by the genius and enterprise of the Greeks, city life was introduced on a scale never previously known. Great trading routes freshly marked out towards the Black and Caspian seas and towards northern India attracted the products and natural resources of distant and unexplored territories. In what had become under the last Persian monarchs a stagnant area, an industrial and commercial revolution took over.

We may readily suppose that Jewish colonists, already domiciled in the many provinces of the Persian empire, were not slow in benefiting from a widened horizon opened to them by the progressive and enlightened Greeks. Soon, as merchants and craftsmen, and to some extent farmers, Jews were to be found in all the newly founded cities such as Antioch, Seleucia, Smyrna, and a hundred others. None the less, their concentration during many centuries, and in fact down to our own time, remained greatest within that geographical area where the two great rivers come more closely together, an area loosely referred to as Babylonia. Within this busy area, lying between the Iranian plateau on the east and the Arabian peninsula on the west, and serving likewise as the funnel for the seaborne trade with India, there were to be found clustered together such great trading centres as Nippur, Borsippa, Seleucia, and, in a later day, Baghdad; all these being the heirs of the vanished "great Babylon." Additionally, there grew up other cities of secondary importance, among them Nehardea, Nisibis, Sura, and Pumpeditha, where the Jewish population predominated. The activities of Jewish merchants of that region, as importers and exporters of a host of commodities, both natural and manufactured is well documented.[24]

Above all was this formidable concentration of Jewish

wealth and numbers linked with the restored Jewish commonwealth in the Holy Land. All but insurmountable obstacles had barred the way of the exiled Jews who, after the edict of Cyrus, returned to the land of their fathers. "The Judaean community did not possess the power to extricate itself from its impotence ... But help was to come from the richer community of Babylon."[25] That the financial resources as well as political influence of the Mesopotamian communities were a decisive factor in the successful repatriation of their brethren is a conclusion not to be resisted.

The Scripture informs us of the aid furnished by these outposts of Judaism. In the year 519 B.C.E., it tells us that gold and silver were forwarded from Babylon to the struggling builders of the Second Commonwealth.[26] This generosity of ancient times was in all respects analogous to the aid afforded to the newly born state of Israel by the contemporary Jewries of the United States, Canada, and South Africa and other countries of the free world.

The progress of Judaism, as distinct from the Jewish economy itself, during the period of the Second Temple does not form part of my theme. It is appropriate none the less to mention in passing that on this level the flow of indebtedness between the two main sectors of the Middle Eastern diaspora tended to be in the opposite direction. The great nurseries of Jewish learning for which some centuries later Babylonia became celebrated, and which served as beacons for the earliest universities of Europe, had their ground prepared for them among the sages residing in the land of Israel.

PART III

The favourable political and economic climate of the Babylonian Jews had its counterpart in their resettled homeland. In both areas, the growth of population on the one hand and of wealth and political power on the other were mutually interactive.

Be it known that the edict of Cyrus which called for simultaneous restoration of both Tyre and Jerusalem was motivated by a large political and military objective. We are to look back to the process of reshuffling the populations of western Asia instituted by the Assyrians. Carried forward by their Babylonian successors, the policy of mass expulsion and resettlement had its own distinct motivation, in the case of Judaea at least.

Significant is the fact that Nebuchadnezzar, having uprooted from their homes the greater part of the Jewish population, both rural and urban, did not see fit to repeople the empty spaces thus created, as his Assyrian forerunners might have done. The Neo-Babylonian Empire, having no more than a fraction of the offensive military power of its formidable predecessor, entertained no expectation whatever of being able to annex Egypt.[27] Apparently, the relatively weak conqueror of Jerusalem preferred leaving a largely unsettled wilderness between his empire and that of a strong neighbour. It was his intention not only to deter the Egyptians by depriving them of a more advanced base of military operations, but likewise to strike at their economic well-being. The desolation of the Palestinian countryside helped to deprive Egypt of its main source of wine and oil, two of the very essential commodities of its civilization. Having to procure these elsewhere the isolationist Egyptians, suspicious of all foreign contacts, were at last persuaded to open their coastal areas to Greek merchant vessels, a quickening of intercourse which had likewise a profound bearing on the furtherance of Helenic civilization and influence.

Unlike Nebuchadnezzar and his feeble successors, the triumphant Persians acknowledged no visible limits to the growth of their empire. For King Cyrus, who foresaw and in all likelihood planned the invasion of Egypt, even though he did not live to carry it out by himself, a depopulated Judaea was no advantage whatever. As in the days of Esarhaddon and Ashurbanipal, vast preliminary preparations were deemed necessary for so ambitious an enterprise as a landward invasion of Egypt across desert territory. A military campaign, far removed from the centre of empire and its bureaucracy, required an advanced base, plus an assured supply of provisions such as oil, wine, fruits, and grains, furnished by a well-disposed population located within an area close enough to the scene of operations. This prescription, the Jews and their country were able to fill to perfection. Jerusalem was once again a scene of preparation in the wars against Egypt, as it had been in the time of the last Assyrian warlords, and as it was to be in the 12th century in the time of the Crusader kingdom.

It should here be interjected that while Jerusalem had been physically obliterated, along with other Judaean cities that had resisted the Babylonians, some life was allowed to remain in the surrounding countryside. We are informed of a peasantry made up of "the poorest of the land" being left behind. Without the foodstuffs grown and supplied by this remnant, who were later returned to their Jewish allegiance, the rebuilding of the Holy City itself could hardly have been undertaken.

Scarcely less needful to the Persian warlords was a body of merchants skilled in the techniques of collecting from the tillers of the soil and the city artificers the required provisions and weapons, storing them adequately, and by land and sea expediting them to wherever needed. Additionally such traffickers were expected to take custody of prisoners of war for the purpose of disposing of them in the known slave markets, such as that of Rhodes. There were at hand such middlemen. Of all the conquered nations that were absorbed into the polyglot Persian empire, none were to prove themselves more submissive and attentive to the requirements of their masters than the Phoenicians. By the aid of their fleet, a rising of the Asiatic Greeks had been crushed in the days of King Darius. A few years later, it was this same fleet that readily enough assumed the burden of transporting to the shores of Attica a Persian army that was to meet with defeat at the battle of Marathon. Xerxes, leading his monster expedition into Greece, had reason to value highly the skills and managerial abilities of these devoted satellites and inveterate haters of the Greeks. It is deserving of notice that of the many dependent nations of the Persian empire, the Jews and the Phoenicians were taxed the least heavily.[28]

To resume. The loyalty of the Phoenicians was first tested during the invasion of Egypt by Cambyses, the successor of Cyrus. By land and sea, the task alloted to them was that of assembling and transporting to Egypt the food grown largely on Jewish farms, Phoenicia itself not being distinguished as a food producing area. The subjugation of Egypt, successful enough in the beginning, proved to be far from easy in the longer run. The entire period of Persian overlordship was punctuated by further uprisings of this westernmost province. In the course of two centuries these entailed repeated expeditions on the part of the Persian warlords. Along with their continued dependence on Phoenician carriers, their demand for the produce of Jewish farms continued unabated. Following a visit to Jerusalem by Alexander the Great, it is probable enough that it was from this same source that food and other supplies reached his camp to enable him to sustain the lengthy siege of Tyre and later of Gaza. All this spelt a continued inpouring of treasure to Jerusalem and to its farmers and merchants.

Such was the growth of the Holy City newly risen from its ashes that within only a few decades of its rebuilding it contained within its walls a large enough mercantile community to permit of its being organized into three distinct guilds.[29] Among these merchants, were such purveyors of luxuries as goldsmiths and perfumers. At the time of Nehemiah's arrival, so far had the city gained ground as a trading centre, that the setting up of a distinct market inside its walls in emulation of other trading centres was warranted. In planning its defensive walls, the farsighted governor caused them to enclose so large an area as to make allowances for its anticipated growth.[30] Several currents of merchant caravans coming from distant places were known to converge on Jerusalem. Reference to its trade with Arabia is to be found in the book of Joel.[31]

The rule of the Persians over Judaea provided an all but blank period in Jewish history. For the Jews themselves, there was, in the absence of kings, prophets, and the waging of wars, almost no recording of public events. The grievances once laid bare by the prophets had apparently fallen away. Old subjects of contention had vanished, while other still to come had not as yet made their appearance.

Among the returned exiles, a relative absence of dramatic episodes and an aversion to all political adventures was their distinguishing characteristic. Within the huge Persian Empire, they constituted a docile element. To the host assembled for the invasion of Greece, they provided their contingent of untrained foot soldiers.[32]

While thoughts of political independence were furthest from the minds of the resettled Jews, conditions were ripe among them for attention to economic development. They had ceased to be a nation of soldiers even prior to the destruction of the first Temple. If not soldiers, what were they to be if not craftsmen and traders? In the so-called Wisdom literature, a creation of the Persian period, is to be found a prizing of material possession as a reward for righteous living. I refer to the sententious utterances about

210

the virtues of thrift, hard work, and integrity to be found in Proverbs, Ecclesiastes, the book of Jesus the son of Sirach, Job, and the Wisdom of Solomon.

Influenced beyond any doubt by the brilliant spectacle of their Babylonian coreligionists, a new attitude towards trade took hold among the men of the Holy City and of the land of Israel. No longer was it held in ill-repute, suitable only for "Canaanites." As long as it was honestly conducted, commerce became respectable. There was praise for the upright merchant: "A just weight and balance are the Lord's, all the weights of the bag are in his hands." [33] There was a new-found respect for those "that go down to the sea in ships, that do business in great waters." Testifying to the importance that trade had assumed among the Palestinian Jews, Strabo, a geographer of the last century before Christ, reported that the Jews of Palestine were in part agricultural and in part commercial.

In both Babylonia and in the land of Israel itself, the rise of a Jewish mercantile community was partly in replacement of a pre-existing Semitic monopoly. As regards the Phoenicians, it was the Hellenization of the entire Middle East that spelt the end of their commercial dominance both on land and on sea. As far back as the middle of the sixth century before the common era, the Greeks had ousted the mariners of Tyre and Sidon from the traffic of the Aegean Sea. The victory of the Athenian fleet over that of Xerxes at the battle of Salamis, proved the death knell of whatever remained of their maritime commerce. Command of the sea passed to the Athenians and their allies, and with it the carrying trade of the eastern Mediterranean. On land, as well, the monopoly long exercised by merchants of Tyre and Sidon was soon extinguished. In the earliest time, all movements of merchandise from India by way of the Persian Gulf and the cities of Mesopotamia and Syria terminated at the coastal cities of Phoenicia, while the alternate

211

route by way of Egypt and the Red Sea remained sealed under the isolationist Pharaohs. But under Greek influence and domination, and after the founding of Alexandria especially, this rival passageway became unlocked.

In both these "great waters," Jewish merchants from Palestine and Babylonia were now to be seen going "down to the sea in ships." With their coreligionists in Babylonia, the trade relationships of ancient Israel was of the closest. To their Babylonian brethren the Palestinian Jews sent much of their surplus production of wine and oil, for which there was a failing market in Egypt and the West. In return, they received such Oriental products as silks, woolen cloth, pearls, drugs, spices and furniture.

Evidence permits us to believe that there was also much closing of the geographical gap between both these twin regions of the Middle East making them more immediately accessible to each other. Jerusalem then as now lay on the western margin of a desert, while Babylon lay on its opposite side. Both cities, it will be noted, lay almost due east and west of each other. At the time of the Second Temple, and perhaps even earlier, it became possible for merchants without great peril to themselves to traverse the space between these cities by a shorter and more direct route than that taken of old.

Roads were little depended upon by the Semitic masters of the Middle East. The pioneer road-builders were the Persians. They built roads in places where only trodden pathways had existed previously. Darius and his successors instituted the lengthy and ambitious highway that linked their capital at Susa with the subjugated cities bordering on the Aegean Sea. Ultimately however, the economic usefulness of such trunk lines depended on a corresponding build-up of transport in areas that were obliged to do with less than artificial highways. The partial conquest of desert areas and vast distances was made possible additionally by

212

the domestication of the camel at some time during the early Biblical period; and later by the building up over the centuries of large enough herds of this drought-resisting beast of burden. Its domestication by the Arabs constituted for the lands of the Middle East a revolution in transportation altogether on a par with the initiation of road building by the Persians, Greeks and Romans.

The sands of Arabia extend far to the north of the peninsula proper. In remote times, these had constituted an impassible barrier between the western and eastern segments of the Fertile Crescent; and made compulsory a wide detour in a northerly arc through cultivated, if dangerous, regions. But across this expanse of empty desert a series of oases were in the course of time discovered. As early as the eighth century before the Christian era, a number of Arab principalities are known to have put down their roots inside this hitherto forbidden territory. These in effect constituted a series of land bridges.[34]

For a beast of burden such as the camel and dromedary that was capable of challenging the fearsome stretches of the Sahara, traversing the relatively short distance from Jerusalem to the cities of Babylonia was no impossible feat. This foreshortened and direct route was by all means more dependable than the ancient roundabout one which was subject to interference by unfriendly cities in transit. Though never one of the major importance, this direct line of communication between the two centres of world Jewry helped in cementing more closely relationships that were both spiritual and economic. Such contact was all the more feasible inasmuch as between Jerusalem on the one hand and the opposite shore of Babylonia much of the intervening territory had become settled and fruitful. Archaeological research carried out by the late Professor Nelson Glueck in Trans-Jordan has revealed that its population has reached a high level of density during the Roman period.[35]

213

The presence of this intermediate population was certainly compatible with the notion of a direct and short route linking together the two halves of the Jewish world.

On the political level, it is a useful exercise to draw an analogy between the rebuilding of the Jewish commonwealth in the time of the Persians and in the time of the British. The Persians, like the English, issued their "Balfour Declaration." Beyond that, their assistance to the outnumbered and straitened builders of Jerusalem was minimal. The Jews then, as in the present century, were on their own; and they had to fight for their existence. Ezra reported that "the people of the land weakened the hands of the people of Judah and troubled them in building." Nehemiah was compelled to divide the people into two groups, those who actually did the building and those who stood guard. Without self-help, Jerusalem then as in our time would not have been built.

Intrigues and calumnies against the returned Jews were plentiful and found a ready enough ear with the authorities. The edict of Cyrus met with opposition from among his entourage immediately after being issued. Ezra reported that it persisted in the Persian capital "all the days of Cyrus king of Persia."[36]

Little is certain as to the attitude of the Jewish population towards its Persian rulers. A barely concealed contempt for them is to be found in the Book of Esther. The Talmud expressed it this way: "The last Darius, the son of Queen Esther, was spotless on his mother's side and unclean on his father's side." (Found in Midrash Rabah, Parsha Vayikra.) There is reason to assume that for some time prior to the visit of Alexander of Macedon to Jerusalem and his warm welcome there, Persian rule had become as odious to the Jews as it was to the Greeks, Phoenicians, Cilicians, and Egyptians.

I cannot complete this portrayal of the times without

some reference to the background of the Maccabaean struggle for religious and political independence. In this connection particular interest attaches to the part Grecian, part Oriental, and part Semitic kingdom of the Seleucidae. Seleucus, one of the generals of Alexander, succeeded in 312 B.C.E. in carving out for himself an extensive empire embracing the territory conquered by Alexander between the Aegean Sea and the Indus river. However, during the reign of his immediate successors, the easternmost provinces of Soghdiana, Bactria, and Susiana soon fell away. This process of attrition began to accelerate further with the onset of the Parthians, a people holding some dominion south of the Caspian Sea. Their westward sweep resulted finally in their becoming masters of Babylonia in about the year 140 B.C.E., at a time about coinciding with the Jewish struggle for independence. That the Parthian invaders were aided by the Jews living in that area is altogether probable.

Also gaining ground at the expense of the diminishing Seleucid kingdom were the Romans. In the notable battle of Magnesia fought in the year 190 B.C.E., the Romans defeated the forces of King Antiochus "the Great" and detached from his kingdom virtually the whole of Asia Minor, leaving him to rule over Syria and Mesopotamia. The explosion of Jewish feeling against his son Antiochus IV came at a time when, thanks to both the Romans and Parthians, the Seleucid empire had been reduced to no more than a shadow of its original self. It would have gone hard with the Jews and Judaism had the religious persecution been instituted at a time when the strength of this empire was still at its height.

Aided both directly and indirectly by their eastern brethren, the Palestinian Jews did succeed in gaining for themselves temporary political sovereignty, exercised however under rulers who were in no wise distinguished. But within a region dominated in turn by Assyrians, Babylonians, Persians, Macedonians and Romans, small and feeble kingdoms had long gone out of fashion. Along with a number of other small states, such as Rhodes and Pergamum, the Hasmonean kingdom was soon swept aside. It is worth noting that the Seleucid kingdom, grown completely senile and decrepit, was gathered up into the Roman empire in the year 64 B.C.E. by the same Roman general Pompey who, three years earlier, had put an end to Jewish independence.

CHAPTER VII

THE DIASPORA—BABYLONIA, SPAIN, POLAND

PART I

Apart from a number of forced deportations by Assyrians, Babylonians, and Romans, the withdrawal of Jews from their ancestral home during the early centuries of the Christian era was an unhurried and prolonged process. Hence, it is by all means difficult to determine the particular century in which the Holy Land ceased being predominantly Jewish. That it continued for a long time to be the heartland of world Jewry following the destruction of the Temple by Titus is certain.

The Jewish revolt, which broke out in the year 66, coincided with the reign of the emperor Nero. Reverses suffered by the Roman armies during the early stages of the rebellion helped terminate the career and the life of the tyrant. Also, Rome, unlike Babylonia in 486 B.C.E., gained no advantage, either political or economic, from Jerusalem's destruction and the submergence of a flourishing

217

outpost of its empire. Paradoxically, it was not so much the loss of statehood as the subsequent decline of the Roman world as a whole which brought it about that the land of Israel came to be largely abandoned by its children, as will now be explained.

The Roman Empire, which coincided with the territories encompassing the Mediterranean basin, could not long have endured by reason of its own lack of a sufficiently balanced and diversified economy. There were at its door no considerable export markets to absorb its one-sided and excessive production of wine and olives. With the lands of the far-away East, its limited exchange of goods was altogether out of balance. In payment of luxury goods brought in from China and India, the Mediterranean world had little to send in return beyond quantities of the precious metals. These stores were all but exhausted in the course of time, even though the temples were gradually stripped of their gold and silver offerings and innumerable statues had been melted down.

But this was not all. Between Marcus Aurelius, who died in the year 180, and Constantine, the first Christian emperor, a period of 125 years, there were no less than 47 emperors. With scarcely any exceptions, each and every one of these was murdered by his own followers or soldiers. Their reigns were featured by continued internecine warfare and incessant attacks by barbarians from without. Think of a population about the size of that of the United Kingdom having to defend its borders, not only along the entire length of the Rhine and the Danube, but also along the Euphrates and the full extent of the Sahara desert. The expense of these extensive chains of defence, added to those of the not-infrequent civil wars, was bound in the long run to prove overwhelming.

At first, Roman military preparedness devoured mainly the poor; but after a time, the wealthier classes too began seeing the menacing shadows, as the rustic population was able no longer to shoulder the entire burden of civil and military government. A point was reached when it became essential for the ephemeral emperors of the third century to gather revenue by means of raids and confiscations. So voracious were the demands of the military machine that taxation became indistinguishable from outright pillage. In every corner of the Mediterranean world, the economics of war and civil commotion took over, with normal economic activity brought to a near standstill, and with famine and disease everywhere triumphant.

Jewish Palestine was not exempted from the effects of this decay, its economy no less than that of the entire region being caught in the downward spiral. One example will suffice. There had grown up in Palestine a large class of artisans engaged in the weaving of the raw silk that was brought to the west by way of the overland route from China. But this raw material ceased coming once the empire's supply of metallic currency had been depleted. To the oppressive imperial tax gatherers this and similar failures being a matter of indifference, entire communities are said to have fled the country. We are also informed of Jews abandoning the farms, towns and villages of their ancestors taking to the hills and leading the lives of outlaws.[1]

With the triumph of Christianity at the beginning of the fourth century, and more especially with the creation of the separatist Byzantine Empire, the lives of those that remained were rendered even more unbearable by an intensified religious persecution. Overwhelmed by vindictive and discriminatory taxation, they broke out in armed revolt in the year 352 during the reign of the emperor Constantius. It was the first such revolt since the days of Bar Cochba some 220 years earlier, and the only reported instance of organized warfare between Jews and Christians. For those compelled to betake themselves to the Asiatic interior, it was

219

however fortunate, if not providential, that they had not too far to wander. The earlier creation of Jewish outposts in Mesopotamia allowed the Palestinian Jews, on observing the omens of decline, to abandon their homes with some degree of gradualness and good order.

Even their defeats of the years 70 and 135 were less devastating to their morale inasmuch as their other bastion in Babylonia had during these troubles remained intact, and was then at the height of its prosperity. But the turn of the latter community as well to taste of the bitter cup of defeat was soon to come. Here likewise, external political and economic changes played their part in bringing about stagnation and gloom.

The affluent period of Babylonian Jewry was at its peak under the rule of the Parthians, a people with whom they seemed to have lived in close harmony during no less than four centuries. The Parthians were a pastoral people, partially Hellenized, originating in that part of the Iranian plateau immediately to the south of the Caspian Sea. Their kingdom, which after 140 B.C.E. took in Mesopotamia, was however of much smaller extent than that of the earlier Persian founded by Cyrus, as well as the Sassanian which fell heir to it, and consequently weaker militarily than either of these. With the determined aid of its Jewish inhabitants, the Parthians managed, with some vicissitudes, to hold off the Romans still grasping after conquest. In return, the Jews were accorded the privilege of managing their own internal affairs and of having a central authority. Unlike their brethren living under the rule of the Romans and Greeks, they were not politically powerless and insignificant. Living for the most part in compact communities, they were able by virtue of their numbers to dominate a number of cities strategically important for commerce and for war. By reason of their great wealth and superior education, they were able as well to lend courage to the scattered communities of Asia and even those of the Graeco-Roman Empire.

The year 226 C.E. saw the demolition of the Parthian kingdom by the Persians who were headed by a new dynasty known as the Sassanian. With apprehension and forebodings of evil times to come was this defeat of their friends greeted within the Jewish communities, both far and near. Among them it was judged that the Parthians resembled the armies of David, while their Persian enemies were compared to the demons of hell. When news of the catastrophe came to a certain Rabbi Johanan, living in Palestine, he is said to have swooned out of fear and sympathy for his brethren; but on coming to, he reassured himself that through their wealth the Babylonian Jews would manage to persuade their new masters to behave in a friendly manner. He proved to be no more than partially right.

Money could not buy off the rancour of the fanatical Magi, who mistreated Jews and Christians alike.[2] They were responsible for numerous acts of rapine, such as destruction of synagogues, forcible delivery of children to the temples of the Zoroastrians, prohibitions of the observance of the Sabbath and the study of the Law, along with a number of massacres. By way of a crowning misfortune, there appeared in the year 501 a certain Mazdak, the founder of a communistic sect called Zendiks, whose doctrine of the community of both property and of women spread horror among Jews and Christians alike. Against these new fanatics, the Jews offered some stout resistance reminiscent of the time of the Maccabees. Details of this unequal contest and the manner of its termination have not been recorded. What is known is that, after seven years of fighting, the Jewish, patriarch and leader in the struggle, Mar Zutra II, was taken alive by the Persians and crucified. What is also known is that when the time came for the Persian Empire to fall before the Moslems, the Jews offered their assistance to the invaders, as did their coreligionists in far-off Spain.

Their security following the Moslem conquest did not last long. More especially did their position deteriorate with the accession of the Abbasids, who extirpated the half pagan and tolerant line of the Ommeyads.[3] It was with the rule of the Abbasids that the Jewish exodus from Iraq became a steady and permanent flow towards the west. "From the third to the fifth century of Islam the movement of the Jewish population was from east to west, from Persia and Iraq to Palestine, Egypt, North Africa, and Spain."[4] Those that stayed on in the east continued to live there more by resignation than by hope.

The region long known as the "Garden of the Lord" coincided in the dawn of history with the heart of the civilized world, and one which in antiquity stretched from the Indus River to the Nile, the entire continent of Europe itself being outside this pale. From the beginning of recorded history, and for several millenia thereafter, the land of the two rivers excelled all others—not excluding Egypt—in fecundity and commercial activity. However, this lofty position was destined to be gradually diminished and forever lost as the centre of gravity of civilization and economic well-being shifted towards the west.

Prior to the inauguration at the end of the fifteenth century of direct sea communication between northern Europe and far Asia, there existed and were known two principal water routes by which goods could be carried from the distant Orient to the lands bordering the Mediterranean. The first and older was that by way of the Persian Gulf. The second and more recent was that of the Red Sea utilizing the Egyptian land bridge. But the latter, at least for Europeans, such as Greeks, Romans and Venetians, en-

222

joyed nearly every advantage over the more primitive Persian Gulf. For European importers and exporters, the cheaper and more convenient access to the markets of India, the Spice Islands, Ceylon and China was by way of the Red Sea. It was much nearer to European ports and involved less carriage over intervening land surfaces. Be it added that throughout antiquity and the Middle Ages Egypt was a relatively stable and peaceful country, in contrast to the lands bordering on the Persian Gulf where civil commotion within and warfare from without were endemic.

On the political side, the inevitable and preordained recession of Mesopotamia was hastened by its early loss of political independence, and the ending of Semitic hegemony in Persian and Graeco-Roman times. From the time of its incorporation into the Persian Empire of Cyrus, the land presently known as Iraq came to be no more than a pawn in the struggle for power among contending empires. The incessant civil disorders and invasions to which it was prone from several directions reached some sort of climax with the invasion of the heathen Mongols under Hulagu Khan in 1258. The Khan, in addition to abolishing the Caliphate of Baghdad, wantonly demolished the entire network of irrigation canals on which the rich agriculture of the area had been long dependent.

Despite its reduced condition, the Jewish population of Mesopotamia long managed to survive. It remained a fruitful source of income, through either taxation or bribery, for a long succession of Moslem rulers and local governors, whose religious fanaticism in a great many instances managed to give way to their cupidity. Only in our own time, after these thousands of years, were the last embers of this valiant community finally quenched forever. It is perhaps more than coincidental that neither in Iraq, Spain, nor

Poland, countries which each in their time served as the principal haven of the Jewish diaspora, is there at the present time any Jewish presence.

Before quitting the subject of the Oriental Jews, it cannot be too greatly emphasized that without their determination to go on living in such countries as Iraq, Egypt and Syria, it would have been next to impossible for their remaining brethren in the Holy Land to have retained their unbroken but precarious foothold. Palestine was now a country which for centuries to come would possess few economic attractions. More especially was its backwardness in common with that of the entire region intensified with the opening of the direct sea route from Northern Europe to the far east. From motives of religion mainly, Jewish exiles from far and near continued to arrive there, and to hang on with matchless tenacity. The various expulsions from the cities of Europe never failed to induce some of the refugees to direct their footsteps to the forsaken land of their ancestors, its bleak economic possibilities notwithstanding. For such settlers hardly any livelihood presented itself other than that of petty trade and some poverty-stricken handicrafts. Yet this pioneer remnant was enabled to draw some limited energy through living at a crossroad, and from the presence of at least a handful of successful coreligionists in the neighbouring countries with whom trade relations were not difficult to maintain. Be it said finally that without this foothold, uninterruptedly and stubbornly maintained, the movement for the restoration of the State of Israel would scarcely have been able to get under way.

PART II

Throughout the many centuries that they were a stateless nation, the scattered Jews found themselves on several occasions concentrated under alien governments as a considerable and influential minority. The first of these, following upon the dissolution of their own independent commonwealth, was of course Babylonia. Its hegemony passed over to Spain at some undetermined century, but probably the tenth. At the close of the fifteenth century, this centre of gravity was moved of necessity, and before long was taken over by Poland.

Next to claim our attention after Babylonia, is the thousand-year connection of the Jews with the Iberian peninsula. During the time that Rome was still in bloom, and for a number of centuries following the blackout of its western half, Mesopotamia and Spain continued to be respectively the antipodes of the the Jewish world. For a long time, those of the Latin-speaking part remained insignificant by comparison with their correligionists of the Greek-speaking East and of the Persian Empire. In this western extension of the diaspora, there were in existence no communities that could have been rated as bastions of Jewish learning; and we seek in vain for the names of outstanding personages in such places. Of the lands contained within the Latinized orbit, only in Italy and Spain were there to be found any considerable concentrations.[5] As between both these peninsulas, Italy was undoubtedly the earlier haven; but the weight of numbers seems to have passed to Spain at some time before the collapse of the empire of the west in the middle fifth century.

For filling up the later settlements north of the Alps, Spain was the main area of both concentration and diffusion. It was the curious destiny of the Pyreneean peninsula to serve as the remote ancestral home, in succession to Palestine and Mesopotamia, of by far the greater number of Jews living at the present time. Those presently residing in the State of Israel, in America, in western Europe, Soviet Russia, and south Africa, can lay claim to being the descendants of persons who at one time or another resided south of the Pyrenees Mountains. That segment of world Jewry commonly referred to as "Ashkenazim" are for the most part the lineal descendants of the Jews of Spain otherwise known as "Sephardim."[6]

Not long after becoming stabilized as Rome's first major colony, Spain became a beacon to ambitious and covetous men. Both Julius Caesar and his opponent Pompey reaped personal fortunes in that country. Referring to its opulence at the time of the Emperor Augustus, a modern historian has written, "Spain was the most flourishing part of the Empire. The inhabitants had become almost entirely Roman in dress, manners, and speech. From the valley of the Quadalquivir, then one of the most fertile and densely populated on the globe, a very lucrative traffic was carried on, along the shores of the Mediterranean with the cities of Italy. The articles transported in this traffic were wool, corn, wine, oil, wax, honey. . . .Spain was also rich in copper, gold, silver, lead, tin, and iron. The present towns of Cordova and Seville were distinguished Roman colonies.[7]

Again it has been testified that "Spain was Rome's chief metal mine. It has been estimated that during the centuries of Roman occupation Spain yielded an annual average of 300,000 ounces of gold. The silver mines of New Carthage (Cartagena) employed 40,000 workers, and the iron deposits of Bilbao were vigorously exploited. Along the coast, grain, oil, wine, and fruits were produced, with improved irrigation methods. Sheep grazed on the central plateau, and hogs found food in the forests. Spain took a long time to conquer, but was well worth the trouble."[8]

Not only was Spain Rome's most opulent province, but after a time its most tranquil. Spain was touched hardly at all by the innumerable civil disorders inside the empire which successively devasted Italy, Illyria, Greece, Asia Minor, and Gaul. So docile were its inhabitants that almost

226

no armed forces were required to hold them in subjection. Among the native Celtiberians, unlike those of Gaul and Germany, there were hardly any memories of national independence. Under the Emperor Claudius, the entire Roman garrison consisted of no more than two legions, by way of contrast to the eight that were deemed necessary to patrol the Danube, the Rhine, and Syria respectively.[9] Vespasian found it safe enough to reduce this force to one solitary legion.

Testifying even more eloquently to the attractiveness of Spain as a country of residence was the fact that, unlike the provinces bordering on the Rhine and the Danube, Spain up to a very late date enjoyed greater immunity from barbarian incursions than any of the other provinces.[10] Inside that province, the authority of Rome diminished more slowly than in other parts of the troubled empire. It was only in the beginning of the fifth century, long after most of the remaining provinces had become a prey to anarchy, that the peninsula suffered serious intrusions, first by the Vandals, who did not long remain in the country, and somewhat later by the Romanized Westgoths, who had for some time been settled in the transalpine province of Aquitaine. While Gaul was for centuries exposed to successive inundations by barbarians coming from the north, the north-east, and the east, such entry into Spain came from one direction only.

The coming of Jews into Spain followed in all probability the common pattern of entry first being made by a small number of adventurous pioneers. The influx that followed came in a series of intermittent and irregular waves resembling somewhat, one might imagine, the successive and irregular migrations of their descendants into North America. But their entry on a larger scale had to await the inauguration of some firm means of access. Like that of the Romans their entry into the peninsula was more probably

227

from the south than from the north. "As early as the first century of the common era a belt of Jewish settlements extended from Babylonia, traversed Egypt, and followed the north shore of the African coast as far as Carthage."[11] It was in all probability by way of the rebuilt city of Carthage that the earliest Jewish settlements in Spain came to be planted.

Carthage had been taken by the Romans in 146 B.C.E. at the termination of a long drawn-out series of wars and completely demolished. Every building inside the doomed city was systematically levelled to the ground, and by decree of the Senate no one was ever to rear another edifice upon the accursed site. But not very long afterwards, Rome found herself mistress of the entire north African littoral. With the expanding volume of transport between the coastal cities of Alexandria and Cyrene at its eastern end and Spain in the far west, the dire need for a convenient halting place for shipping was soon realized. Hence the earlier decree of the Senate forbidding the restoration of Carthage was quietly rescinded. It was Julius Caesar in the year 46 B.C.E. who ordered its restoration as a Roman provincial city.

The connection of Julius Caesar with the first coming of the Jews to Spain can be dimly indicated. He is known to have placed high store in the Jews as collaborators in his plans for a revised Roman state. "The Jews were destined to play no insignificant part in the new state of Caesar."[12] At Caesar's court and his councils, Jews were influential in financial as well as political matters. Their contingent of men in his army was not unimportant. They were helpful to him in his struggle with Pompey, with whom incidentally they had their own scores to settle. Of further historical interest is the aid that he received from the Jews of Alexandria when he showed himself in Egypt with a mere handful of men.[13]

For the successors of Alexander, it had long seemed politically feasible to plant Jewish enclaves in the cities either founded or taken over by them. Jews were then regarded as highly serviceable an forming a link between the new rulers and the sometimes sullen native population. That from a similar motive Caesar induced Jewish migrants from Alexandria or Cyrene to settle in the restored and highly strategic north African metropolis can be conjectured, despite the absence of documentary proof.

From Carthage, as a point of departure, Jews in all probability went forth to plant new communities in Spain. By sea and by land they followed routes formerly taken by the Carthaginians, the first outsiders to colonize the peninsula; and more especially so once the region then known as Mauretania in the far west of the north African shore had been annexed to the Roman Empire.[14] The roads that were soon built linking together all the many cities of the north African shore line, together with the extirpation of piracy at about this time, made it even easier for Jews issuing from Alexandria, Cyrenne and Carthage to adhere to a well-trodden caravan route leading to the settled areas of the Quadalquivir valley.

Parenthetically, it is deserving of note that the very name given by its discoverers to the major portion of the Iberian peninsula derives etymologically from a Hebrew-Semitic word meaning "hidden" or otherwise "northern." To the Carthaginian Semites, whose tongue was close to Hebrew, Spain was in the beginning the hidden or northern country. According to Baron, much of the Carthaginian population not carried away captive by the Romans later on converted to the religion of a nation in whom they discovered a kinship both of race and language. To the earliest Jewish arrivals in such places as Cadiz, Seville, Cordova, and Segovia, the pre-existing Semitic colonists might well have attached themselves.

As in the case of the earlier deportation to Italy by Titus, much of the Jewish settlement in Spain was the result of forcible measures taken against them in consequence of an uprising. What is known about the revolt of the Palestine Jews in the year 131, which was quelled in 135, permits the conjecture that after the crushing of this revolt by the emperor Hadrian, there occurred a large deportation of captive Jews out of their native country and that their place of destination was none other than Spain, where there happened at the time to be a need for labour in the mines. As a source of mineral wealth, the Iberian peninsula excelled all the other Roman dominions. But these resources, unlike those of Greece, Macedonia, Sicily, and Asia Minor, were in that century still in a condition of underdevelopment. Additionally, Spain stood in need of workers for the construction of roads, aqueducts, harbours, arenas, basilicas, porticoes, and temples. The emperor Hadrian was himself a native of Spain; and throughout his reign the improvement of his country of birth was never far from his mind. Not only did the emperor see in his Jewish prisoners a means for carrying out many of his cherished projects, but he also saw the added advantage of carrying them off to a region that was utterly remote from where they might be tempted to participate in further uprisings. In the process of crushing the Jewish revolt, there had been a great convergence of shipping upon the coast of Palestine. With the war's termination, these vessels were now available for transporting the captives to their places of exile.

The gateway into Spain was from the north as well as the south. The first land communication from Italy came about with the building of a roadway as early as 121 B.C. along the north shore of the Mediterranean through a countryside variously designated as Provincia or Narbonnensis.[15] The apostle Paul, who ended his life in Rome, is known to have planned a visit to Spain where he would have met with many of his fellow Jews who had preceded him there. Had he lived to make this voyage, he would undoubtedly have chosen the overland route in preference to another sea voyage.[16] Whether by way of the north or the south, Spain, in the early centuries of the Christian era, was the ultimate haven of Jews, and doubtless others, who thought it well to abandon the strife-torn cities of Italy and the provinces. Incidents such as the partial destruction of Alexandria in the year 273 by the emperor Aurelian added to the migratory stream.

Even in pagan times, Jews must have shown a preference for Spain over Gaul. Roman Gaul and Roman Spain, at opposite sides of the Pyrenees, differed greatly in character. Gaul was not an inviting country for strangers. Its religion prior to the triumph of the Church under Constantine, as the French historian Guizot has pointed out, was dominated by the Druids, an organized and self-centered clergy whose bigotry was without counterpart anywhere in the pagan empire. To Christianity and to Judaism alike it was actively hostile. Even in the last stages of its existence, this hierarchy was not devoid of great vitality.

That with the coming of the barbarians many of the Jews settled in Gaul took refuge south of the Pyrenees we may gather from the following portrayal of the havoc that overtook that province: "Nations countless in number and exceeding fierce have occupied all the Gauls; Quadians, Vandals, Sarmatians, Alans, Gepidians, Herulians, Saxons, Burgundians, Allemanians, Pannonians, and even Assyrians have laid waste all that there is between the Alps and the Pyrenees, the ocean and the Rhine. Sad destiny of the commonwealth, Mayence, once a noble city, hath been taken and destroyed. Thousands of men were slaughtered in the church. Worms hath fallen after a long siege. The inhabitants of Rheims, a powerful city, and those of Amiens, Arras, Tournay, Spires, and Strasburg have been carried away to Germany. The towns, save a few, are depopulated. The sword pursueth them abroad and famine at home." The foregoing dirge, commemorating the events of 410 was written by St. Jerome, living in far-off Bethlehem, and is quoted by Guizot.[17] From such terrifying ordeals Roman Spain was spared by and large, and so presumably were its Jewish inhabitants. "Europe ends at the Pyrenees" was for a long time a current aphorism. These mountains, though generally lower than the Alps, at all times formed more of a protective barrier, since they were more difficult to cross, dropping as they do to negotiable passes in fewer localities.

With the conversion of the Frankish kings to Catholic Christianity around the year 490, the position of the diminished communities within Gaul tended to become even less supportable. The reports of the persecutions that set in soon after leave little doubt that many more departed to find refuge in Visgothic Spain, which, prior to 586, though Christian, was not a Catholic country. The Arian heresy, which had divided the Church for over two hundred years, held out longer in Spain than anywhere else. Spain, under its Arian kings, was thus the last home of religious toleration anywhere to be found within the Christian world.[18]

From Africa, no less than from Europe, the ingathering into Spain accelerated, following the annexation of the neighbouring north African coast by the emperor Justinian (528-565). In the long line of Byzantine emperors, Justinian was the first whose enmity towards the Jews was altogether implacable. Prior to the enactment of the famous code bearing his name, those residing within the empire, along with the remaining pagans, had enjoyed some of the rights of citizenship. Under the new code, they became ethnically strangers and religiously unbelievers. As such they were deprived of all civil rights.

Some thirty years elapsed between the death of this

oppressor and the conversion of King Recarred to Catholicism, an event which dealt the Jews long domiciled in Spain their first blow. The decree that they were to convert to the official religion was repeated by all his successors down to the taking over of the country by the Arabs in the years 717-720. Many pretended to comply; and since the age was not yet ripe for an inquisition, such deception was neither difficult nor dangerous. Some recrossed the Pyrenees to the southern countries of France at a safe distance from Paris, from which the enfeebled arm of the Merovingian kings was unable to reach them. Others reverted to their original dwelling places in neighbouring Africa. The bulk of them stayed on, being sufficiently numerous and wealthy to offer some resistance to the royal edicts. Their wealth in all probability was behind much of the civil disorder and rebelliousness of the nobility that plagued the Visgothic kingdom during the final throes of its existence. In the end, they played a notable part in the lightning invasion of the Arabs and their Moorish auxiliaries. With the Arab conquest, the drift of the Jews into Spain was resumed on a considerable scale. There was now ample room for such newcomers, since many empty spaces had been created both by the enslavement of the Christian inhabitants and the flight of a great many of them to the mountainous region of the northwest which had not fallen into Moslem hands. Though, like their brethren elsewhere under Moslem rule, the Jews were subject to a special tax, the burden due to their increasing numbers was relatively a light one.

Spain, overrun in the years 717-720, was the last major conquest that the Arabs were able to make at the expense of the Christians, following their absorption of Syria, Egypt, and the entire North African coast. The Arab empire stretched out longitudinally over a territory extending all the way from east of the Caspian Sea to the Atlantic seaboard; and managed to endure for about a century. Its day

233

was virtually over when, in the year 750, the Ommeyade dynasty centred in Damascus was overthrown and almost eradicated by its Abbasid rivals. A number of resounding defeats at the hand of the French in the west and the Byzantines in the east had heralded its approaching demise.[19] Their unsuccessful attempts to take Constantinople by sea in 668 and again in 717 resulted in their elimination as a naval power. The immense treasure in gold looted from the palaces of the Sassanid monarchs, as well as from many of the churches, most of which had gone into the building up of their naval strength, had by that time been completely dissipated.

The triumphant Abbasids, who set up their new capital at Baghdad, at a safe enough distance from a revived and aggressive Byzantine empire, had to content themselves with a narrower area than had been ruled by their vanquished predecessors. It did not include Spain, where a member of the defunct Ommeyads, who had escaped the wholesale carnage of his family, was enabled to set up a caliphate of his own, and to bid defiance to his hated rival. The single Arab world founded by the prophet and his immediate successors now became two. Before very long further fragmentation set in. The further disintegration of the Moslem world later began to manifest itself at its eastern extremity, with the steady enfeeblement of the Abbasids. By the year 920, the Baghdad Caliphate began to show signs of going to pieces as well. The Moslem princes of Asia, Arab and non-Arab, ceased being a threat to the Christians, and remained only a threat to one another. With the political fragmentation, came a fresh growth of religious intolerance and fanaticism. In proportion as their threat to the Christian nations lessened so did their threat to the Jews living in their midst grow apace.

The Caliphate of Cordova remained prosperous, united and vigorous for about a century after its eastern rival had tumbled into disorder. "Spain under the Caliphate was

234

one of the wealthiest and thickly populated lands of Europe."[20] During the brief period of its greatness, Moslem Spain attracted to itself a large immigration of Jews from Iraq and elsewhere in the Moslem East, fleeing from crushing taxation, the fanaticism of its imams and cadis, as well as the hostility of its mobs.

The death of Abdul Malik in the year 1008 marked the final end of the Ommeyade dynasty. Cordova was sacked, and Moslem Spain as a single unified state ceased to exist. In its place there arose a number of petty kingdoms and emirates—Malaga, Seville, Murcia, Almeria, Saragossa, Valencia, Toledo. The succeeding decades were marked by rebellions, poisonings, slave mutinies, crucifixions. It was a period of blood and shame, and of departed greatness.

The fall of the Ommeyade dynasty and of the Caliphate of Cordova at the beginning of the eleventh century was a catastrophic event as to which no details are available as to about effects upon Spanish Jewry. That it brought with it an end to further Jewish immigration into Moslem Spain is highly probable. Likewise, the eventual return of the peninsula to Christian rule was as of that time foreordained.[21] During this period of gradual reconquest—*two centuries and a half approximately*—Spain was for the Jews the safest of all Christian lands, as it had formerly been of all Moslem lands. For a period of several centuries they were able to enjoy a position of great strength which permitted them to maintain their existence even against the combined agitation of the two great monastic orders, the Dominicans and the Franciscans.

The strength of the Spanish-Jewish economy was such that it took the Church no less than four hundred years to succeed in breaking it down. For several centuries both canon law and papal admonitions were ignored by Spanish monarchs, who continued to place great reliance on Jewish administrators, on whom they depended for managing their finances, the salt marshes of the country, its silver mines, its excise and custom duties.

Christian Spain during these centuries was a country which placed land, the Church, and warring with the infidel Moslems high on the list of values; with industry and commerce at the very bottom. Hence the Jews enjoyed a free hand in carrying on a lucrative trade with foreign lands as well as inside the country. "By the end of the thirteenth century, Christians and more especially Jewish Europeans were engaged in trans-Sahara trade, dealing chiefly in gold and ivory."[22]

Unlike that in France, Germany and England, Jewish commerce in Spain had a solid industrial base. As producers as well as traders, their economic status was solidly fixed and highly resilient. They were the country's chief producers—in woollens, in silks, in leather, in hardware, and in arms. They were owners and managers of mines, with full access to metallic ores for the needs of their manufacturers. They were growers of fruit, and breeders of sheep and cattle.

I shall not enter into the misfortunes that marked the golden sunset of Spanish and Portuguese Jewry. These have been adequately portrayed by standard works on Jewish history. I would, however, make this observation, which to many might seem paradoxical and startling. The so-called expulsion in 1492 was not really a disaster. Quite the contrary. For the Jewish people as a whole, as distinct from the many personal tragedies, it was an act of salvation, resembling remotely the exodus from Egypt. Had the Jews of Spain not been ordered to leave—and we know that the sovereigns issuing this order were hesitant about it and in all likelihood regretted it later on—the Jews of Spain would in the course of a generation or two have succumbed to a series of pogroms or otherwise forcibly and completely converted to Catholicism. Under no circumstances, during

236

the fiery age of the Reformation and within the crucible of Spanish bigotry and hatred, could they have gone on living as an observant community. The major event was of course the order of expulsion of 1492. But as in the case of Nazi Germany, there had been over many decades a steady departure by those who had been able to read the signs of the times. Likewise, after 1492, a considerable number who had pretended to embrace Christianity managed to escape from both Spain and Portugal and return to Judaism. This further exodus from the peninsula was to be credited to the Inquisition. Had it not been for the Inquisition, with all its cruelty and hideousness, there would have been no Marannos. And without the Marannos, the nascent communities of Amsterdam, Hamburg, London, Leghorn, and even New York, would not have been created in their time. The men who founded these and other congregations, had they not been terrorized into leaving their native country, would in the course of time have developed into sincere enough Christians. The founders in London in 1657 of the Spanish and Portuguese synagogue were the descendants of men and women who for five or six generations had all been baptized at birth and had attended mass regularly.

The ringing down of the curtain on Spanish Jewry did none the less result in damaging blows to the other European communities with which they were in close business contact. Ejection from Provence and Sicily followed almost immediately. Not unconnected, in all probability, were the series of expulsions throughout Germany from such places as Cologne, Nuremberg, Augsburg and Ulm, all occurring within less than a decade. Also broken down was the bridge which had united the communities of transalpine Europe with those of north Africa. Thereafter, Italy with its small number of Jewish inhabitants remained as the frail link between the Jews of eastern Europe on the one hand and those of the Levant on the other.

In the Biblical book of Esther, we note the earliest recognition of an expanding Jewish world. The Persian vizier, addressing his royal master, speaks of them as "scattered abroad and dispersed among the peoples of thy kingdom."[23] Strabo, a Greek geographer of the first century before the common era, again mentions them as inhabiting every known city of the civilized world. Originating within the limited area of the Middle East, the Jewish pale of settlement has tended, in its expansion, more towards the west than towards the east, more in the direction of Europe than towards the Asiatic interior.

Within an illuminating view of a gradual widening and changing Jewish diaspora, Poland furnishes the third major tableau. But the displacement of the centre of gravity to that East European country from Spain ought first to be viewed under the aspect of a transitional period that took in France, Germany, England and certain of the Slavic countries as well.

First, this assertion. Its thousand years connection with the Jews has made of the Iberian peninsula the ancestral home of nearly all members of that nation that in the course of centuries came to inhabit the lands north of the Pyrenees and the Carpathians. It can be asserted likewise that among those early pathfinders issuing from out of Spain and seeking new dwelling places in these northern climes, not all were driven by religious compulsion. Even as pressure of population was the indispensable factor in the eastward expansion of Europe, and the creation of new cities and monasteries, so in like manner, among the Spanish Jews, was there a similar necessity to send forth pioneer settlers into northern lands, settlers of whose memory nothing remains.

Ancient and mediaeval cities were consistently small,

and the ceiling of their growth was soon reached. There was room in any walled city for only a restricted number of weavers or armourers or importers of grain or dealers in money. Young men were even obliged to transfer to other cities by reason only of a shortage of brides in places where they had been raised. For Jews, more than any other group, the shortage of living space was perennially acute, even in cities where they were not compelled to live in ghettoes. In Basle, for example, the special taxes they had to pay was proportionally raised with each new house that they occupied. New land for synagogues and cemeteries was often difficult or impossible to acquire.

Fluidity of residence is at all times to be expected among individuals of a community that is essentially mercantile in outlook. This has been exhibited by many nations starting with the Phoenicians and the Greeks. Jews tended to leave the Spanish homeland to resettle farther afield on much the same grounds as induced their descendants dwelling at ease in Amsterdam to depart for Hamburg, London, or Curacao; or the sons of immigrants established on the Atlantic seabord of North America to relocate in Chicago, the Middle West and the Pacific coast.

It fits in with the facts to suggest that from time to time much of the increment of Spain's Jewish population found its immediate outlet across that country's northern frontier, first into southern France and subsequently farther north. The most commonly used route leading northward out of Spain was by way of the shoreline of the Gulf of Lions and the extreme eastern defiles of the Pyrenees in a line joining the cities of Barcelona and Perpignan. This was the route of Hannibal, Scipio, Caesar, and Pompey, and later of the incoming Visigoths. It was followed as well by the Arab invaders from Spain pouring into southern France. Finally, and in like fashion was it the pathway of Jewish migrants and merchants going from Spain in the direction of northern Europe. Such coming and going on their part resulted in the frontier communities of Marseilles, Avignon, Arles, Lunel, Villefranche, Gerona, Narbonne, and Perpignan.

The relatively narrow passageway linking together southern and northern France has been referred to as "the vertebral column of the land commerce of France throughout history."[24] Equally well adapted for both the marching of armies and of merchant caravans, it was this column of land, along with its main watercourse the Rhone river that served the Roman conquerors of Gaul in maintaining their grip upon the entire prefecture. On its western margin, this accomodating land and water highway is bounded by the Massif Central, a semi-arid and sparsely inhabited mountainous country. Towards the east, it is hemmed in by the Jura range of mountains and farther to the north by the Vosges.

Of vast significance historically has been the opening between both these latter mountain barriers, known as the Trouée de Belfort. Since Gallo-Roman times, and down to this very day, this aperture has been the doorway opening between southeastern France and the Alsacian plain bordering on the west bank of the Rhine. The many forays of Germanic tribes such as the Alemanni and Burgundians into Roman Gaul came by way of this portal. In reverse, it was through this gap near the present city of Belfort that the Roman legions coming up from the south were enabled to secure their entry into and control over the Rhine country. Hence it is a tenable suggestion that the early Jewish settlements in such cities as Basel, Freiberg, Speyer, Worms, Mainz, Strassburg, Cologne were the offsprings of merchant adventurers coming from the verge of the Mediterranean, ascending the watercourses of the Rhone and Saone and then turning towards the right at either Lyons or Dijon.

Likewise, from the earlier communities of Provence

240

and Languedoc, Jewish settlers filtered gradually into the level country of Champagne, at the eastern extremity of the broad northern French plain extending to the English Channel, and drained by the rivers Seine, Loire, Vesle, Aisne, Marne, and Aube. The river system of northern France was in old times far more exploited than now as avenues of communication. Along the banks of these rivers were the important Jewish communities of Paris, Troyes, Rheims, Vitry, Chalons-sur-Marne, Rouen, Caen, Evreux. The county of Champagne's economic importance as a place for merchants coming together from all parts was emphasized further by its easy accessibility by way of the Saverne gap from the river port of Strassburg.

I have asserted that the Jewish population of mediaeval France, and by extension that of England, Germany and the Slavic countries, were the descendants of forefathers who came out of the Iberian peninsula. In contradiction of this thesis, it will be pointed out that Jews in substantial numbers were already settled in Gaul and on the Rhine as far back as Roman times, and that these in all likelihood had come from Italy and not from Spain. To this, I reply as follows:

In France, both north and south, the several streams of Jewish immigrants originating mainly south of the Pyrenees, may well have amalgamated with remnants of Jewish communities of Roman times. However, these latter had been all but eliminated soon after the Frankish nation turned to Christianity. As far back as 624, the expulsion of all Jews living in his realms had been proclaimed by King Dagobert. This Dagobert ruled over a territory that was not merely co-extensive with modern France, but which embraced likewise a portion of Germany as far east as Bavaria. As to the consequences of this decree of expulsion, the English historian James Parkes has written, "It is possible that the absence of all data on Jewish life in France for one

241

hundred and fifty years after this event is due to this expulsion."[25]

Parkes proceeds to express the opinion that during this century and a half of silence, some Jews continued to live, perhaps unobstrusively, in some portions of this large area. There is no reason for disputing this. It is certain, none the less, from all the available evidence, that there was an interval of some duration in which there were no active Jewish communities anywhere in the Frankish dominions. The eclipse of the violently anti-Jewish Merovingians, following the death of Dagobert in 638, in all probability made possible an influx of Jews from Spain, fleeing from the persecution of the Visgothic kings but recently turned Catholic. Under the more reasonable and less fanatical Mayors of the Palace, the ground was undoubtedly prepared for the reconstitution of the Franco-Hebraic communities openly and on an extensive scale. By the time of Charlemagne (768-814), these had become sufficiently numerous and wealthy to occupy a substantial role in the economy and commerce of the Carolingian empire.

A short deliniation of the circumstances attending the Jewish re-entry into Frankish Gaul and western Europe would here be in place. Their re-admission by the Mayors of the Palace was not unconnected with the depressed times which fell upon Christendom following the rise of Islam. The border wars carried on the name of Christianity against the heathen tribes to the north and east of the Frankish kingdom that seemed to go on forever were no mere neighbourly feuds, soon enough climaxed by an ingathering of booty and terminated for the nonce. In these distant and protracted campaigns, there was to be had neither profit nor booty, beyond the taking of captives and the disposing of them in the nearest slave markets. The wars against the Saxons and Frisians not being self-liquidating, much money was required to finance them—a

242

totally new element in the warfare of the Dark Ages. The soldiers of the Cross, being unable to live off the land, and having to stay away from their hearths for many days at a time, required to be paid in money. As the one available source of wealth, the Churches, enriched by the votive offerings of the faithful, soon attracted the speculative gaze of the contemporary Frankish warlords. More especially did Charles Martel, the grandfather of Charlemagne, make free with ecclesiastical possessions, much to the scandal of the faithful and to the peril of his own soul. For avoiding the sacrilegious raiding of Church property, no remedy could suggest itself other than the re-admission of the Jews.

The celebrated Champagne fairs, held once or twice in the year in each of the principal towns of that county, enjoyed great fame throughout the Middle Ages. The area as a whole was conveniently located for the exchange of merchandise and produce deriving from the several points of the compass. Under the immediate predecessors of Charlemagne, these market places began to see much of Jewish dealers, who came there mainly by way of the Rhone and Saone river valleys, bringing with them silks, bales of fine woollen cloth, carpets, furniture, spices, fruits, pearls and rubies, and perhaps even paper. Abandoning the perils of long-distance travel, many of these newcomers soon found it to their advantage to make their homes in these towns together with their families. They were in this way brought closer to both customers and suppliers, and were enabled to participate more fully in local trade as well. Those with surplus funds to lend out at interest found residing in the same neighbourhood as their borrowers an indispensable condition.

What other merchandise did these newcomers bring with them to have recommended them favourably to their new hosts? In addition to tempting them with a display of Oriental luxuries, they did not fail to bring along with them some of the accoutrements of war. To the warlike Charles Martel and to Pepin, one and the other engaged in protracted warfare with heathens and Moslems, they came with larger and stronger horses bred in Persia, that were alone suited for carrying the new order of knights weighed down by their heavy armour. Not least of all did they bring with them articles suitable for the adornment of churches and monasteries.

In the course of overrunning such portions of the Byzantine empire as Syria, Egypt, and north Africa, the Arabs had set about looting their churches on a truly royal scale. Much of this sacred booty found its way into the hands of Jewish dealers. For such articles as crucifixes, chalices, pictures, vestments, along with bones and other relics of the saints, the expanding dominions of Pepin and Charles offered an enlarged and active market.

The worship of relics had been introduced into Christian worship by Pope Gregory the Great (590-604). A new article of commerce being thus presented to the business world of the time, it was one to whose profitability Jews of that and later ages were not unresponsive. Though obliged to share in its distribution with their Greek and Syrian rivals, the fact that these sacred remains were for the most part "discovered" in Palestine, possibly by coreligionists, gave to the Jewish dealer a competitive advantage as a rule. It should of course be added that not invariably was a trader's intervention required for such procurement. After a highly successful raid into northern Italy, the emperor Otto I of Germany in the year 972 returned to his own country with wagon loads of sacred objects for the adornment of the churches of Magdeburg and Quedlinburg. The Venetians, on capturing Constantinople in the year 1204, helped themselves to the contents of its churches both piously and liberally.

What merchandise did these Jewish suppliers receive

in exchange? Worth drawing attention to were two commodities which Jewish suppliers along with their Venetian competitors received in exchange. The Frankish kings, and more especially Charlemagne, were incessantly engaged in a crusade against the obdurate Saxons, who for a long time refused conversion to Christianity. In order to be closer to the scene of this sacred carnage, which consumed not merely masses of human lives, but his own valuable time as well, Charlemagne shifted his capital northward to Aachen, otherwise known as Aix-la-Chapelle, a city founded by him in 794. First, the thick forest covering the eastern reaches of the Elbe river and inhabited by these stubborn barbarians provided a supply of timber for which there was a steady demand among the Arabs. Timber, of which north Africa and the Levant were but poorly supplied, was the essential raw material for the building up of the Ommeyade navy, which for some time claimed the mastery of the Mediterranean.

The slave trade was featured strongly during the rise of Islam. For this particular commodity, the demand among the Moslems was insatiable, and more especially if they were "fair-skinned." Male or female, a slave was among them a highly consumable article, being destined as a rule to only a brief span of existence. Oddly enough, the bulk of the Arab forces came to be made up of slave warriors, the personal army of the Calif of Cordova being known as the Slavonian Guard. Naval vessels were of course dependent entirely on slave oarsmen. Without an almost inexhaustible reserve of servile manpower, the erection would have been impossible of the massive palaces and mosques of Damascus, Aleppo, Baghdad, Cairo, Shiraz, Samarcand, Merv and Bokhara. The famous palace of Az Zahra with its 4,300 marble columns required a mere forty years for its completion by a force of "construction workers" numbering no less than 10,000, whose rate of mortality could only have been appalling. Since fully one-third of the state revenue during his entire reign had to be devoted to this enterprise by Abderrahman III, the bankruptcy of the Califate of Cordova shortly after his death becomes understandable enough.

To sum up this matter, the nefarious business of slavery, in all of its several phases of production, distribution, and consumption, was common at one time or another to Jews, Christians, and Moslems, to white men, black men, and coloured men. It was an occupation of shame and of guilt, of which not a single race or nation has been exempt. Mediaeval Venice was known as the "eunuch factory." Other seaports where slaves were dealt in as a specialty were Naples, Danzig, Bristol, Liverpool.

The piercing of the forest fastness of northern Europe went hand in hand with the task of converting the heathen, and the extension of Church influence. To both early Teutons and Slavs, living inside the forest with its attendant moods meant the preservation of their heathen superstitions. Hence the Church's war against paganism was in effect a war against the wilderness as well.

Christianity is primarily an urban religion, in its organizational features at least. The nucleus of Church organization is the diocese, each having its bishop. Invariably, the bishop has his palace within a principal city. It was with the founding of bishoprics that many of the flourishing cities of Germany were originally associated. Hamburg, whose first bishop was appointed in 834, can be said to have been founded in that same year. The bishoprics of Wurzburg, Freising, Salzburg, and Ratisbon among others were due to the labours of St. Boniface of the eighth century. St. Landolin was the recognized founder of a number of interior cities of Germany, as were St. Firmin, St. Kilian, St. Sebaldus, St. Tecla, St. Lioba, St. Walpurgis. It has been estimated that from the year 900 till 1400, over 2,000 cities were planted throughout central and eastern Germany.[26] All such urbanization bore additional fruit in the creation of fresh farmlands in their vicinity, along with new roads and trading routes.

Even as in earlier times, Jews had been attracted to the newly created Hellenistic cities of Asia Minor and the Middle East, so were they drawn to the episcopal and ducal cities of north and east Germany, in which they in common with all settlers were awarded distinct privileges. These newly created centres of Christian worship thus carved out of the forest stood in need of tools and materials for the erection of churches, hermitages, abbeys, as well as the monasteries of the spreading Cistercian order. They were incipient towns where Jews were at first welcomed as bringers of cloth for priestly vestments, croziers, images, and saintly relics. Likewise were their services required for carting away the surplus wood and logs from the cleared forests. Jews who moved eastward into the European wilderness can be said to have been following the cross.

If we are to except their brief connection with England, the centre of gravity of the mediaeval Jews was from the very outset directed eastward, that is to say from the Seine valley towards the Rhine country, and from the Rhineland towards the Danube and beyond. By the end of the eleventh century, on the eve of the first Crusade, there were probably more Jewish settlements within the German realm than in France, and more German-speaking Jews than French-speaking.

The tendency of the French Jews to betake themselves farther eastward may have been prompted as early as the middle of the ninth century by general disorders which, fully as much as religious persecution, helped in shaping the Jewish diaspora. Thus the depredations of the Vikings were in all likelihood no less a nightmare to the Jews than to the Christians. Likewise, the invasions of the Magyars, until checked in a big battle in the year 955, covered much of the Danube valley, and brought devastation to numerous cities of Bavaria and Austria. From such incursions, the Jewish inhabitants may have suffered almost as much as at the time of the first Crusade, even though they were not singled out by the barbarians as specific targets.

As the Germanized area of Europe continued to expand so too did the area of the Jewish dispersion. Yet a further stage in the eastward movement of the Jews was their crossing over to the territory of the Slavs. A glance at the present-day map will reveal that the German speaking portion of Europe—including Austria—is broad from east to west in its southern part, and similarly broad in its northern flanc; but that it has a relatively narrow waist midway between the north and the south. Jutting into the Germanic world at its centre is the land of the Czechs and Slovaks. Now if we look back a thousand years ago, the separation between Teuton and Slav was almost in a straight line, extending due north and south between the Baltic and Adriatic seas. But in the course of later centuries, both the northern and southern flancs of this line of separation were bent back towards the east by the more warlike Germans. Only at the centre did the defensive position occupied by the Slavonic Czechs not give way to the Germanic tide. Protected from their aggressive neighbours by the mountainous nature of their country, the Czechs and Moravians, though reduced to submission by the German emperors, were successful in preserving their distinct languages and cultures. In so doing, they were aided by the fact that within the entire Slavic family of nations they were the first to accept Christianity, borrowing therewith the more mature political organization of their German-speaking antagonists. Moravia became an organized state as early as 878.

The Slavic peoples, both of the north and south, unorganized as they were politically, were easily trampled by the

248

totally new element in the warfare of the Dark Ages. The soldiers of the Cross, being unable to live off the land, and having to stay away from their hearths for many days at a time, required to be paid in money. As the one available source of wealth, the Churches, enriched by the votive offerings of the faithful, soon attracted the speculative gaze of the contemporary Frankish warlords. More especially did Charles Martel, the grandfather of Charlemagne, make free with ecclesiastical possessions, much to the scandal of the faithful and to the peril of his own soul. For avoiding the sacrilegious raiding of Church property, no remedy could suggest itself other than the re-admission of the Jews.

From the final conversion of all East European peoples to Christianity, there flowed two consequences. First, the slave trade with the Arabs, originating in Europe, was virtually brought to a standstill. Unable any longer to buy slaves that were "fair-skinned," the Arabs turned increasingly to Africa for their supplies. Secondly, the termination of the crusades against the heathens of Eastern Europe paved the way for a new series, this time against the Moslems of the Middle East as well as the Jews settled in Europe.

PART IV

Poland's history can be said to have had its opening date in 963, the year in which her ruler accepted Christianity. Of all the Slavonic nations bordering on the Holy Roman Empire, the Poles were the last to undergo conversion. In so doing, they lagged behind their neighbours, the Bohemians and Moravians, by well over a century. This tardiness was permitted to them by reason of their sheltered geographical position. From the south, Poland was isolated by a mountainous frontier that helped seal her off from the vassal states of Bohemia and Moravia, where German influence prevailed from an early time. A complexity of lakes and marshes afforded her protection at her northwestern frontier as well. Reinforcing this secure position was the added fact that none of the rivers of northern Europe, passing through German territory, flowed in her direction. And finally, the Poles remained isolated for a long time from crusading German armies by a screen of embattled heathen tribes to the west of them who gave the Germans a good deal of trouble.

The acceptance of Christianity by the Poles, while it proved timely in obviating a crusade with all its savage and sanguinary consequences, did not relieve them from the shadow of German expansionism. By the thirteenth century, German influence had reached and penetrated the barrier of the Vistula River, with east Prussia, Lithuania, Latvia, and Esthonia on the verge of becoming absorbed within the Germanic orbit. Throughout the Middle Ages, the eastward trend of the German sphere of influence was spearheaded by the Hanseatic League along with its military affiliate, the Teutonic Order of Knights. Having achieved the mastery of much of the territory adjacent to the Baltic, these commercial and military monopolists reached out for sovereignty over Poland as well. They came close enough to achieving it. But in 1410, in the famous battle of Tannenberg, the Teutonic Order was handed a blow by the Polish defenders from which it never wholly recovered. For the Jews, already settled in Poland in large numbers, this decisive victory was of the greatest moment. Poland, like Denmark, might have become a feudatory of the Hanseatic League, within whose territories not a single Jew was permitted to set foot or to carry on trade.

The ability of the Poles to resist the encroaching Germans was only made possible by their timely alliance with the Lithuanians, who were masters of a territory that stretched from the Baltic to the Black Sea. At Tannenberg,

Poles and Lithuanians had fought side by side. The joinder of both these nations under one crown, late in the fourteenth century, was in effect an enlargement of the Polish state. Originally but a small country, bounded by the Oder in the west and Vistula in the east, Poland in the course of several centuries was enabled to extend eastward and northward into underdeveloped and underpopulated regions, with many new cities waiting to be founded within its sphere of influence. By the middle of the sixteenth century, the area encompassed by the Polish kingdom was not much smaller than that of Germany. The eastward expansion of Poland in a sense repeated the eastward expansion of Germany during earlier centuries. Once again, the eastward expansion of a Christian nation, featured by creation within its borders of new urban centres, benefited the European Jews by opening to them living space not previously available.

The coming of the Jews to Poland dates probably from about the time of that country's adoption of Christianity in the late tenth century. A mere handful of pioneer merchants and artisans heralded the waves of refugees that within a few decades were to begin their flight from the inhospitable lands of the west and south. The first stream of any magnitude arrived from Bohemia in 1098 in the wake of the first Crusade that saw an onslaught by the Crusaders on the community in Prague.[27] Subsequent butcheries and expulsions in the lands of the Holy Roman Empire during the four centuries that followed served to build up the great Jewish centre that was once Poland. I hazard the guess that it was by way of Czechoslovakia, rather than by way of the eastern provinces of Germany, that they came for the most part; and that their entry was usually through the defile between the Carpathian and Sudeten range of mountains, known as the Moravian Gate. My supposition is supported by the fact that it was in the cities that were closest to the

251

Bohemian borderland that the earliest Jewish communities in Poland were created. These major cities were Posen, Kalisch, Cracow, and Breslau. From these pioneer communities offshoots went forth in the course of time in the direction of Galicia, Podolia, Volhynia, the Ukraine, and White Russia, all virgin territories gradually absorbed into an expanding Polish-Lithuanian kingdom.

Lithuania, whose union with Poland was solidified in 1572, became the scene of a fresh knot of Jewish settlements. The number of Jews in Poland, computed at about 50,000 in the beginning of the sixteenth century, rose to 500,000 by 1650. The spreading out of Jewish settlements into the far reaches of an expanding continent implied the advent of new trading opportunities within these regions. It is here that the coming of Russia into the family of trading nations needs to be taken into account. Furs and timber from Russia began to reach the west in substantial quantities by the sixteenth century. For acting as intermediaries in such trade, the Jews of Poland were strategically situated. Additionally, Russia as a result of its expansion towards the east, and by coming into contact with China, served as a channel for the conveyance to European countries of silks, tea, porcelain, sugar, and other Chinese products. Paradoxically, this new empire, despite its extreme anti-Jewish phobia, was on the economic level a positive factor in the life of Polish Jewry.

The sixteenth century was the golden age of Poland's history, and concurrently marked the period of greatest material progress of its Jewish population. However, the year 1572 can be put down as the faint beginning of Poland's gradual retreat from its predominant role in Eastern Europe. It was that year that saw the death of the last member of the Jaghello dynasty, which had ruled the country successfully for over two hundred years, and had raised it to some measure of prominence.

Concurrent with the election of a new king, a new constitution came into effect, one in which sovereignty in the state passed from the king to a parliament dominated by the nobility. To Poland's relapse into the feudal principle of an elective monarchy was traceable its disappearance from the map of Europe some two centuries later. During this period of constitutional flaccidity, Poland was a loser in every war that it engaged in with its neighbours. It was a country of large size which none of its neighbours considered worth having as an ally; but which did offer much temptation to their aggressiveness and rapacity. Russia, as late as the fifteenth century a small and insignificant state built up around Moscow and vassal to the Mongols, developed into a European power primarily through its seizure of what was originally Polish territory.

The kings of Poland, a number of whom were men of ability, were in no position to perform the functions expected of monarchy, among them effective leadership in war. Denuded of their strength on the home front, they were none too effective as leaders in war when defending their kingdom in face of the undivided powers wielded by the despotic rulers of Russia, Austria, Prussia and Turkey.

With the progressive enfeeblement of the monarchy, so likewise grew the wretchedness and defencelessness of the Jewish population. From the time of their first coming into Poland, the Jews had been able to look to the kings alone for protection from the ferocious zeal of the Church, whose hatred of the "enemies of Christ" never slumbered. Also, in the main cities, including Cracow, Lublin, Posen, Lemberg, Kalisch, they had at no time been secure from the animosity of their Christian competitors, who were in firm control of the magistracy and of the courts of law. It was due to royal patronage mainly that Polish Jewry had been built up and was able to endure for hundreds of years. But Poland's kings of the seventeenth and eighteenth centuries, who were no longer in any position to offer resistance to Poland's external enemies, were even less able to come to the aid of the beleaguered Jews, whose indispensability to the nation's economy they alone were willing to concede.

On October 24th, 1795, Poland finally ceased to exist as an independent state. For the Poles themselves this seemed like an irreparable disaster. But for the Jewish inhabitants virtually locked into that country, it heralded a great deliverance. Within several decades a narrowly confined and spiritually backward Jewish pale of settlement was metamorphosed into a broad network of communities covering Europe both east and west, the Americas, South Africa, and ultimately the state of Israel. The several stages of this transformation, I shall now portray.

Without the constructive changes set on foot for the Jews by the partition of Poland, the world Jewish population would not have been able to increase from less than two millions in the year 1800 to seventeen millions on the eve of World War II. On the eve of the first partition in 1772, Poland's Jewish population had been estimated at somewhat less than 900,000, a number exceeding at the time the Jewish population of the rest of Europe, including that of the Turkish dominions. This community, so pivotal to the survival of world Jewry at the time, had been under violent and increasing pressure for many decades emanating from its numerous enemies inside the Polish state. The details of this sustained persecution, which need not here be gone into, are available in any standard history of the Jews, and more especially in Dubnow's "History of the Jews of Russia and Poland." It suffices merely to observe that in all likelihood the Jews of Poland could not for very much longer have endured this fiery ordeal, and that they would have succumbed both physically and spiritually some one hundred and fifty years before their time.

With the loss of their national independence, the Poles

came to be on the receiving end of a "Kulturkampf" instituted by their Prussian and Russian overlords. Subject from time to time to brutal reprisals by their conquerors, the Poles were compelled to abate much of their own persecutory zeal towards their Jewish neighbours. Their privileges greatly diminished; no longer were the city magistrates of Posen and Cracow and Warsaw in a position to lay down conditions as to the residence and occupations of their Jewish rivals. The intensely anti-Jewish Jesuit Order, which for about two hundred years had monopolized the education of Poland's younger generation, saw itself dissolved in 1773, soon after the first partition.

Throughout the dismembered portions of the defunct kingdom, the legal disabilities of the Jews continued for several decades to be unabated, and especially so in that portion grabbed by Russia. But the economic level of their existence was raised almost instantaneously. Under these new masters, what had formerly been Polish territory began to prosper as never before, with economic activity in each of the annexed portions oriented in the direction of the occupying power.

The new occupants were not slow in turning to their own profit the fragments of the exhausted state that had fallen to them. Areas previously all but inaccessible began to be threaded by new roads, these being later supplemented by railways. Mills and factories sprang into existence. In both Austrian and Prussian Poland, unexploited mineral resources added to the sum total of wealth.

Participating as they did in this new prosperity of the annexed regions, the Jews of Poland could no longer be preventing from settling in the wider areas of Europe that lay beyond the superghetto to which they had long been restricted. "With the rise of big industry in the Rhineland, the Jewish and German townsmen of Poland were glad to sell out and to go to these more prosperous fields."[28] Illustrative of the manner in which the Jews living in that portion of Poland annexed to Prussia were enabled to revive Jewish life in the whole of Germany, there were in 1849 in the province of Posen twenty-one localities with Jewish populations of from 30 to 40% of the total. By 1900, this disproportion had shrunk considerably, while at the same time the number of Jews living elsewhere throughout Germany had risen abundantly.[29]

CHAPTER VIII

THE ECONOMICS OF SURVIVAL

PART I

AGRICULTURE

In this chapter, I single out for selective discussion the several dimensions of the Jewish economy throughout the ages, synoptically, and without regard to chronological arrangement and sequence. In the main, this economy, beginning with a predominant reliance on the fruits of the soil, changed in the course of the centuries to one based largely on commerce and finance. Only in more recent times has Jewish enterprise become highly diversified, with production as distinct from distribution taking its rightful place in a total kaleidoscope.

While the surge of the Hebraic economy has been from its original rural character to one concentrated within urban communities, this has not been a consistent evolution. There have been instances when Jews abandoned mercantile pursuits and reverted to agriculture. This was notably the case in the Arabian peninsula, where the first newcomers from Palestine in the time of the second Temple, were for the most part merchants. By the time of the prophet Mohammed, their descendants concentrated near the city of Medina, which they may have founded, were living in compact agricultural units devoted to the cultivation of the date palm.[1]

How did it come about that a migrant nation like the Jews, wandering far from their ancestral base, were able to fix themselves as large landed proprietors in such far-flung places as Cologne, Narbonne, and Tarragona? The records are plentiful enough as to facts, but as is often the case with historical phenomena, the explanation for such facts required inferential deduction. An answer to the anomaly of the Jews abandoning agriculture in the land of their fathers only to take it up again in the lands of their dispersion is to be found in the vagaries of the Roman Empire in whose destiny they were involved.

Circumstances brought it about that land within the Roman dominions became very cheap and easily acquired. The historian Gibbon wrote: "In the course of this history, we shall be too often summoned to explain the land tax, the capitation, and the heavy contributions of corn, wine, oil, and meat, which were exacted from the provinces for the use of the court, the army, and the capital."[2] The story of the later Caesars is indeed one of a constantly gathering burden of taxation, bearing down heavily on the humble tillers of the soil, and eventually devouring as well the rich landowning class.

Sixty years after the death of the Emperor Constantine, some 330,000 acres of once fruitful land in the Italian province of Campania were denuded of its inhabitants. It came to be fallow at a time when this region was threatened by no foreign enemy.[3] This was but a solitary example of the drastic decline in agriculture and the extensive depopulation which overtook the later empire; and whose steep decline was marked by military uprisings, mass executions, large-scale proscriptions and confiscations and epidemics. In the course of time, the amount of empty and abandoned land available for sale to reluctant buyers in all the provinces of the Empire consumed the time and energy of many an imperial auctioneer.

In addition to the gathering disorder and anarchy within the cities, the drying up of trade due to the disappearance of the coinage, one other event was required to complete the discomfiture of all merchants, Greek, Syrian, and Jewish alike. This was the edict of the Emperor Diocletian, late in the third century, that spelt the taking over by the state of virtually all trade in major commodities. Where was the disinherited merchant to betake himself for his further livelihood if not back to the land, either as a tenant farmer or a proprietor?[4]

Jews in Gaul, Spain, Germany, and north Africa came to occupy much land both as "coloni" or free peasants or as "possessores," owners of large estates cultivated mainly by slaves. The barbarian invasions did not at first affect them too adversely. In common with the other Roman proprietors, they were obliged to turn over to the conquerors one-third of their holdings; but this apparently did not ruin many of them. The Christianity to which were converted the invading Visigoths, Ostrgoths, and Vandals was of the Arian heresy, which was not anti-Jewish. In Spain, the Jews were on the point of being entirely dispossessed by the ruling Visigoths turned Catholic; but they were saved by the timely taking over of the country by the invading Moors, under whose rule they continued for several centuries to be undisturbed in their landed possessions.

The period of Jewish land ownership in the Christian part of Europe was destined to be no more than temporary. With the rise of feudalism in the eighth and nineth centuries, tenure of land by those other than the military aristocracy became increasingly anachronistic. This new system, in which land ownership became indissolubly linked to military service and the quasi-religious institution of knighthood, was then summed up in the legal maxim "Nulle terre sans seigneur. Nul seigneur sans titre." Throughout western Europe, until the end of the mediaeval period, there was not anywhere a parcel of land not subject to claim by one feudal lord or another.

It can be declared that at no time throughout their entire period of statelessness did Jews abandon agriculture universally. Not only in their ancient homeland, but in Mesopotamia, Egypt, Greece, Italy, Gaul, Spain, Russia, Rumania, the West Indies, and North America, there were to be found at one time or another Jewish tillers of the soil. It is to be noted that, preceding the admission of a group of Jewish merchants into England by Cromwell in 1657, Jews had for several decades been prominent in promoting the cultivation of sugar in England's West Indian colonies, notably Barbados, and Jamaica. The excellent impression which they created upon the authorities in London contributed no doubt to the tolerance accorded the early settlement of their coreligionists in that city.

For quite some time following the destruction of their state by the Romans, agriculture continued to be the dominant feature of their economy. Even at a time when its practice was not possible, agriculture continued to hold a favoured position in their literature. One of the earliest of known treatises on agriculture is to be found in the Talmud, in a section called "Zeraim," meaning "seeds," while among contemporary Graeco-Romans, to the contrary, agriculture was not considered to be a topic worthy of any literary effort.[5] Among a people crammed inside ghetto walls, so ingrained was the nostalgia for the cultivated fields of its ancestors as expressed in the fervent observance of their ancient harvest festivals, that Disraeli was moved to declare prophetically of his former brethren that a nation which in its exile continues to celebrate its vintages of roomier times will live to do so again. In the dream of a restored Jewish Commonwealth, place was given to agriculture as a calling taking precedence over all others.

The Israelite farmers, like their Canaanite predecessors, whose economy their own largely mirrored, preferred living inside the protected cities allotted to them by Joshua, with their landed possessions lying in zones adjacent to the civic enclosures. Boaz, the ancestor of King David, was a yeoman who had his dwelling in the city of Bethlehem. Gideon's father, who owned a vineyard, had his home in Ophra, and not in the open country. The typical Israelite agriculturist was what nowadays we would term a commuter. He would leave his city home in the morning in order to work his fields, returning by nightfall to the protection of its walls.[6] Considerations of personal safety made it essential for the husbandman in retiring for the night to seek the companionship of fellow townsmen. Some anxiety as to the safety of one's crops there remained none the less. More especially during harvest time was there the risk from uninvited harvesters. Hence, circumstances dictated that for a period of seven or eight days, the Israelite husbandman, together with the members of his family and his helpers, would take up his abode within his fields and orchards in temporary booths known as Succahs, the better not to leave his ripened fruits unattended either by day or night. To this very practical necessity is related the religious observance of dwelling in the Succah as characteristic of the harvest festival of Succoth, or Tabernacles.

The Israelites, though agrarian in vision, were as it happened predisposed to types of farming that were immediately conducive to a dependence on the market place. Agriculture being one of the parents of commerce, this was especially true as regards the agriculture of the Hebrews of old. Among them, tillage, in contradistinction to that prevailing elsewhere, was not generally of a subsistence character. Throughout the lands of the Mediterranean basin, cereals such as wheat and barley rarely averaged more than twelve to fifteen bushels to the acre; and were thus grown for the most part only for the cultivator's own family needs. Contrasting with this self-sufficiency, the mainstay of Israelite farming was rather in the tending of vines and trees. With the strong sunshine of summer imparting a fine flavour to fruits and orchard produce, ancient Israel was a land of fruit trees. By its very nature produce such as grapes, raisins, olives, and pomegranates was not raised to be wholly consumed on the farm, but was intended for entry into commercial channels. From being a seller of your crop or a portion of it, you were but a step away from yourself becoming a dealer on occasion, or at least having one of your sons enter upon a business of buying and selling. Thus, farming, as practised by the Israelites of old, involved some acquaintanceship with currency and prices and the art of bargaining.

Aside from gardening, and even taking precedence over it, the most consistent feature of Jewish husbandry was the pasturing of animals. In the allegorical rivalry of the brothers Cain and Abel, the one personifying tillage and the other pasturage, a preference for the latter's occupation obtrudes itself. Added emphasis was given in the Scriptures to the virtues of the pastoral life by the expressed aversion to the life of the huntsman as typified by such personnages as the rejected Ishmael and Esau.

Animal farming had been the backbone of the patriarchal economy. It remained so during the sojourn in Egypt. Cattle raising conferred upon the Israelites that necessary mobility which permitted them to move effortlessly from the land of the two rivers toward Canaan, from Canaan to Egypt, and from Egypt back to Canaan. It was this livestock economy that also made the Israelites a meat-eating nation, in contrast to their Egyptian hosts.

It was in this context likewise that we are to understand the dietary laws of their religion, under which the imposed restrictions concern food derived only from animals and not from plants. Significant in this connection is the omission from the Mosaic ordinances of religious festivals in any way connected with grazing. No such observance was felt to be needed. Mainly for those who had freshly acquired a calling for the cultivation of harvests were conceived the three festivals of Passover, Pentecost, and Tabernacles. As rustic festivals they bore no relationship to the raising of cattle or the shearing of sheep, or the birth of lambs, but were intended as the counterparts of the fertility festivals of the pagans from whom the cultivation of plants had been taken over. For the growing of field crops, the Israelites were for some time depending for their instruction on the pre-existing population, unlike the pasturing of flocks for which they needed no such instruction.

The land of Israel contained much parched country that was suitable neither for sowing nor for gardening. Hence the pastoral economy prevailed through large portions of the country, on both sides of the Jordan river, and more especially at the extremities of its southern border. The area of grassland was also enlarged by means of improved cisterns for the storing of water, a technology for which, according to Bertholet, the Israelites were to be credited.[7]

The raising of livestock was in early Israel as everywhere else attended by serious risks, there being no adequate means for coping with disease outbreaks among the flocks. Otherwise, it was a more rewarding occupation than the raising of cereal and field crops. Even by comparison with the growing of fruit trees was it more remunerative. For the vine, a good deal of tending was required. Even

263

though the olive with its deep tap root was ideally suited for regions with sparse rainful, its maturity called for a waiting period of some twenty years before producing abundantly. By way of further comparison, taxation fell less heavily on pasture land than on land that was arable. It thus followed that whoever among biblical personages was rated among the rich, it was invariably on account of his ownership of ample herds, rather than as a grower of field produce. Both Saul and David came of families attached to animal husbandry.

Archaeologists have not failed to draw our attention to the fact that the settled area of Eretz Israel was of greater extent during the Israelite period than in the time preceding the conquest under Joshua. For the Israelite newcomers it proved easier to occupy tracts of land previously untended than to engage in battling for possession of farms and gardens already being cared for by the resident Canaanites. That the sum total of cultivable land increased with the arrival of the Israelites is all the more credible inasmuch as the period of the Israelite invasion corresponded somewhat with the introduction of the use of iron, which in turn resulted in better plows and other agricultural tools.

Among the Israelites of both kingdoms, a flourishing and extensive commerce was able to grow up on the foundation of their arboreal and pastoral economy. A breeder of sheep and cattle quite often became a dealer as well. A grower of grapes or olives, or figs, or pomegranates was by the very nature of his calling perennially involved with middlemen who came to buy his crops. Both graziers and cultivators were producers for a market economy, and were thus well acquainted with the feel of currency, whether in the shape of ingots of metal or coinage. Observing their ways, the prophet Isaiah permitted himself to remark that "their land is full of silver and gold, neither is there an end to their treasures."[8] A pregnant observation here suggests itself. The presence in the land of Judah of the gold and silver to which the prophet alludes was indicative of the fact that it exported much produce, but purchased in return very little from abroad. While the exiles to Babylon are known to have carried to their new homes their spiritual treasures, it is a justifiable inference that they were able to transport likewise the accumulation of gold and silver bespoken by the prophet, and which in due course was to serve as the basis of an enhanced commercialism.

It remains to be pointed out that agriculture among the Hebrews of old suffered from handicaps peculiar to this nation alone. Under the Mosaic legislation, it was intended that there were to be no large landowners. To the extent that this was actually the case, it meant that the adoption of more advanced methods of tillage was impeded. Only territorial magnates would have had at their disposal the necessary resources to have permitted them to leave tracts of land fallow for a protracted number of years for them to regain their full fertility. As it happened, the gradual exhaustion of the soil belonging to a host of small proprietors was the true source of that "laying field to field" so deplored by Isaiah. On his crops being sharply diminished, the small homesteader saw himself compelled to borrow; and in the end, either to sell his patrimony, or have it taken over by his creditor.

The institution of Schmittah, or the enforced rest of the land once in seven years, proved to be of no help either to the land itself or to its possessor. Schmittah came at the close of a rigid cyclical period. All too often, the Sabbatical year would fall at the very worst time, such as following a drought or an attack by locusts. At best, one year in seven was never enough time for a given field to lie fallow. With rotation unknown, continuing cropping of the fields for six years caused a loss of fertility which a single restful year could not undo. There were other burdens as well. A writer in the Jewish Encyclopaedia has observed[9] "It required no small share of self-sacrifice and piety to live as a farmer and to observe the Mosaic laws concerning tithes and other gifts claimed by the priests and Levites, the altar and the poor, the Sabbatical year of release and similar precepts, while at the same time many a year's produce was spoiled by locusts, and drought and other irresistible causes."

The inconvenience of Schmittah was perhaps the determining factor in the preference among the Jews for arboriculture in place of field crops. True enough the rule of Schmittah did apply to the produce of trees as well. However, its evasion in such case was a simple matter.[10] During the Sabbatical year you were not supposed to harvest the spontaneous growth of your trees. But how could you prevent some merchant of Jerusalem or Tyre from gathering in your olives and grapes and pomegranates, and rewarding you for the privilege? Trees were the solution to an otherwise severe disability under which Jewish agriculture would have laboured in vain. Also, pasturage was apparently not subject to any Sabbatical year.

Added to these inherent drawbacks, other disadvantages awaited Hebrew agriculture in Graeco-Roman times as well as later; and these I now touch upon briefly. The economic growth under Roman auspices of all the lands enclosing the Mediterranean had a decidedly adverse effect upon its agricultural economy by creating an overabundance of wine and oil, products in which the land of Israel had long enjoyed a virtual monopoly.

Throughout antiquity, the olive had a number of important usages. As a source of food, it was appreciated by rich and poor alike. The oil that was pressed from it was used for cooking, for lighting lamps, for anointing the body as protection against the sun, and for the anointment of kings. Its wood was useful for building, and the making of home furnishings, and not least of all for the carving of idolatrous images. Two centuries after the founding of Rome, both Italy and north Africa were still strangers to this useful and profitable plant. But within the Roman Empire, it became naturalized in every country of the Mediterranean. Other fruits previously known only in Palestine and western Asia, such as apricots, peaches, citrons, and pomegranates, were soon in great profusion cultivated in many of the provinces of the empire, and to the detriment of the original producing areas. In the course of time, the famous wine of the Israelites gave way to superior vintages of Italy, Greece, and Spain. Also, with the introduction into the husbandry of Gaul and Spain of artificial grasses, there disappeared much of the eminence earlier enjoyed by Palestinian herds of sheep and cattle.

To these less than favourable developments from the Jewish point of view was added yet another, one that was even more devastating. The heavy and discriminatory taxes that the Jews of the Roman Empire were compelled to pay became even more unbearable under the rule of the Byzantine emperors. Under the rule of the Koran, the land tax that Jews in common with all unbelievers were obliged to pay varied from one-quarter of its income to one-half. This tax ended by eliminating Jewish farming in both Palestine and Mesopotamia.[11]

PART II

HANDICRAFTS

The standard of value that ruled ancient societies was such as to make craftsmanship even more demeaning than commercial activity. Among the Graeco-Romans, handicrafts were considered as fitting only for slaves, freedmen, and aliens. Ungentlemanly occupations by their standards included doctoring to the sick, teaching of children, acting, and even the practice of architecture. The attitude of the Hebrews was otherwise. While from their sacred writings contempt for trade is by no means absent, in respect to artisanship itself, they contain not a single derogatory passage. As forming part of the fabric of Israelite society, we are to take note of the following evaluation: "All these put their trust in their hands; and each becometh wise in his own work. Without these shall no city be inhabited, and men shall not sojourn nor walk up and down therein. They shall not be sought for in the counsel of the people, and in the assembly they shall not mount on high; they shall not sit in the seat of the judge, and they shall not understand the covenant of judgment; neither shall they declare instruction and judgment; and where parables are they shall not be found. But they will maintain the fabric of the world; and in the handicraft of their craft is their prayer."[12]

The Israelites of old did not see their destiny as being tied to a limited number of occupations. Even among the patriarchs, do we find a well-developed capacity for change. Abraham became a herdsman and peddler, even though in early life he had been neither. His son Isaac happened to be a tiller of the soil. Again, Jacob, pursuant to the training that he had received in the home of his father-in-law, reverted to the grazing of animals. Joseph, born inside a tent, ended his life in a palace. The dying Jacob foresaw multiform callings for his descendants.

At the time of their sojourn in Egypt, artificers in wood and in textile materials were to be found among them. It is certain that in other crafts as well they had some proficiency. "And they built for Pharaoh store-cities Pithom and Raamses."[13] Be it noted, however, that not until our own time have men of the Hebrew nation become prominently engaged in the erection of buildings. By their ancestors no architectural styles were inaugurated.

That the architecture of the classical world was able to attain a development so precocious as to rival and even excel that of our own time was due to a superabundance of slave labour and its merciless utilization. But in old Jerusalem, there rose no stately pleasure domes and no triumphal gates to rival those of Egyptian Thebes and Babylon. Nor was Solomon's Temple of such lofty dimensions as to give it place among the Seven Wonders. If in the cities of Judaea, there were to be found none of the adornments of Antioch and Edessa, Pergamum and Samosata, it was on account of a sound religious and ethical interdiction of towering edifices and the multiplicity of temples. Human life was held in greater reverence than marble structures. It was the relative absence of a servile population among the Jews which permitted their working classes to be held in greater esteem, and to be considered worthy of a number protective measures.

At various times throughout their history, both the fabrication and dealing in implements of war have not been foreign to Jewish men of business. The making of gunpowder, for example, though eagerly pursued from the very moment of its introduction into Europe, was by many considered as too impious and diabolical to be engaged in by true Christians. Also, due to the very high frequency of accidents and fires, it was regarded as a proper enough occupation for Jews. In Venice, the term "ghetto," be it recalled, meant a foundry, or more broadly, that outlying precinct to which guncasting and powder making were relegated. Spain in 1492 deprived itself of a large category of artisans skilled in the making of swords, cannon, and gunpowder, causing a later generation of Spanish warlords to turn for their weaponry to fabricators in Augsburg and Nuremberg. As for the expelled swordmakers, guncasters, and powder makers, they soon enough found an appreciative clientele among their new hosts, the Ottoman Turks. In

1551, a certain Nicolo Nicolai, who had accompanied the French ambassador to Constantinople, reported dolefully that the Jews, "with great harm and injury to Christendom have taught the Turks to make implements of war."

On this question of weapon making, the scripture is not altogether silent. While the Israelite warriors under Joshua had to get along without "chariots of iron"—the tanks of early warfare—it is implied, none the less, that in other war materials they were not deficient. More specifically, Scripture informs us, likewise, of shortages of a later period, when shut out from supplies of iron, the Israelites were hampered in their defensive wars against the encroaching Philistines.[14] Thus, the hero, Samson possessed no sword, but was obliged to rely on the jawbone of an ass for laying about him. Israel's deficiency in arms was in evidence at the coronation of King Saul; but was later on corrected. Beyond any doubt, it was as a result of the close commercial relationship with the Phoenicians that the Philistine embargo was nullified.

PART III

COMMERCE

From an evolutionary standpoint, commerce is the offspring of productive enterprise, such as agriculture, handicrafts, and mining. Regardless of any distinction between the so-called economic systems, there is room in any one city or community for no more than a limited number of merchants, be they wholesalers, retailers, brokers, importers, or exporters. While the ratio between distributors on the one hand and producers on the other may be indeterminate and vary from place to place, it remains true that in a healthy economic situation those engaged in produc-

270

tion must greatly outnumber those whose livelihood is founded on pursuits that are purely mercantile.

The term commerce is generally accepted as denoting the flow of commodities on a considerable scale and over great distances and usually from one country to another. By the subsidiary notion of trade is meant the redistribution of such commodities brought from afar, within limited and neighbourly areas. In connection with the flow of merchandise from one place to another, both by land and by water, the basic concept that we are to start with is that of the geographically allotted lines of transportation which have come to cross and to criss-cross the entire inhabitable globe from end to end, and to bind all regions however diversified into a single unbroken system. These firm and recognizable channels and means of access are basically of a physical character. They were in remote times confined to a few fenced in areas of the known portions of the earth. In pre-Biblical times there was but a simple overland route linking together the two major river valleys, that of the Nile and that of the Euphrates-Tigris. Beginning with a few such tenuous desert passages, together with their connecting navigable rivers and seaways, this primitive system of communication has grown steadily and uninterruptedly throughout the centuries, and is at present time made up of an inexpressibly complex and vastly interwoven confluence of well defined land, sea, and air routes, of navigable rivers, railroads and highways, and not least of all, the interior streets of all the world's cities, towns and villages. It is in close and intimate dependence on this finely developed and intricate network, along with its ancillary facilities for the diffusion of information, that the circulation of both money and commodities is to be understood.

Within this larger matrix of the world's trade and commerce, the Jewish communities of Europe and Asia formed

during many centuries a distinguishable entity. Bound together by mutual fidelity, and carrying on among themselves a large volume of transactions, they were in some
degree self-sufficient and self-contained. Without the benefit of any centralized synod, these widely scattered communities presented a kind of informal confederacy reminiscent to a degree of the Hanseatic League with its eighty
member cities. A near parallel was also the close bond
during the seventeenth century between Amsterdam and
the Calvinist port of La Rochelle which too was based on a
common religious identity. It was natural enough for intercourse between merchants united by ties of faith and charity to rest on a more confidential level in an age when the
generally accepted maxim was "He who does not cheat does
not sell."

Attempts at the complete economic ostracism of Jewish
merchants were often successfully resisted thanks to the
protective influence afforded them by distant coreligionists. Of the important Jewish community of Prague, it was
thus pointedly declared:[15] "If by now the Jews participated
substantially in the trade in spices, colonial products, leather, furs, and other commodities, it was evidence of the fact
that they had broken through the blockade the Old Town
burghers had tried to enforce. The Jewish merchants were
capable of procuring goods and furs from the east of
Europe with greater readiness and regularity than their
rivals."

Now how did it come about, one might ask, that the
Jewish merchants in Prague were able to procure goods and
furs from the east more easily than their Christian competitors? Nowhere has the answer been given explicitly; yet
it may be inferred readily enough. The furs and leather
from the wilds of Eastern Europe were shipped to them by
none other than their coreligionists of Poland. Again, how
was it possible for the Jews of Prague, and Frankfortam-

Main, to obtain more easily than their Christian competitors and at better prices spices and other Oriental products, if not from men of their nation carrying on business in Venice, Leghorn, and Amsterdam, who in turn were supplied by others living in Constantinople, or Cairo, or Bombay?

I am tempted to offer yet a further instance, one of many, of Jewish economic power deriving from such prominence in foreign trade. The Emperor Ferdinand II of Germany, whose intolerance helped to ignite the Thirty Years War, was careful to leave unmolested the Jews of his capital city, Vienna. This community contained a number of large importers of commodities badly needed for the prosecution of a long war. Not of least importance were their imports, by way of the Danube River valley, of gunpowder and other weapons fabricated by Jewish manufacturers located in Brusa, Salonika and Adrianople. Between Vienna and Venice, another emporium where Jewish importers and exporters were well entrenched, there lay only the low cols of the Carnatic and Julian Alps, whose ceiling of less than 4,000 feet did not impede the traffic between these great cities. But my reference to the Austrian capital does not end here. On March 1st, 1760, the Emperor Leopold I issued his edict that "for the glory of God" all Jews living in Vienna were, on pain of imprisonment or death, to leave by the following Corpus Christi day. By August 1st of that same year, the entire community had indeed abandoned the capital.

A few of them found a welcome in a little provincial capital called Berlin, where before that time no Jews had been living, and which a few years later was to open its doors to a stream of Protestants driven out of France by King Louis XIV. For the fatuous Austrian ruler and his grateful subjects, it did not take very long to find out that "the glory of God" required a high price in terms of worldly sacrifices.

The imperial treasury began to miss the taxes, war duties, and special assessments once levied on the Jews, to say nothing of the custom duties on merchandise which they had been bringing into the city from outside places. Also Christian shopkeepers began complaining that certain commodities which Jews had been selling to them, and which had kept them in business, were no longer to be had. The trouble was that while the Emperor could do as he pleased with Jewish merchants residing within his dominions, he could do nothing with their kinsfolk, and coreligionists living in such places as Belgrade, Solonika, Constantinople, Hamburg and Amsterdam. All this having become clear, it did not take very long before the Oppenheimers, the Wertheimers, the Eskeles, the Arnsteins and Aguilars were back in their old places of business.

The members of the Jewish mercantile world enjoyed a further advantage of operating under a legal system that permitted an expeditious and inexpensive means of adjusting differences between them. Disputes arising from the forwarding of merchandise were almost invariably submitted to the decision of well-known and respected rabbis. Their Responsa, based on Talmudic sources and replete with comments on commercial matters, were expedited through the system of mail carriers set up by the Moslem rulers. Such Rabbinical decisions were of no expense to the disputants. Down to about the fourteenth century, the tradition held good that spiritual leaders were to serve their congregants without pay; and were expected to earn their livelihood either through handicrafts or trade. These men, all too often, led lives of penury rather than accept any remuneration out of communal funds. Their only material reward consisted in their being exempt from communal taxes and the enjoyment of certain priorities in the market places.

On its more fragile side, Jewish commerce, aside from

its exposure to hostile and repressive measures, was severely handicapped by the lack of a dependence on a strong and sufficiently diversified productive apparatus. The exception was of course Spain, where, thanks to a highly integrated economy of production, commerce, and finance, it was possible for the Spanish Jews for a period of about four centuries to hold out against the onslaughts of the Church. A source of weakness was the lack of a merchant marine under their control, and their complete dependence on the grace of others to carry their goods over the seas. In this respect the position of the Jewish mercantile communities differed fundamentally from their Phoenician and Greek predecessors, as well as from their Venetian, Hanseatic, Dutch, and Portuguese contemporaries.

As to the origin of commerce among the ancient Israelites as distinct from those of later ages, there is, as with other nations, a scarcity of authentic memorials and an absence of an unbroken narrative. Such Biblical reports as we do possess are excessively concise, leaving the field open to conjecture taking the place of verifiable facts. But such veiled references as are to be found do receive some assistance from analogous situations among contemporary nations, and especially from our knowledge of economic development in the antique world.

The country of the Israelites, misnamed Palestine, though not rich in natural resources, was yet not without its economic advantages. Its upland areas were suited for the production of grapes, olives, wheat, barley, figs, pomegranates, sycamore wood, cypress, oak, along with balsam wood for the manufacture of perfume. It contained extensive steppes where herds of sheep, goats and cattle were able to find pasture. The Dead Sea yielded a harvest of salt, as well as bitumen much in demand among the Egyptians for the embalming of their more distinguished dead. Basalt for the making of the indispensable mill-stones was quarried in the north. Not wanting was clay for pottery and for bricks, as well as limestone for luxury homes and fortifications. There was vitrifiable sand along the coastal area north of Acre. As far to the south as present-day Haifa, the coastal plain yielded a snail from which there came a dye highly prized throughout the Mediterranean world. Haifa was in Graeco-Roman times known as "Purpureon," meaning the city of purple. From all these raw materials scattered throughout the land, along with the industries founded upon them, there proceeded a not inconsiderable trade.

The poet Kipling once referred to this land as "the buckle in the belt of the world." In the circumscribed world of antiquity, this appraisal would have been undeniably accurate. At a period when neither Europe nor India nor China were yet of any consequence in the community of old world nations, the area lying between the rivers Nile and Euphrates was the focus of all attention and was the most central region of the world. Between Egypt and Mesopotamia, respectively the Occident and Orient of the early world, the land occupied by the Israelites was the natural and obvious corridor, for merchant caravans no less than for armies on the march.

"The overall situation of this country was such as to turn its inhabitants in the direction of international trade. Palestine was a natural crossroad for an extensive transit of merchandise, and more especially for the caravan routes forming the connection between Mesopotamia and Egypt. One of the main routes leaving Egypt for the coastal plain was bifurcated at Mount Carmel. One branch continued northward towards the cities of Phoenicia, while the other crossing the plain of Jezreel reached the crossing of the Jordan River, whence it turned northward to Damascus. Damascus was the terminal likewise of another important trunk route, namely the one extending from Elath northward through trans-Jordan valley, the so-called King's Road mentioned in the book of Numbers. Branching westward from this main artery were at least two feeder lines extending across the Jordan River, one going towards Jericho and Jerusalem and the other towards Samaria."[16]

Biblical Israel's economic importance is to be gauged likewise from the fact that it happened to be the next-door neighbour of Phoenicia, the land chosen as the cradle of early commerce. In the twenty-seventh chapter of the book of Ezekiel do we discover an outline of the far-flung trade connections of this nation, with mention made of Ethiopia, Libia, Greece, Italy, Spain, Lydia, and Armenia. From the beginning of their statehood, the small and insignificant body of traffickers among the Hebrew tribes were under the tutorship and direction of the rich and plutocratic Phoenicians settled within the country. In both the internal and external trade of ancient Israel, the Phoenicians were for a long time the dominant influence, so much so that among the people the term "Canaanite" (Phoenician) was synonymous with merchant.[17]

The germ of Hebrew commercialism is certainly traceable to the early Biblical period, perhaps even as far back as the time of Abraham; but it was with the founding of the monarchy that its transient growth began to manifest itself. David in one of his Psalms speaks of one "who heapeth up riches."[18] Doubtless, by exploiting his military successes, he was able to obtain some commercial advantages for men of his nation in respect to traffic by land. But it was in the time of Solomon that for the first time the Israelites heeded the call of the sea. Intent on having his own fleet of ships, Solomon was none the less careful not to affront his Phoenician partners and allies by having it collide with their monopoly of the Mediterranean Sea. He chose instead to have his new fleet ply the coasts of Arabia and Africa, and then only in close association with Phoenician seamen and shipwrights.

This early bloom of Israelite commerce withered with the collapse of Solomon's empire. Its later vicissitudes varied in accordance with the political and military successes of the Israelite and Judaean kings. Do we not read of the victorious Ahab compelling the defeated Syrian king to grant to Israelite merchants the right of trading in Damascus?[19] With trade normally picking up on the heels of military victories, the highly successful reigns of Jeroboam II and Uzziah were undoubtedly featured by some enlarged commercial horizons on the part of their Israelite and Judaean subjects. As to this we have some evidence from what the prophet Amos wrote: "Woe unto them that are at ease in Zion, and to them that are secure in the mountain of Samaria. The notable men of the first of the nations to whom the house of Israel come. Pass ye unto Calneh and see; and from thence go into Hamath the great. Then go down to Gath of the Philistines."[20]

Were there any large traders in Israel during biblical times? It is a reasonable enough supposition that in King Solomon's time co-operation with the Phoenicians was not restricted to the single reported instance of a joint enterprise upon the high seas. It could have been that in the Phoenician caravans going from and to Solomon's dominions, Israelite partners were not excluded. The indications are none the less that no Israelite of the time travelled any great distance from his home base all on his own. I range myself on the side of Werner Sombart, who contradicting Herzfeld (Handelsgeschichte der Juden des Altertums) maintained that Israelite entrepreneurs were bazaar sitters rather than voyagers; and that their role in world trade was insignificant. Had these men ventured beyond the borders of their own country, they would quickly have fallen prey to

278

their voracious and violence-prone competitors. Not least of all, they were without the large concentration of capital needed for setting on foot expeditions to distant places. Their role, for the most part, one may suppose, was that of warehousemen, distributing among fellow townsmen their necessities in the way of wheat, barley, wine and oil. This is not to deny that of these small-scale merchandisers some among them became wealthy enough to lead the lives of callous luxury that so aroused the ire of the early prophets. Then as now, be it remembered, the opportunities for gain were by no means restricted to those engaged in long-distance trafficking. No matter what was the period, the combined import and export trade of any nation has at no times been more than a fraction of its internal commercial activity.

Commerce is essentially a service; and one for which a number of small states and republics have been distinguished for relatively short periods at various times throughout history. A long time ago, and for a span of from one to two centuries, the Jews came close to enjoying a predominant role in international trade, comparable in some respects to that of the Venetians, the Hanseatic League, the Portuguese, and the Dutch in their time.

On a truly ecumenical scale, Jewish commerce can be said to have attained its zenith during a brief period—perhaps no more than a century—following the rise of Islam. Later events in Europe and the world were favourable at times and unfavourable at others to Jewish commercial activity; but in no other era did such activity achieve an amplitude in any degree comparable to that of the early Islamic period. With the rise of Islam came the first iron curtain between east and west. It was one which Jewish merchants were for the time being at least alone in a position to penetrate, since they were represented in both areas, and after a fashion tolerated in both.

In their overrunning of Christian territory, the conquering Arabs, bent upon earthly rewards, were not inattentive to the costly ornaments of the numerous churches that straddled their paths. For the task of disposing of gold and silver crucifixes, chalices and vestments, Jewish men of business were the natural middlemen, since no honest Christian could be induced to lay hands on such sacred loot. Again, articles of Asiatic luxury for which Christian barons and their ladies had some preference were now under the control of men with whom Christians were forbidden to have peaceful dealings. Under such circumstances of mutual exclusiveness, Jews served as the natural intermediaries.[21]

We may take it for granted that such commercial hegemony of the Jews—very temporary though it proved to be—could only have been the end result of a lengthy process of apprenticeship and prior development. In the commercial life of the great city of Alexandria they had long been conspicuous, where they were reputed to have controlled the garment industry, along with the trade in Chinese silk, Indian gauzes, and African cotton.[22] Also other events preceding the rise of Islam lent credibility to their exceptional position. Following the barbarian invasions, the ensuing hostility between the Greek-speaking Eastern empire and the successor states of the West was aggravated by the fact the newly adopted Christianity of the latter was deemed to be unorthodox by the ecclesiastical authorities of Constantinople, Antioch, and Alexandria. If in a situation of this kind trade intercourse was to go on, there was also need of an intermediary that was neither Greek nor barbarian.[23]

To the extent that they had cast their fortunes among nations that were themselves little inclined to mercantile pursuits, the spirit of Jewish commercialism was able to operate most briskly. Persians and Parthians and Egyptians were typical of those nations in which a taste for business was no more than vestigial. Also, early Christianity, in contrast to Judaism, and for a number of centuries at least, was antagonistic not only to moneylending but to all commercial diligence. As noted by the historian Gibbon, Christians were for a number of centuries dead to the business and pleasures of this world, their minds being focused on the delights of the world to come, so that during this extended period, the worldly-minded Jews were in a relatively happy non-competitive position. Troubles awaited them, however, as soon as the anti-materialistic bias of the Christians gave way to a commercial impulse not distinguishable from their own.

Even at the time of its greatest expansiveness, Jewish leadership in world commerce was by no means uncontested. In the vanguard of a nascent Christian commercialism stood Venice, the earliest among the Italian trading republics. The rise of Venice as a commercial metropolis was, as in the case of the Jews, propelled by the Islamic revolution. Its early and advanced prosperity was indeed founded upon a disregard of the Papal prohibition against trading with the enemy. In competition with the Jews, Venetian exporters provided the needy Arab conquerors with wood for their warships, iron for their scimitars, and perhaps above all, human cargoes taken into captivity in the lands to the north of them among an eastern group of peoples designated as Slavs.

Between the Jews and the Venetians, rivals and competitors in their first encounters, there was to be much intertwining in their later destinies. Strategically located at the head of the Adriatic, the port of Venice was for a number of centuries the most notable link between transalpine Europe and the cities of western Asia and north Africa. Between Europe and the Holy Land, there had been prior to the age of the Crusades no regular communication by sea. Christian pilgrims were compelled to follow the long and tortuous overland route by way of the Danube River valley and Constantinople. For European Jews, the route most of all frequented was the equally long and dangerous one by way of Spain and North Africa. It required the sweeping away of both the Byzantine and Moslem navies by the Venetians for an effective and dependable sea route to be opened between northern and eastern Europe and the Holy Land, or what was known in Crusading times as "Outremer."

Following their defeat of the Genoese in a decisive sea battle in 1258, the Venetians acquired a monopoly of the shipping route to the coastal cities of Palestine as well as to Cyprus, Rhodes and Alexandria. Their mercantile houses, to the exclusion of all others, came to be represented at Beirut, Acre, and Jaffa. For the better accommodation of the increased number of pilgrims, both Jewish and Christian, to the Holy Land, the Venetians around the year 1300 introduced a new and enlarged sailing vessel capable of carrying a greatly enhanced number of passengers and their belongings.

In its prime during the fifteenth century, Venice was next to Constantinople, its principal trading rival, by far the largest Christian city. Its population in 1422 was about 200,000, or nearly four times that of Rome.[24] From the time of its founding and throughout its entire existence, this republic remained in the hands of an intelligent and implacable merchant aristocracy, which tolerated neither mob disturbances, nor revolutionary agitators. Of all the European states, its government was the most mercenary and coldly rational in outlook, and least of all moved by sentimental and religious considerations. I have already referred to their rise to eminence through their early disregard of the papal decree against trafficking with the Moslems. Briefly, Venice was a place in which heretics and unbelievers could find a haven for themselves and an opportunity for doing business.[25]

Not surprisingly, to Shakespeare, this metropolis, the New York of the late mediaeval Jews, appeared as the most obvious locale for his obnoxious "comedy." The Jews of Shakespeare's Venice had indeed become a significant factor in helping to stem the declining fortunes of that city. Hard times were in store for the republic as a consequence of being bypassed by the direct sea route between the Far East and Europe. Alexandria, whose commercial affinity with the Venetians had been of the closest, was then in the process of being reduced to a mere village, through being no longer a port of transit for the spice trade of Asia and Africa. In partial compensation, however, a lively trade relationship was then in the course of development between the Jewish merchants of the republic and their coreligionists in Constantinople and other cities of the Porte, along with those of Mantua, Ferrarra, Prague and Cracow. A French-Jewish historian has written about the Jewish participation in the overseas trade of the later republic. Beginning with the early seventeenth century, increasing privileges were accorded by the Signory to Jewish ship-owners and merchants, so that in the Adriatic Sea itself the trade came to almost entirely in their hands. At the beginning of the eighteenth century, somewhat less than one-fifth of the trading fleet, flying the flag of the Republic was owned by Jews.[26]

PART IV

MONEY

Corresponding to the flow of commodities from nation to nation, from city to city and from individual to individual is the circulation of money. A sensitive observer will discern

283

that the circulation of the one, no less than the dissemination of the other, are alike dependent upon and determined by a multitude of passageways, which from age to age have been furrowed across the lands and the seas, joining together all the continents along with regions once secluded from one another. These global lines of communication, both great and insignificant, are in some degree comparable in function to the arteries, veins, and capillaries of the physical organism.

Rulers of states, both ancient and modern, have been concerned about the quantity of the precious metals that flowed into and away from their borders. Since very remote times, and down to this very day, silver and more especially gold have been looked upon as the sinews of war, as well as hoardable materials which neither moth nor rust could corrupt. Throughout the ages Jews, settled in the various countries, have fared well or ill according to their aptitude in influencing this flow.

The origin of coined money, as a factor of some relevancy in the financial story of the Jews, deserves a passing notice. That the use of coined money in place of gold and silver ingots, like most other innovations throughout the centuries, was an answer to some pressing necessity is a statement not likely to be contradicted. This necessity, I would suggest further, was related to warfare.

The invention or discovery of this hugely helpful device for regulating the business of the world is to be credited to a nation once located in the centre of Asia Minor, anciently known as Lydia, a land whose soil was blessed with ample mineral deposits, and particularly of the precious metals. Tempted by the availability of all this substance, the kings of Lydia, around the year 650 B.C.E., from their capital city of Sardis, embarked on a career of conquest, first seeking to incorporate into their landlocked kingdom the many Greek cities strung along the Aegaean coastline.

The slow process of conquest required fully one hundred years of intermittent warfare.[27]

Now at least as far back as the time of King David, the employment of hired fighting men in Middle Eastern warfare had been endemic. Payment of such hirelings, as in other transactions that were purely commercial, was in ingots of gold or silver that required weighing in all instances. Now since not every recipient could be expected to carry about his person the necessary scales for weighing, the suspicion that someone was being cheated was in a great many instances well founded. One might with impunity defraud a peasant, or a hired workman, or even a fellow trader; but the mere appearance of deceptively diminishing that which was owing to a gang of men whose appetite for blood and plunder was never to be tampered with, at times spelt disaster to some unfortunate paymaster. Hence the urgent need for a new system under which each mercenary would be given as his stipend a piece of gold or silver that was the exact equivalent, in weight and fineness, of every other piece of gold and silver so handed out; and one whose weight and fineness, known in advance by the stamp placed upon it, would occasion no disagreeable surprises to the recipient. It soon followed that to nearly all governments the issuing of coined money recommended itself, not only as a means for expediting all business transactions of their subjects but as a new source of revenue for themselves. Hence, the minting of these rounded and imprinted discs could be regarded as the earliest and most basic instance of government ownership of the means of production as well as direct participation of governments in economic enterprise.

Now the advent of coinage, generally placed at around the year 550 B.C.E., during the reign of the fabulous King Croesus, coincided approximately with the overthrow of the Babylonian Empire by Cyrus the Great. Croesus was the last king of Lydia. There followed soon after the incorporation of this kingdom into the Persian empire the construction of the famous highway that linked together Sardis and the Aegean seaboard with far-off Persepolis and Babylon, the seats of Persian power. That Jewish merchants of the time were not slow in taking advantage of both the new horizons that were now visible to them can be safely conceded. No longer were they as a class compelled to bear among their brethren the reproach of carrying about themselves the "balances of deceit." Gold and silver, instead of having to be weighed and tested before the closing of every sale or purchase, was from then onward to be counted only, a method allowing far less occasion for fraudulent dealings. In the eyes of pious Hebrews, the advent of coinage constituted a crucial reform that tended to give respectability to the occupation of merchant. The universal adoption of coined money soon gave birth to the complications of finance.

"The penny has currency only where it is minted" was an early adage governing the acceptability of coined money. As between one sovereignty and another, coinage could not have uniformity as to weight, fineness, and thickness. Hence do we find in the New Testament the first known reference to an organized market of money changers. That this exchange was located inside the grounds of the Temple of Jerusalem may have offended others of that generation beside Jesus. The majority of the nation apparently saw in it no sacrilege; but rather a necessary means for accommodating the throng of pilgrims from many lands bringing with them the monetary units of all the republics and principalities of the known world. It does not seem rash to suggest that the exchange at Jerusalem may have been the first of its kind anywhere in the world. It is also highly probable that, as a full-time occupation, that of moneychanging preceded in time that of moneylending.

Down through the ages, the exchanging of money was a distinctively Jewish business, even to the time of the founder of the House of Rothschild.

In the undeveloped areas of northern and western Europe, including Christian Spain, France under the Carolingian monarchs, Germany, Austria, Hungary, Bohemia, Servia, and Poland, Jews were initially welcomed as bringers of exotic wares connected with warfare, worship, and luxury. But perhaps above all was their coming appreciated for introducing into the host countries the gold which the rulers of these countries had been unable to obtain out of their own natural environment.

Nearly all of this Jewish gold was in the course of time destined to become Christian gold. But all Europe's gold, both Jewish and Christian, was for the most part Moslem gold originally. Some portions of it, to be sure, had first been acquired by Spanish Jewish merchants trading in the depths of black Africa. But by far the greater quantity of this distinguished metal that found its way into western Christendom prior to the discovery of the new world had come from the territories of the Ommeyade and Abbasid Caliphs. It had been dug out of the ground in such remote places as Nubia, Sudan, Khorrasan, and Transoxiana. Much of it had been garnered of old by the tyrants of Persia and hoarded in their palaces at Persepolis, Seleucia, and Ctesiphon whence the Arab invaders had released it into circulation. From the violated churches of Alexandria, Antioch, and Edessa, along with hundreds of others in western Asia and north Africa, much of the consecrated treasures had been looted and melted down. Even the sarcophagi of long dead and buried Pharaohs had been rifled. For all this accumulation of precious metal, the slave dealers of Verdun, Paderborn, Magdeberg, Venice, Naples, and Bristol felt a great hunger.

In an age of increasing refinement, it came about that

throughout western Europe there was not a ducal or baronial family without its collection of golden table service, dishes of ceramics being for a long time to come unknown. Also in due course, the gold standard made its entry, as the monetary supply of Europe ceased to be based solely on silver. Kiev, an important trading post on the banks of the Dneiper, and in close communion with the Moslem east, minted gold coinage as early as the tenth century. The centuries that followed saw the introduction of ducats into Venice, florins into Florence, gulden into Germany, louis d'or into France, pistoles into Spain, and nobles into England.

To be sure, the flow of gold into Europe also had its reversals. The heathen raiders from Scandinavia exacted a heavy toll as ransom for the cities along the Seine, the Loire, the Rhine, and the Garonne; providing thereby a financial infrastructure for the creation of several new states in Europe's far north. Of immediate impact on the fortunes of the Jews of Western Europe was the final conversion to Christianity of all the Slavic and east German tribes. It brought to a virtual end the export of European slaves to the Moslem east, compelling the Arabs to look to Africa for their further needs in this respect. Added to the drying up of this lucrative export trade in which both Jews and Italians had a hand, was a diminution in the supply of exportable lumber with the clearing of much of the forest land of Eastern Germany to make way for the founding of new cities, and the opening of new farms, and the construction of new abbeys and cathedrals. With the consequent reduction in the flow of Moslem gold into Christian Europe, it became increasingly difficult for Jews to qualify as ready-made sources of exploitation by the kings of France, Germany and England.

Some outflow of gold and silver was the inevitable concomitant of every migration of the Jews from one realm to another as, for example, their migration in the middle of the twelfth century from Moslem Spain to Christian Spain. A departure of even a handful of pioneers with much gold and silver in their knapsacks, seeking a new life for themselves in some strange country, such as Poland or Bohemia, or Hungary, or Serbia, unavoidably helped to worsen the situation of those of their brethren who stayed behind. It meant that thenceforth the combined resources of the older communities available for satisfying the avarice of their rulers were diminished.

The Jews of Western Europe who, as far as our limited sources of information permit us to judge, came mainly from Spain and who were in the beginning concentrated within the broad dominions of the Frankish kings tended as time went on to spread themselves out into the forward areas of central Europe. Those among them who for one reason or another decided to move their dwellings to the newly created cities of the Danube, the Main, the Lahm, and the Elbe, took along with them much of the supply of the precious metals previously to be found inside the realm of the Carolingian and Capetian kings. Especially unsettling to the finances of the French king was the departure of a substantial number of Jewish financiers for England in the train of William the Conqueror. The amount of currency thus removed and carried overseas was for that period far from insignificant. Thus Aaron of Lincoln, an English Jew of the second or third generation, through agents located in no less than twenty-five counties, was able to accomodate a host of heavy and importunate borrowers on such security as wheat, armour, estates, and houses. Among these needy ones were the King of Scotland, the Earls of Northampton, Arundel, Aumale, and Leicester, the Count of Brittany, the Archbishop of Canterbury, the Bishops of Bangor and Lincoln, the Prior of the Knights Hospitallers, and the towns of Winchester and Southampton. Additionally, Aaron provided the means for the erection of nine Cistercian abbeys throughout the country along with the cathedrals of Lincoln, Peterborough, and St Albans[28]

At the time of his death in 1186, Aaron of Lincoln was probably the wealthiest man in England in terms of ready cash, while 430 persons of high degree were indebted to him. His entire estate was seized by King Henry II, who left nothing to the deceased financier's heirs. The outstanding claims of the estate amounted to 15,000 pounds sterling, or the equivalent of about three quarters of the royal income for any normal year. To handle their collection, a special branch of the royal exchequer was set up; but some twenty years later one half was still uncollected. The bullion and other treasure that fell into the hands of the royal concessionaire was at once forwarded to France where it was needed for carrying on a war. It never got there. It went to the bottom of the sea in a shipwreck.

The ruin of this great estate from which no one benefited marked a turning point likewise in the relationship of the Jews and the Plantagenet kings. It marked the repudiation of the guarantees that had been given them when they first aided the Norman conquerors with their money.

A similar disaster involving the loss of a treasure repeated itself some decades later, one which even more urgently announced the approaching ruin of the Jews of England. In the year 1216, King John, a few days before his death, was crossing the estuary of the Humber river with his army, from the port of Lynn, when he was surprised by the incoming tide. His baggage with all the royal treasure was carried away. One can easily guess by whom this loss had to be made good.

To the continental Jews along with a great many Christians Anglo-Saxon England had long remained completely unattractive. It was as dangerous and uninviting a place for anyone to settle in as were any of the Scandinavian coun-

290

tries. Its known wildness and poverty—extreme even for that age—finally suggested the feasibility of the country being invaded and taken over by those who considered themselves more civilized. The Jews of Rouen and other French cities, who with their material resources backed Duke William's enterprise, had as their partner, lending him spiritual assistance, none other than the Pope. The Holy Father, who in line with his predecessors had been having his troubles over in Italy, was greatly beholden to the Norman conquerors of Apuleia who had come to his assistance. Hence his strange readiness to declare a crusade against a body of islanders who, however barbarous, were then in the forefront of Christian orthodoxy.

Following the conquest, Jews from France as well as elsewhere were induced to come over to an island which previously they had sedulously shunned. It was for them a haven during the first and second crusades. But their stay was to be both short and unhappy, shorter in fact than in any of the other European states during the mediaeval period. The reason for their very brief sojourn is explainable in part by the fact that from the very beginning their activity was restricted to moneylending. Participation in the agriculture and industry of the country was of course denied them, while such foreign trade as did exist at the time was monopolized by resident merchants from the Hanse. Having neither an industrial nor a commercial base, Jewish finance was before long to shrivel up entirely under the steady impact of royal exactions. The full tale of their spoilation and terrorization, as well as the final expulsion of the handful that were permitted to survive, has been adequately related elsewhere. In a later century, with their resources substantially replenished, their descendants were permitted to re-enter the country.[29]

The Portuguese Jews, who settled in England towards the close of the seventeenth century, were able to find favour with their new hosts by reason of their skill in bringing into the country the gold that was then reaching Portugal from Brazil. It was a highly surreptitious operation, requiring, no doubt, the connivance of friends and relations still living under the shadow of the Inquisition. By 1750, half the gold leaving Lisbon was finding its way to London[30] A regular weekly packet plying between Lisbon and London is said at the time to have carried back to England little but mainland metal.

Paradoxically, the rehabilitation of Jewish finance in the seventeenth and eighteenth centuries was made possible not otherwise than by the heavy importations of oversea metal by their Spanish and Portuguese enemies, as I shall explain more fully in the final chapter.

CHAPTER IX

JEWS, CHRISTIANS, AND MOSLEMS

The time has come to relate the effects of power politics down through the ages upon the fortunes of the Jewish nation, as distinguished from those of economic determinism. Through their aptitude at certain crafts, such as silk weaving, their adroit management of international trade connections, and their occasional monoply of moneylending, the Jews were, in one place or another, and at certain times, successful in weathering the storms of religious intolerance. All this notwithstanding, their creative survival was subject to political winds whose direction it was altogether outside their power to influence. It scarcely needs pointing out that against the unified mediaeval state their economic strength, such as it was, counted for almost nothing. Unlike Spain, England and France suffered no harm whatsoever as the aftermath of the expulsion of their Jewish inhabitants. In both these countries, there were afterwards no shortages of Christian moneylenders to take over the functions of the departed unbelievers. The fact that for hundreds of years there were no Jews dwelling within their borders did not prevent all West European states from making impressive gains in their respective economies. During these centuries, England and France got along without the Jews; while the Jews, for their part, managed to survive without England and France.

Down through the centuries, the Jewish dispersion, otherwise styled as the Diaspora, both expanded and contracted periodically. A point that needs to be made is that at no time did it ever attain world-wide dimensions.

In every age, there have been leading states, in fact entire continents, that were entirely devoid of Jewish inhabitants. Among Hindus, Buddhists, Confucianists, or Taoists, they have mingled hardly at all. For many hundreds of years, and indeed down to our own time, the portion of the earth's surface inhabited by Jews has been limited to areas dominated by the two derived religions. With the advance of the Cross eastward in Europe and of the Crescent eastward in Asia, fresh areas of colonization were simultaneously offered to the children of Israel. But into those areas of farther Asia and farther Africa, untouched by these dominant faiths, the followers of the Old Testament religion failed almost completely to set down any roots.

At no time did their limited number permit them to spread out extensively. An avoidance of great distances between one community and the next was imperative at a time when communication both by land and by sea was beset by difficulties and great perils. It is for this reason that their communities were distinguished for number rather than mere individual size. Ready accessibility from one to the other was vital for the nurturing of commercial relationships between them, for religious and cultural communion, and not least of all for the cementing of matrimonial alliances.

Sundered from other Jewish sources, remote and isolated communities were bound to succumb in the end to the effects of intermarriage and to disappear. Such for example was the fate of a settlement of merchant adventurers, probably from Persia, who came into the Celestial Empire at some unknown time, changing a temporary sojourn into one of permanency at Kai Fung, not far from the Chinese capital of Peking.[1] It managed to retain its distinctiveness for the length of time that the so-called silk route remained open. But this long, dangerous, and tedious passage fell into disuse following the opening of the more convenient sea route between Europe and the East. Cut off from direct contact with their brethren in the west, the isolation of the Chinese Jews was completed by the eastward expansion of the Czarist Empire.

The trek into China, preceding by several centuries the famed voyages of Marco Polo and his father, saw an attempt by Jews to establish themselves in a more genial atmosphere and to place between themselves and their religious opponents as great a physical distance as possible. But for reasons that are difficult to explain, the example of these adventurous pioneers had few imitators among their brethren. Their wandering coreligionists continued to move only within the boundaries of the Christian and Moslem worlds.

Some digression is here warranted concerning the relative strength of these two major confessions. Down to the seventeenth century approximately, the cities of North Africa, Egypt, Asia Minor, and Iran were more opulent and attractive than those of the West. For the nations of Christian Europe, the Atlantic Ocean had long constituted a dead end. Into it there was no venturing forth, much less traversing it to some other land mass. For the successors of the Prophet, to the contrary, no such limiting barrier existed. The one great body of water that confronted them, namely the Indian Ocean, was one which ages before had been made easy to navigate and to overlap. Stretching eastward of their mainland possessions was an all but end-less land surface, giving them first call on the commerce of India, central Asia, China, and the Eastern archipelago. From all direct contact with these fabled lands and their produce, their Christian rivals were effectively repulsed.

But the relative positions of the two sovereign reli-gions, each claiming to offer salvation on an ecumenical scale, were destined to be drastically reversed in the greatest of all revolutions. Not only were the Moslems effectively outflanked in both Asia and Africa by the newly created sea power of the Christians, but the newly revealed overseas land masses were appropriated in their entirety by the Christians, to the complete exclusion of the Moslems. The Atlantic, hitherto an impassible obstacle to progress and expansion, was now turned into a Christian lake, with the Pacific only somewhat less so. The Christian world, once confined to a corner of the immense Eurasian littoral, now acquired giant dimensions of its own.

For the followers of Mohammed, the age of darkness had arrived. For them the revival of learning among the infidels coincided with the decline of learning among them-selves. Not for them was the new age of the printed word, or the birth of astronomy, physics, chemistry, and medicine. On the political level as well, the Moslem world became drastically diminished. Islamic lands which the Crusaders of old had vainly sought to conquer became in the course of the nineteenth century colonies and protectorates of Chris-tian powers.[2]

Parallel with the economic and cultural decline of the Moslem countries was the diminished importance of their Jewish inhabitants relative to that of the rest of world Jewry. Less than ten percent were living in Moslem countries on the eve of World War II. Long before the creation of the State of Israel and the holy war sentiment which it resus-citated inside the entire Moslem world, Jews had acquired a

296

strong aversion to living under Moslem governments. Even while continuing to live in places such as Morocco, Tunis, Algeria, Egypt, Mesopotamia, and Turkestan, they were the first to welcome the colonial administration of the English, the French, and even the Czarist Russians.

I now make the suggestion that the antagonism between Islam and Christianity, enduring for many centuries under varying levels of intensity, was a prime factor in ensuring Jewish survival. By way of a corollory, it could be maintained likewise that Judaism would long ago have disappeared from the earth had it given birth to one only of these religions instead of to both. More specifically, Judaism as an organized religion would have disappeared some time after the seventh century of the common era had it not been for the unexpected appearance of a dynamic and expansive Islam. There is ample evidence to support the contention that without the timely advent of Mohammed's revelation as a challenge and threat to Christianity, the pressure on the frail Jewish population by the militant Church would well have become total and irresistible.

Beginning with what is known as "the peace of the Church" in the reign of the Emperor Constantine and for three centuries thereafter, Christianity found itself without an effective antagonist. By the year 438, the Emperor Theodosius II was able to declare that classical paganism had ceased to exist anywhere within the bounds of the empire. Throughout the length and breadth of the Roman imperium, both east and west, only the stubborn Jews were refusing to fall into line. Hence the closing of the last surviving school of philosophy at Athens by the Emperor Justinian in 529 was followed immediately by a drive against all the synagogues within the imperial territories, a program seconded by much popular violence.

Under Justinian (527-565), the empire was composed of 64 provinces containing 935 cities. It embraced the entire

Near and Middle East, the greater portion of the Appennine peninsula, as well as the whole of North Africa. Nowhere inside this extensive domain and its many urban centres was there a peaceful existence for the Jewish minority, hemmed in as they were by an ever-growing mass of imperial edicts. Their wealth, such as it was, afforded them no protection. The colossal empire was sustained by a vast commerce under bureaucratic auspices, in which the participation of the Jews could have added nothing of great significance. Likewise, teetering on the edge of total annihilation were the communities of Frankish Gaul and Visigothic Spain. Within the empire of the Persian Sassanids, itself under pressure from its more powerful Christian antagonist, the ruling Magi were scarcely less hostile than were the monks.

With the closing down of numerous synagogues by imperial and episcopal decrees, and with no repairs permitted to those that threatened to collapse with age, the heavy hand of the church upon its Jewish rival would appear to have reached the limit of endurance. To human eyes it might well have seemed that the fate of the parent religion was about to be sealed. A miracle prevented this from happening. Such a miracle, from the standpoint of the Jews, was the sudden emergence in the early seventh century of a counterweight to Christianity.

For the first time since its triumph under Constantine, the Christian hierarchy was to taste defeat. Such was the matchless onslaught of the camel-riding tribesmen that in less than a decade about half the territory of the Byzantine Empire was wrested from the sway of the Church. In north Africa alone, two hundred and fifty bishoprices were abolished by the incoming Moslems, by whom innumerable basilicas were razed.[3] Of the four patriarchates of the Christian world, namely Rome, Constantinople, Antioch and Alexandria, the two latter ceased to exist. In Mesopotamia,

Persia, Syria, Egypt, and North Africa, the Moslems were welcomed as liberators not only by the Jews, but by dissident Christians as well.[4] For the sorely beset Jewish communities there arrived an act of salvation. Symbolically, Jerusalem, long forbidden to them by the Byzantine emperors, now stood ready to receive them, following a decisive battle in 634 fought in the vicinity of what is now the city of Tel Aviv.[5]

In Europe, as in Africa and Asia, a Christendom diminished in power and renown was the immediate outcome of the Mohammedan onslaught. Arab incursions at times reached as far to the north as the Loire and the Po. Tidings of setbacks suffered by the Christians at their hands were carried to many heathen nations—Vikings, Saxons, Avars, Hungarians. The two centuries that followed saw Christian Europe under repeated attack by the heathen Norsemen, who on one occasion even entered Paris (845). Indirectly as well as directly and over an all-embracing territory, the Jews, threatened by the all-powerful Church, were benefited by the change to Moslem rule. None the less, the well-being of the mediaeval Jews under these new masters ought not to be exaggerated.

To the immediate successors of the Prophet, a policy of moderation towards all the inhabitants of the conquered territories recommended itself. This toleration was not abandoned until about two hundred years after the Prophet's death. With the exception of Persia and Iraq, all lands taken over in the first rush of Arabic conquest were overwhelmingly Christian. As a matter of sheer prudence, this necessitated some restraint on the conversionary zeal of the victors. Jews along with their Christian neighbours benefited from these necessary concessions to the majority population.

Gradually, however, the Moslem invaders from being a minority were changed into a majority, as the Christian inhabitants of North Africa, Egypt, and Syria found it to their advantage to convert to the dominant faith. In Egypt and Syria, most of the Christian inhabitants had long been persecuted by the Church in Constantinople as adherents of a heretical sect known as Monophysites. These sectaries, whose beliefs were somewhat closer to the monotheism of the conquerors, found it all the easier to become Moslems. The Jews, for the most part clinging more stubbornly to their religion, in time became a more conspicuous minority.

The question has often been argued as to whether the Jewish people, in the course of its long odyssey, fared worse at the hands of the Christians or Moslems. This has become a comparison all the more difficult to make without taking into account the lines presently drawn against the State of Israel by the entire Moslem world. A holy war instituted in our own day against the house of Israel, while providing ample food for thought, should not permit us to distort our estimate of earlier relationships.

During the greater extent of the Christian-Moslem symbiosis, the treatment meted out to "the people of the book" was generally less harsh among the followers of the Prophet. While the poet Judah Halevy, who lived in the eleventh century (1085-1140), once declared that both Christians and Moslems were essentially alike in their persecuting zeal, he did not live to witness the full malignancy of the Church during the thirteenth, fourteenth, and fifteenth centuries. By both Christians and Moslems, Jews were held in varying degrees of disfavour, as having been at one time a nation selected by God, and later proven a disappointment to Him, for having rejected first one saviour and then another. Mohammed likewise had his troubles with them, to be sure. But only in the eyes of the Christians were they guilty of the unimaginable crime of "deicide."

Among the Moslems, there was never an inquisition;

and no judicial horrors such as those instigated by the clergy in eighteenth century Poland. Life for the mediaeval Jews under Islam was easier for yet another reason. Within the Moslem world, political authority was less fractured. It contained nothing that corresponded to the ecclesiastical hierarchy, which in Christian lands enjoyed a great deal of legislative sovereignty. There were thus no church councils, such as those of France, Spain, Germany, and Poland, whose decretals affecting Jews had the force of law. Also, there were few, if any, autonomous "free cities" whose governing councils would have been consistently hostile. Throughout the Moslem dominions, the key figure was the appointed governor, upon whose personal disposition much depended. This powerful individual, far more easily than a corporate body, could more often than not be appeased and manipulated by means of appropriate offerings.

I would be accused of being incomplete were I to omit some reference to the amicable relationships between the majority of the Roman Pontiffs and the Jews of their city, a relationship that helped to some extent in stabilizing the positions of many other European communities. Without a measure of restraint upon the fanaticism of his flock emanating from the Holy Father, their position would have been unbearable in the last degree. The Popes, who were free enough in instigating crusades against Arabs and Turks, and even against Christian dissidents, were at no time responsible for urging attacks upon the defenceless Jews. Pope Urban II, who by his eloquence at Clermont initiated the First Crusade, certainly did not instigate the Rhineland massacres. Of the repeated enormities of the later Crusaders, the Popes were entirely blameless. Also, beginning with Pope Calixtus II (1119-1124) if not before, there went forth a series of bulls threatening Christians with excommunication if they attempted to convert Jews by force, rob them of their possessions, attack them during their devotions, desecrate their cemeteries, or carry off their dead for ransom. By them likewise, the infamous charge of ritual murder was repeatedly condemned.

The easygoing relationship of the pontiffs with the Jews residing under their shadow was in part an outcome of their shared insecurity. The ecclesiastical state, which covered an area between the Tyrrhenian sea and the Adriatic, was even in mediaeval times an anomaly amid the secular powers of the fragmented peninsula. Constantly assailed, its existence was regularly imperilled by neighbours to the north and south of it, for whom religion and politics did not go hand in hand. Hence as a worldly power, the Holy Father had frequently to live and to act in the spirit of Italian power politics, being obliged to undergo the same dark experiences as the upstart adventurers of Milan, Genoa, Florence, Siena, and Naples. Additionally, even within his own dominions, he was compelled to deal with local despots, nominally his vicars, such as the Malatesta, Baglione, and Montefeltri, who from time to time created much disturbance. As a temporal ruler, the Pope was also at the mercy of the Roman nobility. Supreme in the countries beyond the Alps, in his own seat of authority he was habitually defied by the great families of the Colonna, Orsini, Savelli, Anguillera. By these nobles and their riotous followers, the city's ancient monuments were converted into fortified strongholds of which on one occasion there were as many as one hundred and forty. The Eternal City itself was throughout the entire Middle Ages in a condition of endless pandemonium, its streets filled with affrays and deeds of rapine of its turbulent factions, both popular and noble. Rome's populace was distinguished for ignorance, bloodthirstiness, and quarrelsomeness.

That the capital city of the Christian world failed to achieve the status of a commercial centre had also much bearing on the perennial insecurity of the Holy See. Rome, at the time of the Empire, had been a city that imported much and consumed much: but exported little in return. Nor was Rome the natural centre of gravity of the Roman Empire, as the English historian Trevor-Roper has well pointed out.[6] By the third century of the Christian era, it was no longer the empire's capital city. Neither in imperial nor in later papal times was Rome a centre of much importance economically. On the safety of the Jews living in that city, this fact had a significant bearing, as I shall now explain.

The capital city of Christendom, not having the rank of a financial and trading metropolis, the Pontiff, unlike the rulers of England, France, Spain, Austria, and Turkey, saw no great financiers living close at hand and under his wing. Hence, though he could not dispense with their services, he did not at any time hold them in his power. On the contrary, the money barons of Siena, Florence, Venice and Augsburg habitually had him in their power.

Full security was the price exacted of the Holy Father by these magnates to cover whatever credit they condescended to allow him. Commonly required of him was the delivery of the Church's most precious ornaments and most prized relics. By way of added security, Pope Leo X gave to the brothers Bini, the Florentine bankers, the right to sell to the highest bidder certain offices in the Curia. He likewise turned over to them Paul II's jewelled mitre and the tiara of Julius II, along with sacred pontifical vessels. But for the Pope to rid himself of creditors that had become embarrassing to him in the manner of a secular prince was out of the question. No pope was ever in a position of declaring himself bankrupt to outwit his creditors, as did King Edward III of England in the case of the Bardi and Peruzzi of Florence, whose ruin he brought about. Between the Pope and his bankers, the shoe was always on the other foot.

The Pontiff, like any secular ruler, had his money problems. His revenues were princely enough, consisting largely of annates and Peter's Pence payable by both clergy and laity; and which flowed to him from the farthest outposts of Latin Christianity. However, for their collection and transmission to Rome, he was completely dependent on the services of a number of noted mercantile establishments, whose headquarters were successively in Siena, Florence, Genoa, Venice, and Augsburg; with their branches and agencies distributed throughout Europe's principal cities.

Due to the temptation to short-circuit the funds due their principal client, these Papal "campsores" were frequently in default. Century after century was punctuated by the downfall of the financial heavyweights of the Italian cities, with the Holy See the principal victim in each instance. Thus, stricken by a wave of bankruptcies were the Buonsignore of Siena in 1298 followed two years later by the Ricciardi of Lucca. Throughout the Middle Ages, house after house came crashing down, involving the Holy Father in each instance as the main creditor; and invariably leaving him without recourse and without even the possibility of inquiry into the misconduct of his collection agents. A measure of his complete helplessness was the fact that not one among the many defaulters were banking houses originating in Rome itself. Their main scene of operations, and certainly their persons, were well beyond the reach of their outraged and angry patron. It is no cause for wonder accordingly that the Pontiff would find it comfortable to deal with a number of Jews situated in Rome itself, whose individual means were not great, but with whom he was able to do business with far more authority.

Jews living in Rome or even Venice or Florence were certainly no rivals to Christian bankers in the carrying out of large monetary transactions with the princes of Europe. But for the Holy See itself they were a source of revenue that nothing could defeat. For a period of about five centuries, that is to say down to the time of the counter-Reformation, they were permitted to operate under papal license as a privileged class of pawnbrokers, catering to the necessities of the humbler elements of the Italian population.[7]

Rome's Jewish population was in some respects well integrated with its Christian neighbours; more so, in fact, than any of the other European communities. "There were many Jews in Rome at the time of the second Temple. They had so thoroughly adopted the language and civilization prevailing in Italy that even on their tombs they used not Hebrew, but Latin and Greek inscriptions."[8]

This unique community was in all likelihood made up of the descendants of liberated slaves, whose ancestors were carried to the Republic along with the conquered inhabitants of many cities in Greece and Asia Minor. A notable date marking its inception could have been the year 146 B.C. when the city of Corinth was reduced to ashes by Metellus. Corinth was at the time next to Alexandria the largest port of the eastern Mediterranean, and is known to have contained a considerable Jewish population. Alone among the captives of many nations exposed for sale in the Roman forum, Jewish prisoners were promptly and repeatedly redeemed by their brethren, their liberators in all probability visiting merchants from Alexandria. Significantly, the organized community thus set up constituted the only foreign intrusion of its kind inside the imperial city. There were in imperial Rome a large enough number of foreign residents but they were not organized into Greek or Gallic or Syrian communities as such. Most ancient of all the communities of Europe, the Roman Jews of a later period argued that they themselves were not participants in the guilt of the Crucifixion inasmuch as their forebears were at the time of the tragedy living in Italy and not in Palestine.

THE TURKS

The fifteenth century, which has been termed the waning of the Middle Ages, as well as the century of the Renaissance, was one of exceptional peril for the Jews of the entire diaspora. But from further calamities that might have befallen them, not only in Europe but in Asia as well, they were saved thanks to the victorious march of the Turks, who soon cast their mantle over vast stretches of Christian territory.

The first inroad of the Ottoman Turks into Christian Europe began somewhat less than a century before their capture of Constantinople in 1453. They at first crept around this well-fortified metropolis, conquering the entire Balkan peninsula, thereby leaving their ultimate objective effectively isolated from all possibility of aid. The Turkish intrusion into Eastern Europe followed in a reverse direction the march towards Constantinople along the Danube River valley originally undertaken during the first, second, and third crusades.

Unlike the Mongols of an earlier century, the Ottoman Turks were far from being invincible warriors. From the very beginning of their onset, they suffered as many defeats at the hands of their Christian enemies as they scored victories. Nor were the Christian nations altogether incapable of being roused to a united effort against the invaders. But as it happened, the two strongest military nations of Europe, the English and the French, were engaged in a century of warfare one against the other, and were thus in no position to respond to appeals for a crusade such as those issued by Popes Pius II and Calixtus III. Only the Germans, who were themselves partly diverted by a long war against the heretical Hussites (1416-1434), were in some position to engage the intruders, but they were by themselves too weak to drive them away, even though they did score a number of victories.[9]

With the reign of Murad II (1421-51), there began the friendly liaison between Jews and Turks that was to last until the waning of Turkish power some two centuries later. Especially were refugees from the Iberian peninsula welcomed before and after the apocalyptic year 1492. By reason of their contacts with friends, relations, and commercial representatives, they proved to be a unique source of information about the sayings of princes, the movements of armies, and the complexities of international intrigues. Seaborne attacks upon the Spanish coasts undertaken by Moslem allies of the Turks were aided by intelligence supplied by Jews still remaining within the country. Of no less importance were the skills supplied by these refugees, of which the nomadic sons of the desert were still in short supply. Under their auspices gunpowder was for the first time manufactured within the cities of the Porte.

Prior to the arrival of the Jews, the Turks had been dependent for their war material on Europeans, and more especially, it would seem, on the French. In 1453, the year in which Constantinople fell, Jacques Coeur, the richest man in France—one to whom incidentally, the French king was heavily indebted—was stripped of all his possessions and cast into a dungeon "because he had wickedly sent armour and arms, and caused them to be presented to the Sultan, the enemy of the Christian faith and of the King." This Jacques Coeur, it is worth mentioning, was the same financier who had previously come to the assistance of Joan of Arc, and who had later supplied his countrymen with the canon which had made it possible for them to drive the English back across the channel.

The capture of Constantinople by the Turks in 1453, one of the terminal episodes of the mediaeval period, was in Jewish history likewise one of vast significance. A portent of disaster to Europe, it was glad tidings to the whole of Jewry. Abandoned by much of its Christian population, the eastern metropolis immediately became a haven for exiles from Spain as well as from other areas of Christian Europe, as were other major cities such as Adrianople, Salonika, Belgrade, and Brusa. Constantinople, located at the crossing between two continents, was likewise the doorway to the Black Sea with its confluence of trade routes reaching towards India, Russia, the interior of Asia, and the Persian Gulf. Following their victory, the Turks quickly possessed themselves of the entire shoreline of the inland sea, where for a long time Venetian and Genoese traders had been entrenched in the enjoyment of privileges accorded to them by Byzantine rulers. These were quickly expelled, with their monopoly divided between Jews and Greeks.[10]

The Ottoman Empire by the end of the fifteenth century took in the whole of southeastern Europe, including the Balkans, a portion of Hungary, and what is now Rumania, as well as the whole of western Asia. In all these territories, the Jews were made welcome. Without the refuge afforded them inside the newly annexed territories of the Turkish empire, it is certain that well over half a million Jewish refugees from Spain and Portugal and Germany would either have perished or been compelled to go over en masse to Christianity and Islam.

By also turning their assault upon the Arabs, the Turks did much to alleviate the distress of the Oriental Jews as well. Arab rule over the Jews of Mesopotamia was such as to result in their decline from their proud position as the cultural and economic centre of world Jewry. It was invariably discriminatory, capricious, and depended largely on the disposition of each ruler. Much of this insecurity was ended once the Turks took over. The Turks like the Arabs were Moslems. But here the affinity between them ended. The Turks revered the Arab prophet but they had a low opinion of the nation from which he sprung. In this respect their attitude resembled somewhat that of the Christians, who worshipped a Jew, but hated his brethren. The Turks, as devout Moslems, were certainly not free from the fanaticism inherent in that religion. Nevertheless to them the mental discomfort which the prophet had had to endure on account of the impenitent Jews was less a subject for vivid recollection than to the prophet's own kinsfolk and descendants.

Through their conquest of Egypt in 1517, the Turks also made themselves masters of Palestine. It is my suggestion that their four hundred years rule be viewed as preparatory to the creation of the State of Israel, and as a constructive stage in that direction.

The rule of the Arabs which preceded that of the Turks offered very little encouragement to a Jewish return to their ancient homeland. Under the Egyptian Mamelukes, Jerusalem's status as one of the holy cities of Islam became greatly accented, so that within it madrassas and hospices for pilgrims were multiplied, while at the same time, theologians abounded, all crying out for the expulsion or suppression of unbelievers. Persecution of both Jews and Christians at intermittent times was both legal and violent.[11] In the year 1474, the only remaining synagogue in the city was demolished on orders of the Cadi. Here as elsewhere the coming of the Turks was a great relief.

By the Turks, Jerusalem's sacredness was hardly insisted upon; while by none of the Moslems was the country outside the city ever considered as being holy. Hence, during the remaining period of Turkish greatness, and while its administration was still in some condition to inspire respect, no obstacles were placed in the way of Jewish return.

Not a few of the refugees from Spain, finding the cities of the Porte overcrowded, decided to go on to the land of their ancestors. Others came from Egypt and Iraq, countries whose economies had been undermined by blockades instituted by the Portuguese in both the Red Sea and the Persian Gulf, as well as by the opening of the direct sea route to Europe. A certain number came from Italy, where under the pressure from the Spaniards their number had been reduced by two-thirds. From the Papal dominions alone, they were expelled from one hundred localities by the bigoted Pope Pius V (1566-1572). These latter had only to cross from Ancona to the port of Durazzo on the eastern side of the Adriatic in order to find themselves inside Turkish territory, whence a well-travelled highway took them to Constantinople. And finally, Jews of Poland and elsewhere in eastern Europe, desiring to travel to the Holy land, or to forward money there, were now able with comparative safety to make use of the overland passage, inasmuch as from Belgrade to Jerusalem the entire distance was under a single sovereignty. During the centuries that were to follow, and despite much insecurity and lawlessness, the size of the Jewish return to the land of Israel continued to grow. It was under the Turkish regime, be it remembered, that in Jerusalem itself Jews came to be more numerous than any other ethnic group.

Having maintained that the conflict of Christianity and Islam was on critical occasions instrumental in preserving the Jewish identity, my final contention is that this same rivalry helped in a remote way towards bringing into being the restored state of Israel.

That Jerusalem, along with a few other cities of the

neighbouring countryside, was able to retain some measure of economic attractiveness was due largely to the fact that by the Christian world these places were not forgotten as having been the scene where their Saviour had his earthly existence, and whence he had been removed. Not a century went by that did not witness a pouring into the Holy Land of streams of money from Christian Europe for the erection and maintenance of churches, convents, schools, hospitals, hospices for the reception of pilgrims, along with permanent dwelling places. The circulation of such funds, never ceasing, enabled the country at large to enjoy at least a low level of economic viability.

The tangible interest thus shown in the ancestral land of the Jewish people by the entire Christian world was not without effect on the secular side of things. It made it possible for a modest number of merchants and handworkers to maintain themselves, among whom were Jews in appreciable numbers. Hence the paradox arose that, while in the countries of Europe it was often the Church that was responsible for the Jews being driven forth, in the Holy Land, to the contrary, it was the Church that helped make it possible for them to come and to live.

The extension into that ancient land of monastic Christendom did not fail to give some economic viability during the barren centuries. It is none the less a tenable thought that had the Christian settlers been permitted by the Moslems to fix a firm grip upon the country, all Jewish hopes for an eventual restoration would have been frustrated. No room would have been left for a massive Jewish immigration, much less for the renewal of Jewish sovereignty. Under the Byzantine era and prior to the Moslem conquest, this all but happened. Again, when at a later period the Crusaders succeeded in setting up a French-speaking kingdom which endured for about ninety years, had they been permitted to consolidate their position, it is altogether probable that in the course of a century or two the land would have become as thoroughly Christian as France itself, or Spain, or Italy. It would have been filled up with settlers from these countries, its wastes would have been reclaimed, and its cities rebuilt—but not by Jews. There is nothing that the Jews have accomplished in recent decades in restoring the country to fruitfulness that the enterprising and pioneering spirit of the west European nations could not have done equally well.

It was the reaction of Turks and Arabs—mainly the former—to the aggressiveness of the Christians that in the end made possible a large scale Jewish entry into a country that remained largely unoccupied. By not permitting the Christians to take root and to dominate the country, the Moslems, in effect, preserved its status quo, which was that of a semi-derelict territory in a condition of suspended animation. Had there been left no such vacuum, a Zionist movement would have been inconceivable; there could have followed no Jewish mass immigration, with all hope for a redeemed Jewish nation on its own soil abandoned forever.

Bringing the discussion closer to our own time, it should be acknowledged that it was with the support of innumerable Christians of all denominations that the Zionist movement was able to attain its objective. During the past century and even before, the prophecies of the return of the Jewish people to Zion which adorn the Old Testament have found a sympathetic echo among a vast number of them—a response, be it noted, nowhere to be found among any of their Moslem contemporaries.

Not to be overlooked as well was the protection given by Christian governments in the course of the nineteenth century to the growing Jewish population of the country. From the declining Turkish regime there was wrested the so-called capitulations, by virtue of which the consular representatives of several Christian nations were enabled to exercise judicial authority. Through the special powers thus conferred upon them, these officials from overseas were able to give shelter to many Jews and to save their communities from the mercies of predatory local governors. It has been claimed rightly that the creation, within the Holy Land, of extraterritorial rights in favour of the Christian powers marked the end of its mediaeval period.[12]

THE REFORMATION

To the surviving Jews of Europe, the religious changes that were unleashed over the continent during the sixteenth century might have seemed altogether extraneous and of little moment. This was all the more so since by that time they had become concentrated in areas such as Italy and Poland where conditions did not favour the efforts against Rome on the part of reformers and prophets. All this notwithstanding, the cosmic effects of the Protestant Reformation upon the destinies of the Jews were really very great, and merit some consideration.

Unlike the earlier revolt against Rome by the Bohemian Hussites, the movement inaugurated by Luther depended greatly on princely and aristocratic support. It was perhaps not altogether coincidental that it met with its most favourable response in those parts of Germany where Jews were entirely absent, either as a result of massacre or deportation. Territorial lords such as the Elector of Saxony, the Margrave of Brandenburg-Ansbach, the Duke of Brunswick, and the Duke of Wurttemberg, who quickly aligned themselves on the side of Luther, had for some time been in financial difficulties resulting from the need of maintaining standing armies and expanded bureaucracies in a time of rising prices. Increased taxation was the apparent answer.

However, the absence of Jews who might have been a superb source of quick revenue caused these evangelical princes to be more than ever dependent on the authorization of their Estates, that is to say, the town burghers and the landed nobility. Hence by espousing the Reformation, it became possible for them to lay hands on the rich possessions of the ecclesiastical orders.

At the very outset, it could be declared of the Protestant Reformation that as a world remade it helped pioneer events that enabled the Jews of Europe to recover from the depths of affliction and eventually to rekindle their creative energies. Quite obviously, tending to divert attention from them were the rivalries and enmities between Catholics and Protestants. Likewise was the suppression of the monastic orders of immediate benefit to them. Many of the troubles of the preceding century had been instigated by such wandering friars as John of Capistrano, and Vincent Ferrer. As those who denied Christ, Jews continued to incur the contempt of Protestants and Catholics alike. None the less, the darkness of the Middle Ages which had insured a favourable reception of every calumny against them was to some extent lifted, even in the violent society of the sixteenth century. Not any longer were they made subject to massacre by reason of having insulted the cross, or stabbed holy wafers, or poisoned wells, or made use of Christian blood. Even in those countries that remained Catholic—with the notable exception of Poland—these inventions of fanaticism were soon to go out of fashion. And, finally, the translation of the Scriptures and their widened readership soon permitted a display of some amity towards a people who were after all descended from the patriarchs and the prophets.

In England, Holland, and the Calvinist areas of southern France, it became safe for refugees fleeing from the Iberian peninsula to announce their return to Judaism.

The appearance of a nuclear community inside Holland was all the more epochal inasmuch as throughout the Low Countries all traces of Jewry had long ago disappeared. In the cities of Flanders, they had all been killed back in 1349-1350, during the time of the Black Death. In 1370, in consequence of an accusation of having done violence to a consecrated host, all the Jews of Brabant had been burnt alive. But only in the state of Holland turned Protestant were Jews permitted to settle and to flourish. In the rest of the Low Countries, they were not permitted to reside prior to the late eighteenth century.

Not to be divorced from the benefits accruing to them from the Reformation were the salutary effects flowing from the discoveries of the New World. These latter gains, however, were to present themselves more slowly. While the discovery of fresh continents opened up new vistas of wealth from which they could not be excluded, the dawn so heralded was one out of which full daylight was slow in coming. In both North and South America, no professing Jew was permitted to set foot in any part dominated by the Catholic powers. Their settlement overseas did not commence until a century and a half had elapsed after the voyage of Columbus; and then only in regions ruled over by Holland and England, both Protestant nations.

Through a complex chain of causation, world Jewry was to benefit from a combination of highly charged episodes born of the Reformation and the discovery of America. In the year 1520, the Spanish king Carlos I made the disastrous blunder of getting himself elected Holy Roman Emperor, becoming better known as the Emperor Charles V. It would have surprised him greatly had some soothsayer come forward to inform him that he was doing his share in setting in motion a train of circumstances that would in the long run make possible the return of the Jews to Western Europe, and the overseas territories.

In the course of this monarch's reign of thirty-five years, he was involved in wars with France no less than on five separate occasions. He had his troubles of course with the Turks on the eastern frontier of his empire, as well as the Schmalkald League of Protestant Princes. The cost of all these wars, along with sundry rebellions that he was called upon to suppress, had to be paid for out of the gold that flowed into Spain from the Indies, and as rapidly flowed out again.

Bereft of much of its manufactures in consequence of the recent expulsion of a large number of Jewish craftsmen and mechanics, Spain had to turn elsewhere for the repertory of her warmaking capacity. Small wonder that all preferential purchases were made in Germany, tied as that country was to Spain by a common allegiance to the House of Habsburg. Germany, where much of the fighting was going on, happened to be the most highly industrialized country in Europe, as well as the largest producer of war materials. Thus while Nuremberg was famous for its printing presses and pocket watches, musical instruments, cutlery and grinding machines, it was so likewise for its pikes, spears, helmets and gauntlets. The best muskets were made in Augsburg. Also, turned out by skilled and industrious craftsmen of Ulm, Esslingen, Erfurt, Lunefeld, and Passau were such appurtenances of Spanish domination as instruments of torture for the dungeons of the Inquisition, axes for the purposes of decapitation, pulleys for the gallows, compasses and sextants for ships going to the Indies, and chains for the African slave trade.

To a greater or lesser extent, the whole of Europe participated in the shower of the precious metals dug out of the ground in Mexico and Peru, and then funneled through Spain. Of the new monetary resources flowing into France, for example, much of it was brought in surreptitiously by exiles from Spain who were permitted to entrench themselves in the border provinces. Fleeing the Inquisition, they compensated themselves for fixed assets that they were obliged to abandon by not paying off their creditors. The amounts of ready money that they were enabled to carry away on their persons in this way was not inconsiderable. It was small, nevertheless, by comparison with what passed openly and legally into Germany through the medium of the accredited Fuggers, Hochstetters, Walsers, Tuchers, and Grimaldi. Germany, by the late sixteenth century, was a land with a superabundance of currency, not of paper, to be sure, but of metal.

An unceasing rise in the cost of living which accompanied this steady influx of Spanish-American gold and silver made for a new proliferation of starving people. Coupled with the turmoil engendered by the doctrinal hatreds of the Age of the Reformation was the social misery of the population, a misery attributable mainly to the violent dislocation of price levels. Diverted into religious and millenial channels were pressures that were in part economic and social in origin. Within this whirlpool of a crumbling society, working men, whose wages were immutably fixed by custom, rioted in the cities; while in the countrysides were the sporadic uprisings of peasants whose taxes had been elevated to unendurable levels. In a Europe, wasted by fire and sword, the dread of universal dissolution was in the air. Convinced that the end of the world was in sight, the dying Pope Clement VII instructed Michelangelo to depict on the upper wall of the Sistine Chapel the apocalypse of the Last Judgment.

Culminating a long period of weakness and decline inside Germany, the Thirty Years War (1618-1648) was a fearsome eruption brought on by a combination of religious, political, and social motives. As the struggle drew to its close, Germany was all but denuded of her previously swelled liquid capital. Emblematic of this downfall was the

317

eclipse of the established financial oligarchies, whose own affiliates were in turn the victims of the multiple disorders. To sum up, this prolonged and sanguinary contest entailed the extinction of most of the nation's armament ateliers, resulting in a dependence on foreigners by all the combatants for muskets, canon, and gunpowder. "The Thirty Years War not only destroyed craftsmanship, capital and initiative, but sealed up the Germans within an economic tomb . . . At last, they had so little manufacture left that as a bitter jester said, their principal export was sand."[13]

While Europe, in the sixteenth and seventeenth centuries, and Central Europe more especially, was wearing itself out in protracted warfare, first during the age of the Emperor Charles V, and later in the Thirty Years War, the way was being cleared for the return of the Jews first to Germany, and by way of Germany, to France, England, and finally to the oversea extensions of western Europe. Poland, during this period, where they had long been concentrated, and to some degree locked in, remained a relatively quiet country, even though among the several classes of its population there seethed an abounding hatred. For the merchants of Poland, both Jews and Christians, there was to be had a goodly amount of soldierly booty and at low prices. Also in return for supplies to the warring factions, they were the recipients of much of the gold and silver of which Germany was denuded. The termination towards the middle of the seventeenth century of the exhaustive struggle saw Germany divided even more than before, into a host of little states, all of them controlled by authoritarian regimes, and all desperately short of money.

The institution of "Hof Jude," under which during the seventeenth and eighteenth centuries every German princeling, small or large, had at his court a Jewish advisor in charge of his finances, was an outcome of this advantage

318

gained by the uninvolved Jews coming mainly from Poland. These were men of no great financial resources, but sufficient for the petty affairs of Germany's three hundred principalities. What the Court Jew lacked in monetary resources, he was generally able to make up for in shrewdness, knowledge of the world and versatility. He was at the same time court treasurer and a caterer of luxury items, such as furs, jewels, and pictures to his royal master and his family.

Among his multifarious duties, the court treasurer had to be a purveyor of war supplies as well. For such trafficking were required talents of the highest order. The trade in armaments was a more challenging business than, for example, the dealing in rosary beads. Especially difficult and ticklish was the procurement of gunpowder. There were only a limited number of European cities where it was being made; and it was for a very long time a chemical process that only a few were able to master. Those who knew how to make it were not necessarily willing to sell to all comers. Nor was secrecy connected with it easily breached in all instances.

The post of royal treasurer, for which the Jews of Spain had shown aptitude in earlier centuries, was a distinguished one, but not devoid of peril and much anguish to the holder of the office. It required much suppleness in an age when responsible budgeting was even less known than it is nowadays, when revenues were uncertain, and when no distinction was made between the personal extravagances of the sovereign and the needs of the impersonal state. Embarrassing moments that were tests of a good treasurer's nimbleness often came thick and fast. His princely master might be fond of taking to the road; and, as was often the case, absent-mindedly overlook the payment of small bills incurred while getting around. The emperor Maximilian I of Germany once had himself thrown into jail by the heart-less townspeople of Bruges through not having enough cash in his wallet to pay for his previous night's lodgings.

Finally, for the aspirant to royal favour, Jew, Christian, or Moslem, the adage held good that "He who sups with the devil must have a long spoon." Only in rare instances was a rich man, brought to his ruler's attention, richer at the end of the acquaintanceship than at its beginning. If he was not to be soon to run out of funds in servicing his royal patron, he had to become a tax collector. As such, he was almost certain to incur the hatred of the ratepayers. The vicious system of farming out the public revenues for private gain never failed in this respect. Hence, as a convenient scapegoat, whenever things went awry, his life expectancy was not of the highest. The wise and cynical Calif Haroun-al-Raschid had once remarked that the man was happy whom he did not know and who did not know him.

The part played by these "favourites" during what is known as the Baroque period, both in the recovery of Germany and the reintegration of the Jews, ought not to be minimized. Their wealth helped succor the exhausted treasuries of the many territorial potentates which a nation broken by its numberless woes could not otherwise have managed to bring about. Also, by special arrangement, each of these men of financial muscle was empowered to bring with him out of Poland a retinue of "Shutz-Juden," or "protected" Jews consisting of at least ten other adult males with their dependents, for the maintaining of a religious quorum and otherwise providing for the ritual needs of the magnate and his own family, such as a rabbi, a ritual slaugh-terer, a circumciser, and a synagogue beadle. Hence the debut of the "Hof-Jude" by way of the money route coin-cided with the founding in various parts of Germany of a considerable number of small communities, some of them susceptible of becoming larger in the course of time. Not

320

least of all, from this period dates the infiltration of wealthier Jews into the French border cities of Metz and Strassburg, and even into the forbidden city of Paris.

The classes of Court Jew, in conjunction with other select individuals whose wealth and standing were such as to give them access to court circles, were otherwise in a position to further the interests of their co-religionists living in a hostile world. These intercessors, or "Shtadlanim" as they came to be called, were actually of no particular century, but were to be found in all the generations of Jewish exile and dispersion. They epitomized a non-democratic and highly expeditious method for acting in an emergency and getting things done. Here to be evoked is an instance—perhaps unprecedented—where men of wealth and influence acting in concert were able to muster the full weight of international sympathy on behalf of a beleaguered community threatened with dissolution.

The accession to the throne of Austria of the Empress Maria Theresa precipitated the dynastic conflict known as the War of the Austrian Succession (1744-1748) which ended in the loss to Prussia of the rich province of Silesia. A convenient scapegoat for this disaster were the Jews of Bohemia and Moravia, where most of the fighting had taken place. Suspicion of disloyalty raised against them provided a pretext not only for the Austrian soldiery to perpetrate outrages upon them, but for the Empress to issue a decree of expulsion against the entire community of Prague, following in the steps of her grandfather Leopold I towards the community of Vienna in 1670. To the protests of her own councillors, who urged upon her the economic disaster that would result, and the ruin that it could bring to Christians who were in business relationships with the threatened Jews, the good lady at first replied: "Yes, it is true that the Jews are honest, but we have our objections and do not want them in our realm." The crisis called forth the concerted efforts of prominent and wealthy Jews living in the major communities of London, Amsterdam, Vienna, and Venice, who were able to enlist the support of the governments of both Britain and Holland. Where economic considerations alone would have been unavailing, political pressures achieved the annulment of the hostile decree.

This is a convenient place for mentioning yet another outcome of the post-Reformation period that tended towards Jewish emancipation. The undermining of the monopolistic guilds, like that of military feudalism, was not unconnected with the new military technology of the fifteenth century. The invention of gunpowder which altered the map of Europe was not a pivotal factor in Jewish survival; but a contributory one nevertheless. There were in Germany in the late mediaeval period about 150 "free cities," all dedicated to commercial privilege and all bristling with hostility to Jews. Their impregnable walls, like the castles of the feudal baronage, were in the course of a few decades battered down by the canon of the absolutist princes in their vicinity, who thus paradoxically helped usher in the age of free enterprise, the indispensable condition of Jewish commercialism.

The absorption of these self-centered communes into the system of despotic states heralded an end to the baleful supervision of the coercive guilds. Soon free to disregard all fixing of prices, their Jewish competitors were not slow in undermining their authority, contributing thereby to their final disintegration.

Not to go unmentioned, is the exceptional role of Amsterdam in helping to bring about the return of the people of Israel to the non-Slavonic part of Europe. In the Middle Ages, Holland was a small and unattractive expanse of lowland, sand, silt, and water, dotted with only a few fishing villages. Amsterdam, in the fourteenth century was

322

no more than an insignificant commune, while by 1650 it had become the chief commercial port of Europe, if not of the entire world. Its rise to trading eminence, marked by dominance of the North Sea and Baltic coastal trade, was made possible in the beginning by the many blows struck at the monolithic Hanseatic League by powerful neighbours and rivals. Also, the end of Spanish domination of the seas following the defeat of the Armada in 1588 announced Amsterdam's supplanting of Lisbon as the main emporium of the oversea trade in spices and other products. Unhindered, the Dutch were now able to send their ships to the Cape of Good Hope and beyond. Coincidentally the end of Spanish sea power also witnessed the founding of the Amsterdam Jewish community. No longer compelled to operate out of Lisbon, Jewish merchants and ship-owners now found it to their advantage to abandon a city where they were under continual threat by the Inquisition; and from then on carry on their trade in oversea products from a city where they could avow their religion in safety.

The founding of this community by Portuguese Marannos, along with the selective admission into Germany, from Poland, of the more affluent "Juden" marked the restoration of Jewish life in western Europe. With the trade relationships of these wealthy magnates radiating in many directions, there arose in the course of time a fresh network of Jewish mercantile and financial houses in Hamburg, Vienna, Berlin, Frankfort-am-Main, Metz, Strassburg, and Leghorn. The singular community of Amsterdam can be justly referred to as the parent and grandparent of the later settlements of Jews in London, Hamburg, Curacao, and New York. These communities, all founded by men of wealth, paved the way for their brethren in large numbers who were anything but wealthy.

It was following the reconstruction of Europe in the wake of the Napoleonic wars that the Jewish population of the Western World began to make strong headway. Prior to the nineteenth century, famous and historic Jewish communities such as Venice, Amsterdam, London, Vienna, Hamburg, Paris, Berlin, New York, and Warsaw rarely numbered more than two or three thousand souls. The fact should not be overlooked that, beginning with the patriarchs, they were until quite recent times a Middle Eastern people, even though no longer concentrated within that particular segment known as Palestine. The swing of the Jewish scene towards the West and the shifting of the centre of gravity of both their population and their material resources westward could be regarded as a vital step towards insuring their survival. It was the necessary step tending to their final restoration in Zion. It was only in Western Europe and places beyond the seas, such as North America and South Africa, that a suitable soil existed for the planting of a Zionist movement. Under conditions surrounding Jewish life inside Moslem countries, or even in the Slavic lands, a reaffirmation of this kind would have been unrealizable.

EPILOGUE

Following the reconstitution of the state of Israel, the status of the Jews among the nations underwent a transformation. Within Christian communities, there resulted a diminution of hostility, both secular and religious. Among Moslems, to the contrary, their situation quickly became intolerable. Inside the changeless civilization of Islam there was heard once again the cry of the Holy War, this time directed at the risen state of the Jews.

Among Christian nations of the late twentieth century there have become visible moods of self-doubt, hesitancy, and defeatism previously unknown in any of their histories. We take note of church establishments of Western Europe and North America siding with the enemies of their faith in Africa, urging on their governments to turn against their own coreligionists, and observing a discreet silence at the agony of their brethren in Lebanon.

Towards the Jewish state, in its unequal struggle with the massed array of Moslem, Communist, and third-world nations vowed to its destruction, the attitude of virtually all the Christian powers could be summed up as one of "even-handedness," a term definable as each of the hands not knowing what the other is doing—or not doing. Following

325

on the heels of the Six Day War of 1967, in which they piously remained uninvolved, they have been highly critical of Israel's retention of several insignificant parcels of land, previously ruled over by Arab dictators, and by them lost in a war which they alone had provoked. Their conception of "a just and lasting peace in the Middle East" is one of Israel making all the concessions, satisfying each and every one of its adversaries, and dismantling its natural defensive borders. Then, hopefully, by the grace of its erstwhile antagonists, coupled with the "guarantees" of its uncertain wellwishers, a truncated and diminished ghetto state will somehow manage to "survive".

NOTES

Notes to Chapter 1

[1]E. H. Carr, "What is History?" Penguin, p. 55.

[2]Solomon Grayzel, "A History of the Jews," Jewish Publication Society of America, Philadelphia.

[3]See in this connection articles in Studia Semitica, Cambridge University Press, 1971. Articles "Anti-Christian Polemics in Mediaeval Bible Commentaries," also "Judische Antworte."

[4]Andre et Renée Neher, "Histoire Biblique du Peuple d'Israel," Adrien-Maissoneuve, Paris, 1962.

[5]History of the Jews, p. 236.

[6]Sura of the Cow, Verse 96.

[7]As to this generalization there could be some dispute.

[8]Werner Sombart, "The Jews and Modern Capitalism," Leipzig, 1911, p. 261.

Notes to Chapter 2

[1]At one time, the two preceding books of Samuel are believed likewise to have been included under "Kings." Grant & Rowley, "Dictionary of the Bible," p. 255.

[2]"Histoire de la Civilisation d'Israel," Payot, Paris, 1953.

[3]Abba Hillel Silver, "Moses and the Original Torah," Macmillan, New York, 1961, p. 78.

[4]"Zemach David" was the first history of the world attempted by any Jewish writer. First printed in 1592, it was reprinted several times.

[5]W. F. Albright, "De l'Age de la Pierre à la Chrétienté," p. 14.

[6]31:26.

[7]Deuteronomy 20:19.

[8]Genesis 36:31.

[9]Numbers 33: 1, 2.

[10]Exodus 34:28.

[11]Exodus 25:16.

[12]II Kings 11:12.

[13]I Kings 8:9.

[14]Deut. 28:69.

[15]Deut. 31:2.

[16]Deut. 27:2.

[17]Joshua 8:32.

[18]J. H. Hertz, "The Pentateuch and Haftorahs," Soncino Press, London, p. 862.

[19]P. 108.

[20]Judges 5:14.

[21]I Samuel 11:14.

[22]2 Kings 10:1.

[23]Isaiah 29:11.

[24]See for example Berthelot, p. 110.

[25]Grote, "History of Greece," vol. 2, p. 143, Peter Fenelon, Collier.

[26]Isaiah, 8:16.

[27]"The New Bible Dictionary," editor J. D. Douglas, p. 957.

[28]See in this connection article by J. Philip Hyatt, "The Writing of an Old Testament Book" in "The Biblical Archaeological Reader," Doubleday, Anchor Books.

[29]See article by C. C. McCown, "Codex and Roll in the New Testament," Harvard Theological Review, October 1941.

[30]Umberto Cassuto—"Commentary on the Book of Exodus," p. 158, Magnes Press, Jerusalem.

[31]2 Kings 22:13.

[32]Jeremiah 8:8.

[33]Numbers 24:21-24.

[34]Max W. Ball, "The Fascinating Oil Business," Bobbs-Merrill, New York, p. 292.

[35]11 Chronicles 32:5.

[36]Cambridge Ancient History, Vol. III, p. 75 et seq. This same authority further informs us, "There can be little doubt that the prosperity of Syria and adjoining lands was very considerable at this period."

[37]Interpreters Dictionary of the Bible, Vol. III, p. 254.

[38]2 Kings 15:20.

[39]Ezekiel, 38:13.

[40]Pickthall, "The Glorious Koran," New American Library, p. 31.

[41]James 2:2, Acts 11:30, 1 Peter 5:11.

[42]Chambers Encyclopaedia, Vol. 10, page 543.

[43]2 Kings 22:10 et seq.

[44]Jeremiah 8:8, 9.

[45]2 Kings 23:2, 3.

[46]Deuteronomy 17: 16, 17.

[47]Genesis 10:18.

[48]Ezekiel 27:10 and 38:5.

[49]Cambridge Ancient History, Vol. III, p. 1.
[50]Genesis 9:27.
[51]Genesis 10:8-12.
[52]J. H. Hertz—"The Pentateuch and the Haftorahs," p. 36.

Notes to Chapter 3

[1]Encyclopaedia Britannica, Vol. III, p. 509.
[2]Vol. 14, p. 868.
[3]For an elaboration of this far-out scholarship see "The Book of Books: An Introduction" by Solomon Goldman, Harper, New York, 1948.
[4]"Prolegomena zur Geschichte Israels," 1878.
[5]According to the version given credence in Chambers Encyclopaedia, both "J" and "E" came in the eighth century..
[6]C. H. Gordon, "The Ancient Near East," Norton.
[7]C. H. Gordon, "The Ancient Near East," p. 247.
[8]2 Kings 14:6.
[9]Joshua, 1:8, Joshua, 8:31, Joshua, 23:6.
[10]See in this connection Claus Westermann, "Handbook of the Old Testament," London, S.P.C.K., 1969.
[11]I Kings 15:12.
[12]2 Kings 18:4.
[13]Deuteronomy 12: 13, 14.
[14]Leviticus 17:8, 9.
[15]2 Kings, 23:21.
[16]Deuteronomy 32:15-17.
[17]Numbers 24:21-24.
[18]Exodus, chapt. 13.
[19]1:10.
[20]Deuteronomy 1:8.
[21]There is nothing to be found in the books of Ezra and Nehemiah to indicate that either of these builders was preoccupied with temple worship and the regulation of the sacrificial cult.
[22]Prolegomena to the History of Ancient Israel," Introduction, p. 8, World Publishing Co.
[23]Had Wellhausen read Leviticus more attentively, he would have discovered that it also deals with matters concerning ethical conduct, laws of marriage, prevention of diseases, sale of houses, etc.
[24]P. 37.
[25]40:1-43:27.

[26]Ezra 3:2.

[27]In the seventh book of Vergil's Aeneid are rules enunciated for burnt offerings of oxen that are not unlike those contained in the Pentateuch.

[28]Ezra 7:6, 10.

[29]Werblowsky and Wigoder, "Encyclopaedia of the Jewish Religion," 1966, Holt, Rinehart and Winston, New York.

[30]The tell-tale word is "aperion," meaning a chariot. It occurs in Chapter 3, verse 9.

[31]Jewish Encyclopaedia, Funk & Wagnalls, Vol. 5, p. 322

Notes to Chapter 4

[1]Isaac D'Israeli, "Curiosities of Literature."

[2]G. H. Barrow, "The Bible in Spain."

[3]Genesis 6:4.

[4]Andre Parrot "Abraham et son Temps," p. 7, Delachaux et Niestle, Neuchatel, Suisse, 1962.

[5]Genesis, 6:9.

[6]The equivalent word in Hebrew is "Ir."

[7]W. F. Albright, "De l'Age de la Pierre à la Chrétienté," p. 110.

[8]Genesis 11:31.

[9]W. F. Albright, "De l'Age de la Pierre á la Chrétienté," p. 174.

[10]Genesis 12:1.

[11]Max Weber, "General Economic History," Greenberg, p. 195.

[12]Aside from Joseph, at least one other man of Semitic extraction is recorded as having been raised to high office by one of the Pharaohs. See in this connection report by Daniel Rops in "Histoire Sainte," Paris, Antheme Fayard, p. 277.

[13]Grote, "History of Greece," Vol. 5, p. 230.

[14]Genesis 41:51.

[15]William Lyon Phelps, "Reading the Bible."

[16]Genesis 47: 5, 6.

[17]"Letter of Aristeas" quoted in "A Treasury of Jewish Letters," Vol. I, Editor Franz Kobler, Jewish Publication Society, Philadelphia, 1954.

[18]Genesis 46: 2, 3.

[19]Genesis 14:14.

[20]See in regard to their confinement within a restricted area Genesis 36: 6, 8.

[21]Genesis 48:27.

[22]Exodus 1: 7.

[23]Genesis 50: 24.

[24]W. F. Albright, "Archaeology and Religion," p. 96.

[25]Joshua 24: 25, 26.

[26]A. Alt, "Die Ursprunge des Israelitischen Rechts," 1935.

[27]Deuteronomy 29:28.

[28]"Decline and Fall of the Roman Empire," Vol. 2, p. 68.

[29]Acts 7:22.

[30]Exodus 7:16, Exodus 8: 25, 26, 27.

[31]Deut. 23: 10-14.

[32]Exodus 18:21.

[33]Abba Hillel Silver, "Moses and the Original Torah," Macmillan, 1961.

[34]Amos 5:25.

[35]Joshua 8:30.

[36]Deuteronomy 8:15.

[37]Leonard Cottrell, "Anvil of Civilization," Mentor Books, p. 98.

[38]Exodus 1:9.

[39]A reference to this connection is to be seen in the story of the Tower of Babel.

[40]Exodus 1:13, 14.

[41]Exodus, 10:14.

[42]Exodus 1:7.

[43]C. H. Gordon, "The Ancient Near East," Norton, p. 7.

[44]Exodus 12:38.

[45]Menzel, "History of Germany," Vol. 1, p. 465.

[46]1 Samuel 13:5.

[47]1 Samuel 13:5.

[48]"Lettres Persanes," no. 112.

[49]Hollingsworth, "Historical Demography," Cornell University Press, p. 31.

[50]G. Ernest Wright, "Biblical Archaeology," 1957, pp. 66, 67.

[51]Numbers 11:22.

[52]Matthew 4:2.

[53]"De l'Age de la Pierre à la Chrétienté," p. 188.

[54]Leviticus 16:10.

[55]"The Ancient Near East," Norton, New York, p. 116.

[56]"De l'Age de la Pierre à la Chrétienté," p. 188.

[57]Sallen and Watzinger, "Jericho," p. 21.

[58]Joshua 13:1.

[59]Joshua 17:16.

[60]Joshua 11:19.

[61]Joshua 22: 1-3.

[62]Joshua 11:25.

[63]An energetic ruler of Hazor by name of Jabin is mentioned as having

organized a counteroffensive against Joshua. Are we to take note of some textual confusion between Joshua 11 and Judges Chapter 4?

[64]Samuel 7:14.

[65]Judges 18:1-10.

[66]Kings 9:11.

[67]Judges 2:1-5.

Notes to Chapter 5

[1]Deuteronomy 11:18.

[2]Judges 17:6.

[3]Thomas H. Huxley, "Essays Upon Some Controversial Questions."

[4]Jeremiah 22:13.

[5]1 Samuel, 9:2.

[6]1 Samuel 11:7.

[7]1 Samuel 14:21.

[8]1 Samuel 11:7.

[9]2 Samuel 5:3, 4.

[10]1 Chronicles 22:3.

[11]See 2 Samuel 18:18.

[12]See the following: 2 Samuel 15:18, 2 Samuel 22:18, 2 Samuel 20:7, 2 Samuel 21:25, 1 Kings 1:38.

[13]Psalm 69, 27:30.

[14]Psalm 41, 7-10.

[15]Psalm 69:22.

[16]Psalm 60. Also mentioned in 2 Samuel 8:3 and 2 Chronicle 18:3.

[17]1 Samuel 22:2.

[18]Psalm 144, 1, 2.

[19]Psalm 108:8, 9.

[20]Psalms 18:42, 44.

[21]Psalm 31:10, 11.

[22]Psalm 33:5.

[23]Psalms 6:6, 30:10, 39:13.

[24]See for example article on "David" in Jewish Encyclopaedia, Funk & Wagnalls.

[25]Rivalry and hatreds inside families are more especially distinctive of those which are polygamous.

[26]2 Samuel 15:2, 3.

[27]2 Samuel 14:11.

[28]1 Samuel 16:9, 10.

[29]2 Samuel 23:1.

[30]1 Kings 4:26.
[31]1 Kings 4:30.
[32]1 Kings 4:33.
[33]1 Kings 4:32.
[34]1 Kings 4:31. Heman, by the way, was the author of Psalm 88, and Ethan his brother of Psalm 89.
[35]1 Kings 9:26, 28.
[36]The average duration of any of the Egyptian dynasties was a little over one hundred years.
[37]King Josiah's defeat and death at the battle of Megiddo was also noted by the early Greek historian Herodotus.
[38]Grote, History of Greece, vol. III, p. 332.
[39]Julius Wellhausen, "Prolegomena to the History of Ancient Israel," p. 458.
[40]Joshua 11:13.
[41]Judges 3:5, 6.
[42]Judges 6:29-31.
[43]1 Kings 12:28.
[44]Grote, "History of Greece," vol. III, p. 322.
[45]2 Chronicles 11:13-15.
[46]2 Chronicles 11:16.
[47]2 Chronicles 14:1.
[48]2 Chronicles 16:1.
[49]Significantly, he is not mentioned in the text as belonging to one of the Israelite tribes. Neither is the name of his father given.
[50]2 Kings 16:21.
[51]His eldest son Ahab married into Phoenician royalty.
[52]Amos 1:9.
[53]Jewish Encyclopaedia, Vol. V, p. 238.
[54]2 Kings 10:35.
[55]Hosea 12:8.
[56]Amos 6:4-6.
[57]Amos 8:4.
[58]Hosea 12:8.
[59]Joel 4:6.
[60]Nehemia, 5:1-12.
[61]2 Chronicles 17:9.
[62]Prolegomena, p. 501.
[63]John 2:13, 5:1, 7:10, 10:23, 12:12, Luke 2:42, Mark 11:15-17.

Notes to Chapter 6

[1]Jeremiah 2:28.

[2]Jeremiah 44:17-19.

[3]Daniel 4:30.

[4]25:15-29.

[5]Ezekiel 16:3.

[6]Malachi 1:11.

[7]Zecharia 2:11.

[8]Isaiah 29:18.

[9]Iliad 9:447-457.

[10]See for a discussion of this question Article to be found in Encyclopaedia of Religion and Ethics, Vol. 8, p. 819.

[11]André et Renée Neher, "Histoire Biblique du Peuple d'Israel," Adrien-Maissoneuve, Paris, 1962.

[12]Article by Arthur Ruppin, "The Jewish Population of the World," in Vol. 1, p. 348 of series "Jewish People Past and Present."

[13]Theodore Mommsen, "Romische Geschichte," Vol. 5, p. 549.

[14]Kiddushim 71A, quoted in Graetz, "History of the Jews," Vol. 4, p. 273.

[15]Jewish Encyclopaedia, Vol. IX, Article on "Statistics."

[16]29:5-7.

[17]Cambridge Ancient History, Vol. 111, p. 4.

[18]See in this connection Article by Naim Dangoor, "The Jews of Irak," in Bulletin of Canadian Jewish Congress, June 1971.

[19]Keller, "The Bible as History."

[20]Kohler & Peiser, "Aus dem Babylonischer Rechstleben" 1: 1 et seq.

[21]History of Greece, Vol. IV, p. 232.

[22]Landersdorfer, "Die Kultur der Babylonier und Assyrier," 1913, p. 75.

[23]Droysen, "Geschichte des Hellenismus," Vol. III, p. 6, Hamburg, 1836.

[24]See for example Articles in Jewish Encyclopaedia under "Babylonia," and "Commerce."

[25]C. H. Gordon, "Ancient Near East," p. 275.

[26]Zechariah 6:10 et seq.

[27]A glance at a topographical map will indicate that Nineveh, like Moscow, standing in the midst of an extensive plain, was well located for becoming the capital of a far-flung empire. Babylon, to the contrary, a city hemmed in by mountains on one side and a desert on the other side, was not.

[28]Grote, "History of Greece," Vol. IV, p. 238.

[29]Nehemiah 3:31 et seq.

[30]Nehemiah, 7:4.

334

[31]4:8.
[32]Josephus, "Contra Apionem."
[33]Proverbs 16:1.
[34]Encyclopaedia Britannica, Vol. 2, p. 176, under "Arabia."
[35]W. F. Albright, "From the Stone Age to Christianity," p. 39.
[36]4:5.

Notes to Chapter 7

[1]H. Graetz, "History of the Jews," vol. 2, p. 465.

[2]The intolerant spirit of the Magian religion was noted by Gibbon in "Decline and Fall of the Roman Empire," vol. 1, p. 436.

[3]The most famous of the Abbasid Califs, Haroun-al-Raschid, originated the idea of a yellow badge to distinguish Jews from true believers.

[4]Goitein, "Jews and Arabs," Schocken, p. 113.

[5]James Parkes, "Conflict of Church and Synagogue," p. 276.

[6]Sepharad is the Hebrew name for Spain.

[7]John Abbot, "History of Italy," p. 295.

[8]Herbert Heaton, "Economic History of Europe," Harper, p. 48.

[9]W. G. de Burgh, "Legacy of the Ancient World," p. 281.

[10]Spain suffered from a disastrous invasion by the Franks during the reign of the emperor Gallienus, 260-268.

[11]Salo Baron, "A Social and Religious History of the Jews," vol. 1, p. 169.

[12]Theodore Mommsen, "Romische Geschichte," vol. III, p. 549-550, Berlin, 1889.

[13]Jewish Encyclopaedia, Vol. 3, p. 485, article on "Caesar."

[14]42 C.E.

[15]W. G. deBurgh, "The Legacy of the Ancient World," Pelican, p. 294.

[16]The story of Paul's narrow escape from shipwreck on his way to Rome is narrated in the twenty-seventh chapter of the book of Acts.

[17]History of France, vol. 1, p. 105.

[18]The Arian kings had no recourse but to follow the path of toleration inasmuch as the bulk of their subjects as well as the clergy adhered to orthodoxy.

[19]After conquering Spain, the Arabs immediately penetrated deeply into France. For a time, they were in occupation of Lyons, Bordeaux, Avignon, Narbonne, and Arles.

[20]P. Hitti, "The Arabs," p. 138.

[21]Spain's return to the Christian fold was in effect accomplished in the year 1248 with the capture of Seville by King Ferdinand III of Castile.

335

Only in the extreme south a small and powerless Moslem enclave remained.

[22]"An Encyclopaedia of World History," Houghton-Mifflin, p. 363.

[23]Esther 3:8.

[24]Heaton, "Economic History of Europe," p. 157.

[25]"Conflict of Church and Synagogue," p. 335.

[26]Miriam Beard, "History of the Businessman," Macmillan, 1938, p. 60.

[27]S. M. Dubnow, "History of the Jews in Russia and Poland," Vol. 1, p. 41.

[28]Chambers Encyclopaedia, Vol. II, p. 14, article on "Poland."

[29]B. Breslauer, "Die Abwanderung der Juden aus der Provinz Posen," 1909.

Notes to Chapter 8

[1]S. D. Goitein, "Jews and Arabs," Schocken, p. 48.

[2]"Decline and Fall of the Roman Empire," vol. 1, p. 206.

[3]Gibbon, 2, p. 73.

[4]Merchants have on numerous occasions throughout history shown their readiness to transfer their capital to land as, for example, the Fuggers of Augsburg in the sixteenth century.

[5]M. Cary and T. J. Haaroff, "Life and Thought in the Greek and Roman World," University Paper Back, p. 295.

[6]See for example "Judges," 19:16.

[7]Alfred Bertholet, "Histoire de la Civilisation d'Israel," p. 51.

[8]Isaiah 2:7.

[9]Vol. 1, p. 264, under "Agriculture."

[10]Leviticus 25:15, 16.

[11]Isaac Schipper, "Economic History of the Jews," Warsaw, vol. 1, p. 49.

[12]Ecclesiastes, 38:31-34.

[13]Exodus 1:11.

[14]1 Samuel 13:19.

[15]"Prague Ghetto of the Renaissance Period," publication of the government of Czecho-Slovakia under its series "Jewish Monuments in Bohemia and Moravia," Vol. IV.

[16]Alfred Bertholet, "Histoire de la Civilisation d'Israel," Payot, Paris, 1953, p. 32.

[17]Isaiah 23:8, Proverbs 31:24.

[18]39:7.

[19] 1 Kings 20:34.

[20] Amos 6:1, 2.

[21] W. Cunningham, "Western Civilization," p. 49.

[22] Miriam Beard, "A History of the Businessman," Macmillan, 1938, p. 46.

[23] For a portrayal of the commercial enterprise of the Jews of the Graeco-Roman period, see Article by Kaufmann Kohler entitled "Die Weltgeschichtliche Bedeutung des Judischen Handels," in the series "Jahrbuch fur Judische Geschichte und Literatur," 1909.

[24] Jacob Burckhardt, "The Renaissance in Europe," Vol. 1, p. 97.

[25] It was the only city in Christian Europe that permitted the erection of a mosque.

[26] Leon Poliakov, "Les Banquiers Juifs et le Saint-Siège," Calmann-Levy, Paris, 1967, p. 246.

[27] Cary & Haaroll, "Life and Thought in the Greek and Roman World," p. 33.

[28] Cecil Roth, "History of the Jews in England," p. 16.

[29] Two main invasions of Britain were made possible by the aid of Jewish money, that of Duke William in the year 1066, and that of William of Orange in 1688.

[30] Heaton, "Economic History of Europe," p. 370.

Notes to Chapter 9

[1] We hear of no other white community ever settled in any interior Chinese city.

[2] Such dominance of the Christian powers proved to be of very short duration.

[3] H. Trevor-Roper, "The Rise of Christian Europe," p. 135.

[4] In Spain they were welcomed by the Archbishop of Toledo.

[5] S. D. Goitein, "Jews and Arabs," Schocken, p. 113.

[6] "The Rise of Christian Europe," London, 1965.

[7] See in this connection the extensive coverage of this subject in Leon Poliakov, "Le Saint-Siège et les Banquiers Juifs entre le Douzième et le Seizième Siècle," Calmann-Levy, Paris.

[8] Jacob Burckhardt, "The Civilization of the Renaissance in Italy," p. 208.

[9] The Turks were themselves repeatedly called back from their holy war against the Christians by the irreconcilable Shiite Iranians in their rear.

[10] The conquered Greeks soon accommodated themselves to their new

337

rulers, and developed their aptitudes for business and administration. Their power inside the Ottoman Empire came to overshadow that of the Jews.

[11]Encyclopaedia Judaica, Vol. 9, p. 435.

[12]A. Yaari, "A Goodly Heritage," Jerusalem, 1956.

[13]Miriam Beard, "A History of the Businessman," Macmillan, 1938, p. 330.